T

The Magical World of Aleister Crowley

Francis X. King

ARROW BOOKS

Arrow Books Limited
62–65 Chandos Place, London WC2N 4NW

An imprint of Century Hutchinson Limited

London Melbourne Sydney Auckland
Johannesburg and agencies throughout
the world

First published in Great Britain
by Weidenfeld & Nicolson 1977
Arrow edition 1987

Printed and bound in Great Britain by
Anchor Brendon Limited, Tiptree, Essex

ISBN 0 09 951570 9

Contents

Illustrations

The author and publisher are grateful to the following sources for their kind permission to reproduce the illustrations: The Radio Times Hulton Picture Library for illustration numbers 1, 2, 3, 7, 8, 9, 10, 11, 12, 13, 14, 15, 16, 17, and 18; The Fogg Art Museum, Harvard University (Grenville L. Winthrop Bequest) and Sir Caspar John and Romilly John for illustration 4; *Equinox* magazine, illustration 5; The Harry Price Library for illustration 6; The National Portrait Gallery and Sir Caspar John and Romilly John for illustration 19.

Acknowledgments

To G.A.D. and G.J.Y. for giving me access to rare Crowley manuscript and printed material. To C. W. Daniel and Co. Ltd. for permission to quote from *Crowley on Christ* and *The Secret Rituals of the OTO*. To Michael Horniman of A. P. Watt and to Barbara Gough and John Curtis of Weidenfeld and Nicolson for helpful suggestions given at the manuscript stage of this book. To the staffs of the British Library, the Harry Price Library and the Library of the Warburg Institute for their willing assistance. To the publishers of the magazine *Agapé* for their excellent Crowley Cross-Index. To Stephen Skinner and Isabel Sutherland for useful suggestions. To Elizabeth Lewis for her patience in typing.

1

The Magical Decade

ON THE EVENING of 18 November 1898 a twenty-three-year-old poet named Aleister Crowley waited impatiently in the ante-room of the London masonic temple situated at Mark Masons' Hall, Great Queen Street. He was convinced that he was about to have the ultimate secrets of life and death revealed to him.

He was wearing an ankle-length black robe, his eyes were blindfolded, and around his waist was a triple-coiled cord. By his side, holding the ends of the binding cord in his right hand, was another man who was to be his guide during part of the ceremony which was to take place. The guide was more spectac-ularly dressed than Crowley. He too wore a black robe, but over it he wore a billowing white cloak with a red cross on its left breast. Round his neck he wore a broad band of white ribbon from which hung a large cruciform badge and in his left hand he carried a red and gold sceptre surmounted by a carving of a miniature episcopal mitre.

With a blast of hot and incense-laden air the doors which the two men faced were flung open from the inside and the blind-folded Crowley was led through them. He felt himself sprinkled with water, his nose wrinkled from the astringent tang of smouldering perfumes as a censer was waved over his head, and he heard a voice address him: 'Child of Earth, why seekest thou to enter our sacred hall? Why seekest thou admission to our Order?' His guide answered on his behalf: 'My soul wanders in darkness and seeks the light of the hidden knowledge, and I believe that in this Order knowledge of that light may be obtained.'

Crowley, still blindfolded, was led forward, guided into a kneeling position before a cubical altar on which lay a red cross and a white triangle, and his right hand placed on the triangle. Then at the prompting of his guide he swore an oath that he would:

... keep secret this Order, its name, the names of its members, and the proceedings that take place at its meetings. . . .

... not suffer myself to be hypnotised, mesmerised or placed in such a state of passivity that any uninitiated person or power may cause me to lose control of my thoughts, words or actions.

... persevere with courage and determination the labours of the Divine Science even as I shall persevere with courage and determination through this ceremony which is their image, and I will not debase my mystical knowledge in the labour of evil magic at any time tried or under any temptation.

The oath concluded with a statement that 'if I break this, my magical obligation, I submit myself, by my own consent, to a deadly and hostile current of will set in motion by the Secret Chiefs of this Order, by which I might fall slain and paralysed without visible weapon as if slain by the lightning flash'.

Crowley was then led around the temple, 'purified with water and consecrated with fire' – in other words further sprinklings and censings – had an invocation of 'the Lord of the Universe' recited over him, and was told: 'Child of Earth, long hast thou dwelt in darkness, quit the night and seek the day!' With these words the blindfold was removed from his eyes and he was at last able to see his surroundings.

He was standing in the midst of a trio of robed magicians, two of them holding sceptres, the other a sword, over his head. Before him was an altar on which stood, in addition to the cross and triangle previously mentioned, bread, salt, wine, a red-shaded lamp and a bowl of dried rose petals. On the other side of the altar were two pillars, one white and one black, and beyond them was a dais on which sat three immobile figures, one clad in yellow, another in bright blue and the third in flame scarlet. The three who surrounded Crowley addressed him in unison: 'We receive thee into the Golden Dawn.'

The rest of the ceremony was something of an anti-climax. Crowley was instructed in the secret step, signs, grip and word of the grade of neophyte in the Order of the Golden Dawn – quite as banal as the equivalent 'secrets' of other occult societies – and given an explanation of the symbols used in the initiation he had just undergone. He was told for example that the white triangle on the altar was an image of 'that triune Light which moved in darkness and formed the world out of darkness', while the altar itself was an emblem of 'visible nature, concealing within herself the mysteries of all dimensions'.

Finally the meeting closed with a sort of mock communion – each participant in the rite eating a morsel of bread and salt, 'as types of Earth', and swallowing a mouthful of wine, 'the consecrated emblem of elemental Water' – followed by a prayer: 'May what we have partaken maintain us in our search for the quintessence, the Stone of the Philosophers, the Summum Bonum, True Wisdom and Perfect Happiness.'

Such was Aleister Crowley's initiation into the Hermetic Order of the Golden Dawn, the most influential of the many occult societies which flourished in the last quarter of the nineteenth century.

Who was Aleister Crowley, and what personal and social factors had induced him to seek the wisdom of the Golden Dawn? Originally given the forenames of Edward Alexander (it was only in his late teens that he adopted the name Aleister) he was born at Leamington, not far from Shakespeare's Stratford-on-Avon, on 12 October 1875. His parents were both 'Darbyites', members of the most extreme wing of the ultra-Protestant sect known as the Exclusive Brethren. The young Aleister – it is perhaps best to refer to him by the name by which he preferred to be known – was taught his parents' fundamentalist beliefs; that any regular ministry was a denial of the spiritual priesthood of all believers, that all non-members of the Darbyite Sect were destined for hell-fire, and, above all that every single word of the Old and New Testaments had been fully inspired by the Holy Ghost. So strongly were these doctrines imposed upon him, that for the first eleven years or so of his life, he was quite unable to believe that anyone seriously doubted them, and he was forced to conclude that those who belonged to religious bodies such as the Church of England or the Methodists, did so out of a pure delight in wickedness.

Early in 1887 however Aleister's father died and shortly afterwards he was sent away to a Darbyite school in Cambridge. The experiences he underwent there at the hands of the headmaster, who seems to have been a mixture of religious maniac and sado-masochist, were so vile that his strong belief in the Darbyite version of evangelical Christianity was transformed into an undying hatred of the sect and those who upheld its doctrines.

The headmaster in question, a former Anglican clergyman named d'Arcy Champney, encouraged every form of tale-bearing. Informers were regarded as 'instruments of the Lord Jesus', and any story they told, however intrinsically improbable, was taken as the truth, as 'the Lord bringing to light that which was hid in darkness'. The result was inevitable; young boys sought the headmaster's favours by telling him of (imaginary) crimes committed by one or other of their contemporaries.

One such informer was a boy named Glascott, who told d'Arcy Champney that he had visited Crowley in the previous holidays and found him lying in a drunken stupor at the foot of the stairs. No attempt was made to check the story by for example asking Crowley's mother whether there was any truth in it. Instead the miserable boy, still only twelve years old, was subjected to a fearsome regimen of boycott and semi-starvation. He was put on a diet of bread and water, no one was permitted to play with him and his fellow pupils were forbidden to speak to him. Even the masters were forbidden to engage him in conversation save for instructional purposes.

This brutality continued for a term and a half until, threatened with the disgrace of expulsion, Crowley 'confessed' to the truth of Glascott's absurd invention and other equally imaginary sins – that he had held a mock prayer meeting and that he had attempted to corrupt another boy. Eventually an uncle intervened and Crowley, by now physically and mentally ill as a result of the tortures he had suffered, was removed from school. For the next two years he was educated at home by a series of tutors, all of whom he found 'surpassing prigs' save for a certain Archibald Douglas, who won his pupil's gratitude and admiration by introducing him to bridge, billiards and women.

In 1892 he was sent to Malvern, a public school which he hated and where, so he said, 'sodomy was the rule' and his study-mate actually made money by selling homosexual favours. Crowley told his family of this, was removed from the school and sent to Tonbridge, where his health broke down for a reason which, as he himself rather mysteriously expressed it, 'would have been my own fault or misfortune if I had been properly educated but in fact was the direct result of the vile system which . . . handed me over bound and blindfold to the outraged majesty of Nature'.[1] What actually happened was that, ignorant of sexual hygiene, he had caught gonorrhoea from a Glasgow prostitute.

More private tutoring followed until in the autumn of 1894 he went up to King's College, London, in order to study chemistry and other pre-medical subjects. He evidently changed his mind about a medical career for in October 1895 he went up to Cambridge, originally with the intention of reading Moral Sciences (that is, philosophy, psychology and economics) but rapidly switching to classics.

Crowley's three years at Cambridge were happy ones. He had plenty of money, his father having left a considerable fortune in trust for him, and he was able to eat and drink well, have luxuriously furnished rooms, buy limited and finely bound editions of his favourite poets and spend each vacation either climbing in the Alps – he was a good though unorthodox mountaineer – or engaging in winter sports.

Throughout this period he maintained a vigorous sex life, at first fairly normal, conducted with the aid of prostitutes and girls he managed to pick up in pubs and cigar-shops, but extending into homosexual activities in which he played the passive part. These probably commenced during the course of a brief holiday at Kiel – there is a poem in *White Stains*, Crowley's first and

pseudonymous publication, which certainly seems to imply that
such was the case. Most of these homosexual affairs were free
from any emotional involvement, Crowley's enjoyment of them
being derived from the satisfaction of the strongly masochistic
element in his own psychological make-up. For one man however,
a friend of Aubrey Beardsley's named Herbert Charles Jerome
Pollitt, a female impersonator who called himself Diane de
Rougy,[2] he seems to have felt a genuine affection, and as late as
1910 published a flattering poem about him.

At Cambridge Crowley was a romantic of the romantics. He
affected a vaguely poetical appearance, wearing floppy hats and
even floppier ties; he wrote much verse, mostly imitative of
Swinburne and Browning, which he published at his own expense;
he was a profound admirer of Beardsley's art and Pater's prose.
He even concerned himself with the seedier doings of the
European ultra-Right, supporting Don Carlos, Pretender to the
Spanish throne and joining a Carlist volunteer group in which he
learned to service and fire a machine-gun. Fortunately for himself
he was not aboard *The Firefly*, a British yacht loaded with rifles
and English Carlists when it was captured by the Spanish Customs
in 1899.

The English Legitimists – an extraordinary mixture of
Carlists, Jacobites and supporters of such eccentrics as the
claimant to the Imperial Throne of Byzantium – tended to be as
curious in their religious opinions as they were in their politics.
Many of them for example were members of the Order of
Corporate Reunion, a tiny body whose leader F. G. Lee, an
extreme Anglo-Catholic who claimed to have been consecrated
as a bishop, made it his business to re-ordain 'validly' as many
Episcopalian clergymen as he could persuade to undergo the
ceremony.

Crowley was no exception to the religious eccentricity that
characterized his fellow-Legitimists. He joined the 'Celtic
Church', an organization tinier and even more mysterious than the
Order of Corporate Reunion, and for a time took its antics very
seriously indeed. He lived and moved, as he himself later
admitted,[3] in a mystical haze of fairies, seal-women, glamour and

magic, and when a Carlist knighthood was to be conferred
upon him, spent the previous night in prayer and meditation
before his sword and spurs.

The murky intellectual twilight of the Celtic Church did not
satisfy Crowley for long. He began to feel that behind it – indeed
behind all religious groups which had something of the truth in
their teachings – must lurk one true church, a Secret Sanctuary
of the Saints. Inspired by hints about such a Secret Sanctuary
which he found in one of the publications of the occult writer
A. E. Waite, Crowley wrote to him asking for advice. Waite's
reply was characteristically vague, urging Crowley to read
mystical literature, particularly *The Cloud Upon the Sanctuary*, and
to await the coming of a 'Master'. Crowley followed Waite's
advice and studied mystical tracts. This soon led him into an
interest in alchemy and its symbolism on which, with typically
youthful arrogance, he soon began to regard himself as an expert.

In the summer of 1898, when Crowley was mountaineering at
Zermatt, he went into a beer-house and, with a desire to impress,
began to demonstrate his alchemical expertise by talking about
the subject at great length. To his surprise one of those present, a
young man named Julian L. Baker, seemed to know a great deal
more about alchemy than Crowley himself. Was this, Crowley
asked himself, the Master whom he was seeking? A day or two
later Crowley plucked up courage to ask Baker the same question.
No, said Baker, he was not, but on his return to London he
would introduce him to one who was.

The 'Master' in question turned out to be George Cecil Jones,
an industrial chemist who lived in Basingstoke, Hampshire, but
had a small office and analytical laboratory in the City of London.
Jones was impressed with Crowley, introduced him to the
Golden Dawn, acted as one of the officers at the initiation
described earlier in the chapter and assured his protegé that, in
spite of the not very impressive instructions given him at the end
of the rite – Crowley complained that his instructors had bound
him with terrible oaths of secrecy and then confided the Hebrew
alphabet to his safe keeping – he had taken the first step of the
journey which could lead him to the Sanctuary of the Saints.

In spite of such claims however the Golden Dawn was *not* a particularly saintly organization. Its real function was the practice of what its initiates referred to as 'the mediaeval occult sciences', particularly ritual magic, the supposed art of 'causing change to occur in accordance with will'. There is no call to be astonished by this. The last twenty years of the nineteenth century – and particularly the last ten – were a period when many Western European intellectuals, particularly the so-called decadents, re-acted against the materialist certainties of contemporary scientists and philosophers by showing an interest in the occult in general and ceremonial magic in particular. Such an interest was dis-played by Oscar Wilde when he based the whole plot of his novel *Dorian Gray* on a magical interaction between a portrait and the individual it delineated, by Beardsley when he drew his portrait of the fiend Asmodeus and 'how he revealed the Black Art to a Neophyte', and by Arthur Machen when he wrote his story 'The Great God Pan'. It is not surprising then that there were some who desired to go further than this, actually to *practise* magic. Interestingly enough one of these was Oscar Wilde's wife Constance who like Crowley underwent initiation into the Golden Dawn.[4]

The association between decadence and magic began in France as early as the 1840s and 1850s when the poet and novelist Adolphe Esquiros produced a novel in which the protagonist was a hermaphroditic magician who wrote love letters to the moon, and Alphonse-Louis Constant, under the pseudonym Eliphas Lévi, wrote two books[5] in which the magical tradition was presented in a highly romanticized form and yet, at the same time, ration-alized by the presentation of three principles which according to Lévi brought magic into the domain of science.

Lévi's three principles were simple enough and soon captured the imaginations of many European occultists. The first of these theoretical assumptions was that the material universe was only a part and by no means the most important part of total reality – in other words that there were other 'planes' of existence and other modes of consciousness besides the physical. The second, which Lévi probably derived from Mesmer, although more than one Renaissance writer had suggested the same thing, was that human will-power was a real force and that the trained and concentrated will was capable of producing apparently supernormal effects. The third was a rehashed version of the mediaeval theory of the macrocosm ('the great world', the universe as a whole) and the microcosm (the 'little world', that is, man himself). Every factor present in the macrocosm, Lévi asserted, is also present in man himself and by the use of the appropriate magical techniques it would be possible to link up the two.

Lévi, always the romantic theoretician rather than the practitioner of magic, made only one attempt to put his principles to the test of experiment. It was not very successful – he received some gloomy answers to questions he put to 'the other world' and he seems to have suffered a mild attack of carbon monoxide poisoning from the fumes of the charcoal he was burning in a brazier.

In spite of this it is simple to see any magical ritual in terms of Lévi's principles. Suppose a magician wishes to obtain knowledge of some obscure occult science, a matter which is traditionally one of the attributes of the god Hermes (Mercury). His task then is to supplement his psychic hermetic (that is, mercurial) deficiencies by drawing upon the hermetic qualities of the universe as a whole – to use the terminology of the magician, he must 'invoke the god Hermes'. He carries out this ceremony by surrounding himself with things, numbers and substances traditionally associated with Hermes. The number of Hermes is eight, so he has an eight-sided altar standing in an octagon; his temple is illuminated by eight lights; he has eight dishes of burning incense and he eats fish and drinks white wine, foods associated with Hermes since classical times. Having designed his ceremony with the appropriate correspondences, the magician uses his will-power to send up a 'ray' which extends into other planes and taps the hermetic energies of the macrocosm, thus giving himself the qualities appropriate to gaining a knowledge of obscure sciences.

At first Lévi was regarded as no more than an amusing eccentric. Few read his books and the first editions of them were still in print a quarter of a century after their publication. In 1875 Lévi died almost forgotten. Within ten years however he had a small but impressive band of French intellectuals as his posthumous disciples. This came about through the influence of the poet and novelist Catulle Mendès, a man who had known Lévi and had in fact introduced him to Victor Hugo. Sometime around 1884 Mendès met the Marquis Stanislas de Guïata, a young poet of great promise, and urged him to read Lévi. The Marquis took his friend's advice, read Lévi and was immediately subjected to what he himself referred to as the *coup de foudre occulte*, 'the occult thunderstroke'.

He changed his way of life completely, read magical and alchemical works rather than poetry, attempted to contact the gnomes, undines, and other 'elementary beings' of whom the sixteenth-century physician Paracelsus had written, and in his scarlet draped study-cum-alchemical laboratory experimented with hashish, cocaine and other drugs in an attempt to 'loosen the girders of the soul' – that is, to enable his soul temporarily to leave its earthly tenement and wander the universe as it willed.

Soon de Guïata had surrounded himself with a small band of like-minded literary and artistic individuals and in 1885 they founded the kabalistic Order of the Rose-Croix with the objects of studying and practising magic, spreading a knowledge of occult principles among the French public and revivifying the artistic life of Western Europe. Its leading members included not only the Marquis himself but Erik ('esot'-Erik) Satie, the composer and pianist whose works are sometimes still performed today; Joséphin 'Sâr' Péladan, wizard, novelist, fanatical Wagnerian and unorthodox Catholic; and Oswald Wirth, an expert on tarot cards who considered it important to devote his life to curious 'occult battles' against those he considered 'black magicians'.

While Guïata was most interested in traditional occult practices, Péladan was more intent on creating a genuinely mystical 'Rosicrucian' art and made frantic efforts to achieve it. So in addition to writing his own novels, such as *The Supreme Vice*, and curiously entitled works of occult instruction – one was entitled *How to Become a Fairy* – he organized six art exhibitions,

'*Salons de la Rose-Croix*', between 1892 and 1897. The presiding
genii of these exhibitions were the more 'decadent' painters of
the time – Gustave Moreau, Félicien Rops, Georges Rouault and
the Comte de Larmandie. The magical artistic theory which
dominated these exhibitions was summed up by Péladan in a
manifesto issued by his order.

> Artist! You are a priest: Art is the great Mystery. . . .
> Artist! You are a king: Art is the true Empire. . . .
> Artist! You are a magician: Art is the great miracle. . . .

Similar occult interests to those of the French decadents were
displayed by a surprisingly large number of English writers of the
eighties and nineties. Take for example F. W. Rolfe ('Baron
Corvo'), the author of the enchanting Toto stories and since the
publication of A. J. A. Symons's *Quest for Corvo* in 1934 something
of a cult figure. Rolfe was not only a complete believer in
astrology and a competent astrologer in his own right but he also
dabbled in ritual magic. Indeed on one occasion he actually
managed to involve R. H. Benson, a son of the Archbishop of
Canterbury who had managed to become both a Roman Catholic
priest and a best-selling popular novelist, in a magical experiment.
A description of this was given by Vyvyan Holland,[6] the younger
son of Oscar Wilde:

> Father Benson . . . had been deeply impressed with Rolfe's casting of
> horoscopes. . . . He said that Rolfe had evidently devoted a vast amount of
> time to the study of the stars, had found a number of very obscure books on the
> subject, including one quite unknown book by Albertus Magnus, and that he
> probably knew more about astrology than any living man.
>
> The most interesting story, by far, that Father Benson told me was of an
> experiment in White Magic which he had carried out at Rolfe's request. Rolfe
> wrote to him one day in a state of great excitement and told him that he had
> discovered, either in his Albertus Magnus book or in some mediaeval manuscript,
> instructions as how to bring about a certain event. He would not, at that
> juncture, reveal what the event was, but he implored Father Benson to make
> the experiment.
>
> As the experiment consisted mainly in the repetition of certain prayers and in
> certain periods of religious contemplation, Father Benson saw no harm in
> carrying it out. Certain rules were also laid down concerning hours of rising and

retiring and the avoiding of certain foods and drink. I remember that no alcohol of any sort was allowed! The period of this regime was to be from ten days to a fortnight.

At the end of the period stated, Father Benson told me that he distinctly saw a white figure whose features were quite indistinguishable, mounted on a horse, ride slowly into the middle of his room and there halt for about half a minute, after which it slowly faded away. He immediately sat down and wrote his impression to Rolfe, who replied by return enclosing what purported to be a transcription of the passage from the book containing the instructions. This said that, if the instructions were faithfully carried out, at the end of ten days or a fortnight the experimenter would see 'riding towards him the White Knight with visor down'. Benson showed me this at the time and was deeply impressed by the last words, which seemed to explain why he could not distinguish the features of his horseman.

Far more obscure literary figures than Corvo displayed a similar interest in magic and other occult beliefs. Thus Count Stenbock, a poetaster and occult short-story writer who, had he lived longer, might well have developed into another Aleister Crowley and whose interest in diabolism and occult eroticism may be taken as characteristic of the decadents. Eric Stenbock was born at Cheltenham in March 1860, the son of the Anglo-German wife of an Estonian aristocrat who died when Eric was only a year old. Little is known of Stenbock's childhood and adolescence save that he hated his step-father, Francis Mowatt, and his half-brothers, but his four terms at Oxford were eventful enough. He was, nominally at least, converted to Catholicism, he fell in love -- totally unrequited -- with Charles Fowler, the consumptive son of an Oxford clergyman, and he produced a volume of poems (*Love, Sleep and Dreams*, 1881) which induced his family, shocked by the transparent homosexuality of such lines as:

> And if some maiden beautiful
> Become thy love and joy
> Think on that passionate male heart
> That loved thee when a boy.

to insist on a lengthy visit to Kolk, his grandfather's estate in Estonia.

In February 1885 the grandfather, Count Magnus Stenbock, died and Eric inherited both title and estate. For two years he lived in Kolk, spending most of his time in the scarlet-draped apartments at the top of the house. Here he attended to the physical needs of his toads, lizards and other unusual pets; here he lounged, loosening the girders of the soul by smoking opium and hashish, on pseudo-oriental sofas; here he carried out his eccentric devotions before the great altar erected over the chimney-piece of his bedroom.

John Adlard, Stenbock's biographer, has given a description of this altar and the room it was in. The altar, he says, was

tricked out with oriental shawls, peacock feathers, lamps and rosaries. In the middle stood a green bronze statue of Eros. There was a little flame that burned unceasingly and resin in a copper bowl that scented the air. The floor was covered with thick Smyrna carpets, and over his bed hung a big pentagram to keep the evil spirits at bay. (He had, in fact, evolved a religion of his own, compounded of Buddhism, Catholicism and idolatory.)

In 1887 Stenbock returned to London, taking a lease of 21 Gloucester Walk, described by Arthur Symons as 'a certain house, rather out of the way, one of a row of houses where degenerates lived'. It was here, if Ernest Rhys is to be believed, that Stenbock fainted on seeing Oscar Wilde lighting a cigarette from the sanctuary lamp that burned before a bust of Shelley. Wilde, added Rhys, stepped unconcernedly over the body of the prostrate Count.

In spite of poor physical health made even worse by an excess of drink and drugs Stenbock made a genuine attempt to understand his own homosexuality in terms of traditional occultism, eventually coming to view his condition as an aspect of vampirism and lycanthropy. He expressed his conclusions in two short stories, 'The True Story of a Vampire' (originally included in *Studies in Love and Death*, 1894) and 'The Other Side', a contribution to Lord Alfred Douglas's strongly homosexual magazine *The Spirit Lamp*.

In the first of these stories the vampire, a nobleman named Vardalek, is Stenbock himself; Gabriel, the boy-victim of

Vardalek's symbolic sexual corruption, is a younger version of Charles Fowler, the schoolboy with whom Stenbock had been in love; and his death in a last embrace from Vardalek would appear to reflect Charles Fowler's final consumptive haemorrhage.

A boy named Gabriel is also the protagonist of 'The Other Side', a story printed with the sinister sub-title '*A la joyeuse Messe noire*'. Gabriel, an idealized version of Stenbock himself, is torn between the life of his village, a life centred on the festivals of the Catholic Church, and its hellish obverse, the life that flourishes on the other side of the river which bounds the village, notably Lilith, a mysterious wolf-woman, and a veiled wolf-keeper. Eventually Gabriel chooses the life of the village – but 'once a year for nine days a strange madness comes over him'. Thus did Stenbock symbolize his own fate, torn between Catholicism and diabolism; he died, deluded that a huge doll was his son and heir, in 1895.

When then one considered the intellectual ambience of the nineties there is nothing surprising in Crowley joining a magical order. But what were the origins of the order he joined? Whence came the Golden Dawn and who were its leading members?

2

The Golden Dawn

ONE OF THE items circulating in manuscript form among the Golden Dawn neophytes which Crowley must have received shortly after the initiation described in the last chapter was called 'The History Lecture'. According to this the order had its origins in dim antiquity; pompously the document claimed that:

During the early part of the second half of this century several eminent Adepts and Chiefs of this Order in France and England died. . . . These and other contemporary Adepti of this Order received their knowledge and power from predecessors of equal and even of greater eminence, they received indeed and handed down to us this Doctrine and System of Theosophy and Hermetic Science and the Higher Alchemy from a long series of practical investigators, whose origin is traced to the Fratres Rosae Crucis [that is, the Rosicrucians] of Germany which was founded by one Christian Rosenkreutz about the year 1398.

There is not a single word of truth in this account! Christian Rosenkreutz never existed as an historical personage, the first of those who have styled themselves Rosicrucians appeared in the seventeenth century, not the fourteenth, and the Golden Dawn was in no way the inheritor of a secret oral tradition derived from the Rosicrucians. In fact the grades – the supposed degrees of occult wisdom – of the Golden Dawn were based on those of the masonic Golden Rosicrucians of the eighteenth century and the actual rituals used displayed a fusion of religious beliefs which, because of the knowledge of Egyptian archaeology displayed in them, cannot be dated before the second half of the nineteenth century.

The actual origin of these rituals is something of a mystery, but it is certain that they were derived from certain cipher manuscripts which gave the rituals in skeletonic form and have survived to the present day. Where these documents originally came from is unknown, but various stories have circulated among occultists according to which they were discovered by a masonic clergyman, the Rev. A. F. A. Woodford, either on a bookstall in London's Farringdon Road, or among the papers left by the occultist Frederick Hockley who died in 1887.[1]

From Woodford these cipher manuscripts[2] passed into the possession of Dr Wynn Westcott, a North London coroner whose hobbies embraced both high-grade freemasonry and the study of every sort of occult theory. Westcott employed a young occultist who called himself G. S. L. MacGregor Mathers – although he was born plain G. S. L. Mathers – to decode the manuscripts and when this had been done found that he was in the possession of initiation rites to Rosicrucian grades called Neophyte, Zelator, Theoricus, Practicus and Philosophus. The symbolism of these rites was largely Egyptian, although there were Graeco-Roman undertones to them, but the names of the grades were identical with those of the German eighteenth-century masonic-alchemical rite of 'The Golden and Rosy Cross'; this must not be taken as an indication of any actual connection between German occultism and the manuscripts, for not only do these latter decode into English but the 'Words of Power' used in them are derived from the writings of John Dee, the sixteenth-century English mathematician and occultist, who was a semi-official court astrologer to Queen Elizabeth 1.

Together Westcott and Mathers padded out the rites into a form which could be worked, added to each a 'Knowledge Lecture' on some aspect of occult lore and in 1888 founded in London what they called the 'Isis-Urania Temple of the Golden Dawn in the Outer'.[3] Soon this London temple had established subsidiary temples in Edinburgh, Paris and various English provincial centres.

At first the Golden Dawn was little more than another pseudo-masonic order whose members studied occult theory and which was distinguished from other secret societies of the same sort only by the fact that it admitted women as well as men into its ranks.

In 1892 however Mathers claimed to have created a link between himself and certain super-human, immortal teachers, whom the Theosophists called 'Mahatmas' or 'Masters' and the Golden Dawn membership referred to as 'the Secret Chiefs of the Order'. On the basis of the teachings he claimed to have received from these Secret Chiefs Mathers composed a new ritual, which he called that of Adeptus Minor, compiled numerous manuscripts giving details of practical occult working and founded a new Inner (or Second) Order whose members were dedicated to the practice of ritual magic.

Mathers has left his own description of how he contacted the Secret Chiefs and of his subsequent dealings with them in a manifesto issued in October 1896:

Concerning the Secret Chiefs of the Order, to whom I make reference and from whom I have received the Wisdom of the Second Order, which I have communicated to you, I can tell you *nothing*. I know not even their earthly names. I know them only by certain secret mottoes. I have but very rarely seen them in the physical body; and on such rare occasions *the rendezvous was made astrally by them*. They met me in the flesh at the time and place appointed beforehand. For my part I believe them to be human and living on this earth; but possessing terrible super-human powers.

When such rendezvous has been in a much frequented place there has been nothing in their personal appearance or dress to make them out as differing in any way from ordinary people except the appearance and sensation of transcendent health and vigour (whether they seemed persons in youth or age) which was their invariable accompaniment; in other words, the physical appearance which the possession of the Elixir of Life has traditionally been supposed to confer.

On the other hand when the rendezvous has been in a place free from any access by the Outer World they have usually been in symbolic robes and insignia.

But my physical intercourse with them on these rare occasions has shown me how difficult it is for a mortal, even though advanced in occultism, to support the presence of an Adept in the physical body. . . . I do not mean that in such rare cases of physical converse with them that the effect produced on me was that of intense physical exhaustion which follows depletion of magnetism; but, on the contrary, the sensation was that of being in contact with so terrible a force that I can only compare it to the continued effect of that usually experienced momentarily by any person close to whom a flash of lightning passes during a violent storm; coupled with a difficulty in respiration similar to the half-strangling effect produced by ether; and if such was the result produced on one as tested as I have been in occult work, I cannot conceive a much less advanced initiate being able to support such a strain, even for five minutes, without death ensuing.

Almost the whole of the Second Order Knowledge has been obtained by me from them [the Secret Chiefs] in various ways, by clairvoyance – by astral projection on their part and mine – by the table, by the ring and disc – at times by Direct Voice audible to my external ears and those of Vestigia[4] – at times copied from books brought before me, I knew not how – and which disappeared from my vision when the transcription was finished – at times by appointment *astrally* at a certain place, till then unknown to me; an appointment made in the same manner and kept in the same manner as in the case of those rare occasions when I have met them by appointment in the physical body.

The strain of such labour has been, as you can conceive, enormous. In especial the obtaining of the Z ritual, which I thought would have killed me, or Vestigia, or both, the nerve prostration after each reception being terrible from the strain of testing the correctness of every passage thus communicated; the nerve prostration alluded to at the time accompanied by profuse cold perspirations, and by severe loss of blood from the mouth, nose and occasionally the ears.

You know the extreme and sustained attention, and critical judgment, requisite to obtain any reliable and truthful answers through the Table or Ring and Disc. Add to all this the Ceremonies of Evocation, almost constant strife with opposing Demonic Forces endeavouring to stop the delivery and reception of the Wisdom; and the necessity of keeping the mind exalted towards the Higher Self. . . .

This extraordinary account which Mathers wrote in 1896 needs a little explanation: by 'the Table' Mathers meant a slightly sophisticated version of the table-turning so much in vogue at Victorian spiritualist séances; by the 'Ring and Disc', which needed so much 'extreme and sustained attention', he meant a technique which curiously combined the pendulum swinging engaged in by some dowsers (the sort of thing usually called radiesthesia) with something very like the ouija board

which is so popular at the present day. The ring, made of card-
board and symbolically coloured for the elements of Earth, Air,
Fire and Water, was suspended from a silk thread held by
Mathers or his wife, and from its gyrations over a disc marked
with the letters of the Hebrew alphabet meaningful (sometimes!)
words were spelt out which answered questions or conveyed
instructions.

As for the 'Z ritual' – the reception of which, it will be
remembered, was so difficult that Mathers claimed to have
believed that it might lead to the death of himself and his wife –
this was unquestionably the most influential of the many instructional documents produced by Mathers. It gave details of how
the Golden Dawn's Neophyte ritual (described in chapter 1 of
this book) correlated with Egyptian symbolism, of what was
supposed to be happening on the astral plane while the ritual was
being worked and, most important of all from the point of view
of those who wanted to engage in ritual magic, the way in which
the rite could be adapted to almost any occult technique, from
the evocation of spirits to visible appearance, to ceremonial
divination and alchemy.

With the exception of Crowley, who for a time was to become
his most ardent disciple, and of W. B. Yeats, Mathers was
perhaps the most interesting of the two hundred or so initiates
who made up the Golden Dawn as it existed in the 1890s. Not
much detail of his early life was known to even his closest
associates. Westcott recorded what little he knew in an undated
memorandum:

Samuel Liddell Mathers, son of William M. Mathers a commercial clerk; his
mother was a Miss Collins. He was born at 11 De Beauvoir Place, Hackney, on
January 8 1854. His father died early and he lived for some years with his
widowed mother at Bournemouth until her death in 1885. He was initiated[5] in
the Hengist Lodge in 1877 but never became a Lodge Master. While at Bournemouth his studies were directed to mystical ideas by his acquaintance with
Frederick Holland, a deep student of mystical philosophy. He was admitted to
the Rosicrucian Society,[6] and so became associated with Dr Woodman and Dr
Westcott, and pursuing his studies under their tuition he made considerable
progress and proved so apt a pupil that he translated von Rosenroth's *Kabalah*

Denudata, a work which has run through several editions and gave him a recognised position in occultism.[7]

On the death of his mother he was left in very poor circumstances and removed to London where he lived in modest lodgings in Great Percy Street, King's Cross, enjoying the hospitality of Dr Westcott for many years.[8]

Westcott's account concentrates on Mathers's occult interests, but in fact Mathers was also strongly interested in military and political matters, on both of which he had decided opinions. Indeed his first publication was not the *Kabalah Unveiled*, which appeared in 1887, but *Practical Instruction in Infantry Campaigning Exercise*, published three years earlier. In his *Autobiographies* W. B. Yeats referred to Mathers as a man whose 'studies were two only – magic and the theory of war' and gave some details of his extraordinary political ideas. He was a Jacobite who believed in the overthrow of Queen Victoria and the restoration of the Stuarts and 'imagined a Napoleonic role for himself, Europe transformed according to his fancy, Egypt restored, a Highland Principality, and even offered subordinate posts to unlikely people'.

Yeats had first met Mathers in the Reading Room of the British Museum,[9] probably in about 1889, and has left an interesting account of the magician and would-be arbiter of Europe in his *Autobiographies*:

A man of thirty-six or thirty-seven, in a brown velveteen coat, with a gaunt resolute face and an athletic body, who seemed before I heard his name, or knew the nature of his studies, to be a figure of romance. Presently I was introduced, where or by what man or woman I do not remember. He was called Liddell Mathers, but would soon, under the influence of 'The Celtic Movement' become MacGregor Mathers and then plain MacGregor. . . . I believe that his mind in those early days did not belie his face and body – though in later years it became unhinged as Don Quixote's was unhinged – for he kept a proud head amid great poverty. One that boxed with him nightly has told me that for many weeks he could knock him down, though Mathers was the stronger man, and only knew long after that during those weeks Mathers starved.

In fact Mathers had adopted the name of MacGregor long before Yeats met him – his masonic certificate of initiation dated 1878 refers to him as 'MacGregor of Glenstrae'.

Mathers claimed that he was perfectly justified in adopting this title. According to him the name Mathers was an anglicization of the Gaelic words *Mo Athair*, meaning 'the posthumous one', and was one of the names adopted by the MacGregors after the proscription of their clan. This claim was an odd one, but not so odd as another claim which some asserted Mathers made – that he was in reality James IV of Scotland, not killed at the Battle of Flodden, as historians supposed, but an immortal adept. Mathers claims to be a MacGregor and the possibility of James IV having survived the Battle of Flodden were brought out in the high court in an amusing cross-examination which took place in 1910 in the course of the libel action *Jones v. the Looking Glass* and was reported in a contemporary newspaper:

'Is it a fact that your name is Samuel Liddell Mathers?'

—'Yes, or MacGregor Mathers.'

'Your original name was Samuel Liddell Mathers?'

—'Undoubtedly.'

'Did you subsequently assume the name of MacGregor?'

—'The name of MacGregor dates from 1603.'

'Your name was MacGregor in 1603?'

—'Yes, if you like to put it that way.'

'You have called yourself Count MacGregor of Glenstrae?'

—'Oh, yes!'

'You have called yourself the Chevalier MacGregor?'

—'No, you are confusing me with one of Crowley's aliases.'

'Have you ever suggested to anyone that you had a connection with James IV of Scotland?'

—'I do not quite understand your question. Every Scotsman of ancient family must have some connection with James IV.'

'Have you ever stated that King James IV never died?'

—'Yes. That is a matter of common tradition among all occult bodies. Alan Cunningham wrote a novel based on this tradition.'

'Do you assert that King James IV is in existence today?'

—'I refuse to answer your question.'

'And that his existence is embodied in yourself?'

—'Certainly not!'

'Do you claim that Cagliostro never died and that you are him?'

—'Certainly not. You are again confusing me with one of Crowley's aliases.'[10]

The poverty in which Mathers lived after his mother's death, and which was so marked that both Yeats and Westcott commented upon it, was alleviated in 1890 when Annie Horniman, an initiate of the Golden Dawn who was a member of a family who had made a fortune from the tea trade – she was later to become famous as the builder of Dublin's Abbey Theatre and the owner of the Gaiety Theatre, Manchester – got her father to appoint him as Curator of the Horniman Museum. In May 1892 Mathers and his wife moved to Paris where for a time at least they lived fairly comfortably on an allowance of £200 a year from the accommodating Annie Horniman.

As we have seen Yeats referred in his *Autobiographies* to Mathers as being 'unhinged'; elsewhere he wrote of him as being 'half lunatic, half knave'. But Yeats's own occult beliefs and activities were strange enough. He had been intrigued by the occult since adolescence – his interest in the world of the unseen had first been aroused by Irish stories of ghosts and fairies – and while still a young man he had become fascinated by black magic and devil worship. This interest was sufficiently strong to induce him not only to read occult literature but to get to know those who, in Yeats's own words, 'try to communicate with evil powers' and 'keep their purpose and practice wholly hidden from those among who they live'.

From a worldly point of view most of these Irish sorcerers were rather unimpressive – 'small clerks', recorded Yeats – and even their magical activities were hardly such as to inspire admiration. Yeats himself attended at least one such occult gathering and gave a detailed account of what took place at it. The meeting, which took place in a small back room, was conducted by a sorcerer who, clad in black gown and hood, sat at a table on which stood a smouldering censer, a symbol-decorated skull, crossed daggers, an empty bowl, some curious implements shaped like the grinding stones of a handmill and a large book. A black cockerel had its throat slit, its blood being drained into the bowl that stood on the table, and the magician opened his book and read an invocation in some unknown language.

For some time nothing happened. Then another of the

magicians, a young man seated to Yeats's left, called out 'Oh God! Oh God!', became extremely excited and claimed to see a great serpent moving about the room. Yeats himself was affected by the heady psychic atmosphere; he saw no serpents but sensed that black clouds were forming about him and threatening to entrance him. Such a trance would, he felt, be 'evil', so he struggled against it until he had 'got rid of the black clouds'. Meanwhile the sorcerers began to see more wonders, among them black and white pillars moving about the room and the ghostly figure of a monk. Yeats did not share these visions, but the black clouds returned and he felt a tide of darkness threatening to overwhelm him. With a great effort he once more drove off the clouds, asked for lights and then 'after the needful exorcism' returned to the world of ordinary life.

In spite of the unsatisfactory nature of this experience Yeats continued to be fascinated with diabolism and those who 'try to communicate with evil powers'. At times indeed he would talk about diabolism – which he apparently pronounced 'dyahbolism' – to the exclusion of anything else, and Max Beerbohm has left an amusing account in a broadcast talk of one such occasion:

[Yeats] had made a profound study of it [diabolism] and he evidently guessed that Beardsley . . . was a confirmed worshipper in that line. So to Beardsley he talked, in deep vibrant tones, across the table, of the lore and of the rites of Dyahbolism. . . . I daresay that Beardsley . . . knew all about Dyahbolism. Anyway I could see that he, with that stony common-sense which always came upmost when anyone canvassed the fantastic in him, thought Dyahbolism rather silly. He was too polite, however, not to go on saying at intervals, in his hard, quick voice, 'Oh, really, how perfectly entrancing'.

Yeats's interest in diabolism seems to have determined the magical motto he adopted after his admission into the Golden Dawn in March 1890 – '*Demon est Deus inversus*', 'the Devil is the reverse side of God'. The Golden Dawn and Mathers's teaching exerted a permanent and powerful influence on his intellectual and emotional development and these influences have been described and analysed at length by Kathleen Raine and George Mills Harper. Yeats was an active recruiter for the order bringing into membership, among others, Maud Gonne – whom for many years he hoped to marry – his uncle George Pollexfen and the actress Florence Farr, who ended her life as a Buddhist nun but always retained her ready wit: while the saying has been attributed to others it would seem that it was she who remarked at the time of the trial of Oscar Wilde, 'I don't care what they do as long as they don't do it in the street and frighten the cab-horses'. Initiated into the order in July 1890, Florence Farr rose rapidly through the grades and in 1894 became an official of the London temple. She not only avidly studied the theory of ritual magic but became an active practitioner of the art. On 13 May 1896 for example she attempted, with what success is unknown, to evoke the spirit Taphthartharath to visible appearance by means of a ritual which involved the boiling of a pickled snake in a 'hell broth' of various supposedly magical substances. Her companions in this curious rite were Charles Rosher, a former Court Painter to the Sultan of Morocco and the inventor of a new type of water-closet, F. L. Gardner, a stockbroker who studied alchemy and had a remarkable flair for making disastrous investments, and Allan Bennett, an asthmatic electrical engineer.

Bennett, who as will be seen later exerted much influence on Crowley, was reputed to possess extraordinary magical powers. It was said for example that he possessed a consecrated glass 'lustre' – a glass rod from a chandelier – which he had endowed with magical powers; one day a Theosophist whom Bennett had met and who was jeering at the legend of the 'magical blasting rod' was subjected to the rod's influence and was paralysed for a period of fourteen hours. . . . Crowley first met Bennett at a Golden Dawn meeting which took place at some time in the spring of 1899. He was immediately impressed with Bennett, feeling a tremendous 'spiritual and magical force' emanating from him. Bennett was also impressed by Crowley but for a different reason – by some process of spiritual diagnosis he came to the conclusion that Crowley was being attacked by black magic. Crowley affirmed that this was so and that the attacker was none other than W. B. Yeats who he claimed was jealous of his superior poetic genius. Together Bennett and Crowley carried out the necessary occult rites to defeat this attack[11] and shortly afterwards the former went to stay with Crowley in his Chancery Lane flat.

Crowley had not then reached the grade, that of Minor Adept, in which he became entitled to copies of Mathers's manuscripts dealing with the practice of magic as distinct from its theory. Bennett however cheerfully broke his initiation oath, supplied Crowley with copies of all the relevant material and proceeded to tutor him in the magical arts. It is possible that Bennett had Mathers's permission to follow this course. Crowley proved an apt pupil and soon was applying the Z manuscripts, which Mathers and his wife had obtained with so much difficulty, to such ends as the manufacture of a talisman, a magical 'mascot' intended for a particular purpose. This was intended to cure a certain Lady Hall, who was the mother of Mrs Elaine Simpson, a Golden Dawn initiate, of a serious illness. The effect of this talisman, technically referred to by Crowley as a 'Flashing Tablet of the Eagle Kerub of Jupiter', was somewhat alarming:

Extraordinary were its results. For having carefully celebrated the ritual he instructed Soror Q.F.D.R. [Elaine Simpson] to feed the talisman with incense and water it with dew. This she neglected to do, the result being that when she placed the talisman on her sick mother, this venerable old lady was seized with a violent series of fits, and nearly died. Q.F.D.R., however, reconsecrated the talisman, the result being that Lady [Hall] speedily recovered the whole of her former strength, and survived to the ripe old age of ninety-two.

Crowley's consecration of the 'Flashing Tablet' would have been carried out at the White Temple in his Chancery Lane flat. This was a large room, lined with huge mirrors and dedicated to the practice of white magic. Besides this there was a more sinister Black Temple in which the altar was supported by the image of a negro standing on his hands and which contained, as a sort of tutelary deity, a skeleton which Crowley anointed with blood and to which he sacrificed sparrows. Not only the black activities but those which took place in the White Temple seem, if Crowley's account of them is to be accepted, to have been productive of a sinister psychic atmosphere. One night Crowley and his friend G. C. Jones – the man who had introduced him to

the Golden Dawn – went out for dinner, locking up the White
Temple before they did so. On their return they found the door
opened, the temple furniture in disorder and magical symbols
flung about the room. Crowley and Jones restored the temple to
order and then observed that 'semi-materialized beings were
marching around the main room in almost unending procession'.[12]

Towards the end of 1899 Crowley became convinced that
unless Bennett had the funds to move to a warmer climate his
asthma would ultimately prove fatal. Although Crowley was at
the time a comparatively rich man he did not give his friend the
required sum – to do so, he felt, would have violated the occult
axiom that magical knowledge should be given, not bought.
Instead he decided to evoke on Bennett's behalf the demon
Buer, an entity whose appearance and attributes are described as
follows in the Goetia, a sixteenth-century magical text: 'He
appeareth in Sagittary, and that is his shape when the Sun is there.
He teaches Philosophy, both Moral and Natural, and the Logic
Art, and also the Virtues of all Herbs and Plants. He healeth
all distempers in man, and giveth good Familiars. He governeth
50 Legions of Spirits. . . .' Accordingly Crowley and Jones
carried out the evocation of Buer, who duly appeared not under
the appearance of the astrological symbol of Sagittarius but in the
form of a cloudy and vague figure of which only a helmeted head and
part of a leg was clearly visible. In spite of this success Bennett's
asthma continued and eventually a former mistress of Crowley
supplied the necessary funds, either as Crowley affirmed because
Buer influenced her actions in the desired way or as a later
newspaper report claimed because Crowley threatened to inform
the woman's husband of his affair with her unless she did so.

Throughout 1899 Crowley was fascinated by a late magical
text entitled The Sacred Magic of Abra-Melin the Mage which
Mathers had translated and published in 1898 with funds supplied
by F. L. Gardner. The type of ceremonial magic taught in this
volume is curiously unlike any other European text on this
subject. Its approach verges on the quietistic and is more
reminiscent of mystical religion than of the flamboyant magic
taught in such texts as the mediaeval Key of Solomon, which

demanded that the practitioner should wear strange garments, wave wands and swords, chant for many hours, draw strange geometrical figures and threaten the spirit evoked with the pains of hell. The Abra-Melin magician does not even use the traditional magic circle. Instead he is told to select and purify a 'holy place' – either an altar constructed in an isolated wood and surrounded by shrubs and flowers or a consecrated room leading on to a terrace. In this holy place the disciples of Abra-Melin are instructed to carry out the processes which supposedly lead to the attainment of 'the Knowledge and Conversation of the Holy Guardian Angel'.

For six months the devotee is instructed to follow a way of life laid down by Abra-Melin. He is to 'enflame himself with prayer', burn a particular type of incense, invoke the assistance of the Angels and read 'holy books'. Then a young child – a favourite medium of occultists from Ptolemaic Egypt to the present day because of its supposed purity of vision – is to be introduced into the proceedings. The magician and the child are to kneel before the altar on which has been set a silver plate. The Holy Guardian Angel will then manifest himself, the child seeing it write a message on the silver plate. If this six-month invocation has been properly carried out a week of extraordinary phenomena will then supposedly ensue. The Holy Guardian Angel instructs the magician how to evoke both good and evil spirits. When this has been done the magician proceeds to prepare his 'Abra-Melin talismans', mysterious lettered squares designed to produce such wonders as an ever-full purse, overwhelming sexual attractiveness and even an army of phantom soldiers.

Crowley was determined to enjoy all these things and early in 1900 took up residence in a house in Scotland, which he had found in the previous August, with the object of commencing the Abra-Melin operation at the following Easter.

Meanwhile quarrels had broken out among the adepts of the Golden Dawn; not only were a majority of them unhappy with the autocratic tone of Mathers's encyclicals from Paris but they disapproved of their chief's growing friendship for Crowley, and at the end of 1899 had shown their dislike of the latter by refusing to initiate him into the grade of Adeptus Minor – an initiation to which he was formally entitled by reason of his successful completion of the course of study laid down for members of the Outer Order. The reason for this refusal was simple enough; the London adepts had heard that Crowley was a practising homo-sexual and decided that, in the words of Yeats, a mystical society was not a moral reformatory.

Mathers was furious at the decision of the London members and showed his contempt for it by inviting Crowley over to Paris and, on 16 January 1900, initiating him as an Adeptus Minor in the Parisian temple of the order. This Adeptus Minor ritual, which was derived from Mathers's researches and not from the cipher manuscripts, was at the very least a superb piece of theatrical ritual. It combined the use of magnificent temple furniture – notably a seven-sided wooden 'Vault' with a white and gold ceiling, a black, yellow and red floor displaying the dragon of evil and walls decorated with symbols in the seven colours of the spectrum – with sonorous if somewhat mannered language and an exalted teaching. The Vault was intended as a reproduction of that of the legendary occultist Christian Rosenkreutz, and it contained both a round altar and a highly decorated coffin, always referred to in the order documents as the 'Pastos'. The high point of the ritual was the symbolic death of the Chief Adept conducting it (in the case of Crowley's initiation this would have been Mathers) and his resurrection to a new life. The underlying mystical intentions of the rite were conveyed in its second point:

Buried with that Light in a mystical death, rising again in a mystical resur-rection, cleansed and purified through Him, our master, O brother of the Cross and the Rose. Like Him, O Adepts of the Ages, have ye toiled. Like Him have ye suffered tribulation. Poverty, torture and death have ye passed through. They have been but the purification of the Gold.

In the Alembic of thine heart through the athanor [an alchemical furnace] of affliction, seek thou the true Stone of the Wise.[13]

After his initiation Crowley made his return to London, applied to the secretary of the London temple for copies of the manuscripts to which as an Adeptus Minor he was formally entitled and then went on to Scotland with the object of continuing preparations for the carrying out of the operations of Abra-Melin magic. The London Adepti Minores regarded Mathers's initiation of Crowley with great displeasure, refusing the latter copies of any manuscripts and making it clear that they did not regard him as an authentic adept. Florence Farr, who was officially Mathers's representative in London, wrote to her Chief stating that she wished to resign from this office but was prepared to carry on until a substitute was found. Mathers reacted badly to this, regarding it as indicative of disloyalty to himself, and an increasingly heated correspondence eventually followed which ultimately led to the London Adepti holding a meeting on 29 March 1900 at which they voted to depose Mathers of his headship of the order.

Mathers retorted with an extraordinary letter threatening to employ a punitive magical current against the rebels:

I have always acknowledged and shall always maintain the authority of the Secret Chiefs of the Order, to whom and the Eternal Gods I bow, but to *none* beside!

I know to a nicety the capacities of my human brain and intelligence and what these can of themselves grasp, and I therefore know also when the Forces of the Beyond and the Presences of the Infinite, manifest, and when the Great Adepts of this Planet, the Secret Chiefs of the Order are with me. . . .

You have seen the development of the Theosophical Society, and that since the death of Madame Blavatsky nothing but turmoil and strife have arisen, and that the association is tottering to its fall. And I tell you plainly that were it *possible* to remove me from my place as the Visible Head of our Order (which *cannot* be without my own consent, because of certain magical links) you would find nothing but disruption and trouble falling upon you all until you had expiated so severe a Karma as that of opposing a current sent at the end of a century to regenerate a Planet.

And for the first time since I have been connected with the Order, I shall formulate my request to Highest Chiefs for the Punitive Current to be prepared, to be directed against those who rebel; should they consider it (after examination of the Status of the London Order) advisable.

Crowley, at the time still a fanatical admirer of Mathers, wrote to Paris offering his services against the rebels, and left Scotland for London in order to investigate the situation. It was beyond his worst fears; the London temple of the Adepti, situated at 36 Blythe Road, Hammersmith, was locked against him, few of the Adepti would speak to him and those who did were either despondent about the affairs of the order or personally hostile to himself and Mathers. Thus for example Julian Baker, the man through whose introduction Crowley had been led into the Golden Dawn, described the order's documents as 'all rot', particularly the much-prized Z manuscripts.

Shortly afterwards Crowley heard from Mathers that his services were accepted and he hastened to Paris, arriving there on 9 April. Mathers authorized him to return to London as his personal representative and gave him much magical advice together with instructions on how to deal with the rebels. Crowley's instructions and material from Mathers included a list of new Chiefs for the London temple – those few adepts who had remained loyal to Mathers were to be suitably rewarded; instructions to seize the London Vault and the premises, 36 Blythe Road, at which it was held, using legal processes should these appear desirable; a new warrant for the London temple which Mathers, as the only link between the order and the Secret Chiefs, would sign in due course; and instructions to interview each adept separately and ask various questions of him and her – the answer to these questions would decide whether or not the person concerned was to be expelled from the order.

Most of the London Adepti regarded Crowley as 'an unspeakable mad person', in the words of W. B. Yeats; they declined to have interviews with him and to defeat his objects they resorted to an 'occult attack' upon him. Yeats described this attack in a letter to George Russell – the poet A.E. According to this, two or three of the rebels' most competent magicians called up on the 'astral plane' one of Crowley's mistresses and instructed her to have nothing more to do with him. Some two days later she contacted the rebels and agreed to go with them to Scotland Yard where she would give evidence of 'torture and mediaeval iniquity' on the part of Crowley. Crowley's own records give a totally different account of the results of the occult assault of which he believed he was a victim. The Rose Cross – a large multi-coloured occult symbol – which Mathers had supplied for his protection turned white; his rubber mackintosh burst into flames; he found himself losing his temper without good reason; most extraordinary of all at least five horses bolted at the sight of him.

Whatever may have been the truth about what was happening to Crowley and his opponents on a magical level there is no doubt that there was much happening in the mundane sphere of ordinary existence. First of all Crowley broke into the Blythe Road premises and seized possession of them on behalf of Mathers. Then, in the early morning of 19 April, the rebels repossessed them, changing the locks so that Crowley could not gain admittance. At 11.30 am Crowley himself arrived. He was wearing full Highland dress, had a black mask over his face, a dagger at his side and a large golden cross on his breast. This romantic appearance did nothing to overawe the rebels – instead W. B. Yeats called a policeman and had Crowley removed from the premises.

Four days later Crowley attempted to use the law against his enemies. Under the name of 'Edward Aleister', one of the many aliases he was using at the time, he took out a summons against Florence Farr alleging that she was 'unlawfully and without just cause detaining certain papers and other articles the property of the Complainant'. The case did not however come before a magistrate, probably as Ellic Howe has suggested because the property concerned was worth more than £15 and therefore such a case was not within the jurisdiction of a magistrates' court. But Crowley did have to pay £5 costs, which prompted Yeats to make the inaccurate remark that 'the other side was fined five pounds'. Crowley did not bother to take the case to a higher court.

Suddenly and quite inexplicably Crowley withdrew from the whole affair and set sail for New York. Before he did so however he paid a brief visit to Mathers in Paris. Here he found his Chief baptizing a number of dried peas with the names of the members who were in revolt. Then by 'the formulae of the Great Enochian

Tablet of Spirit', Mathers evoked the demons Beelzebub and
Typhon-Set and shaking the peas in a sieve called upon the devils
to work upon the rebels so that they might confound each other
with continual quarrels and disturbances. Crowley with his
departure to New York ended his formal connection with
Mathers and the Golden Dawn. But the influence of both was as
we shall see to persist upon him to the end of his life.

3

The Book of the Law

BETWEEN 1900 AND 1903 Crowley travelled widely, losing for a time his interest in ceremonial magic but becoming fascinated by Hindu and Buddhist philosophy. His activities and interests during this period were summed up by himself in a memorandum he wrote in May 1903.

In 1900 I left England for Mexico[1] and later the Far East, Ceylon, India, Burma, Baltistan, Egypt and France. It is idle here to detail the corresponding progress of my thought; passing through a stage of Hinduism, I had discarded all deities as being unimportant, and in philosophy was an uncompromising nominalist. I had arrived at what I may describe as the position of an orthodox Buddhist; but with the following reservations.

(1) I cannot deny that certain phenomena do accompany the use of certain rituals; I only deny the usefulness of such methods to the White Adept.

(2) I consider Hindu methods of meditation as possibly useful to the beginner and should not therefore recommend them to be discarded at once.

... as I so carefully of old, for the Magical Path, excluded from my life all other interests, that life has now no particular meaning; and the Path of Research, on the only lines I can now approve of, remains the one Path possible for me to tread.

A few months after writing the above memorandum Crowley got married to Rose Kelly, sister of Gerald Kelly, a friend of Crowley's who was ultimately to become Sir Gerald Kelly, President of the Royal Academy. Their honeymoon, which extended over several months of globe-trotting, was in Crowley's own words an 'uninterrupted beatitude'. In the course of it they spent a night in the King's Chamber of the Great Pyramid and

Crowley carried out his first attempt at ceremonial magic for several years – he wanted Rose, not the most intelligent of women, to understand what Western occultism was all about. By the light of a single guttering candle on the edge of the royal coffer Crowley read aloud the Preliminary Invocation of the *Goetia*.[2] As Crowley chanted the words of magic power – '*Modorio: Phalarthao: Doo: Ape:*' – he noticed that he was no longer stooping towards the candle to read the words. He realized that the whole chamber was glowing with 'astral light' of a pale lilac colour. Blowing out the candle he continued to read the invocation by means of the mystic illumination; after he had finished it remained, though lessening in intensity.

After a visit to the Far East Crowley and his wife returned to Egypt in February 1900. They were posing as Persian aristocrats, calling themselves Prince and Princess Chioa Khan for no better reason, as Crowley himself admitted in his *Confessions*, than to swagger about in Eastern robes and have 'gorgeous runners' clearing the path for their carriage through the streets of Cairo.

This tendency to adopt curious aliases which recurred throughout Crowley's life – at various times he called himself by such names as 'Lord Boleskine', 'Oliver Haddo' and 'Count Vladimir Svareff' – may have been imitative of both MacGregor Mathers (who eventually called himself Comte MacGregor of Glenstrae) and of other occultists, such as Cagliostro and St Germain, who went under numerous false names at different periods of their lives. On the other hand, while one must not underestimate Crowley's life-long and habitual imitation of doings of well-known occultists of the past, his changes of name may have had a deeper cause and been indicative of a well established psychological insecurity about the nature of his own identity.

In the middle of March 1904 the two took up residence in a Cairo apartment. Once again Crowley dabbled in magic in order to please his wife; he recited an invocation in order to enable her to 'see the sylphs', the elemental spirits of water. Rose saw nothing, but got into a curious dream-like state in which she kept repeating 'They are waiting for you', '[it is] All about the child', and 'It is all Osiris'.

Crowley, desiring to know more, invoked the god Thoth,[3] the Egyptian Lord of Wisdom, and Rose, still in a trance-like state, informed him that the 'waiter' was the god Horus whom, she said, Crowley had offended and should invoke. She added details of how this invocation should be carried out; these were magically unorthodox and Crowley was suspicious of their validity as they seemed to break the principles of invocation as he had learnt them in the Golden Dawn. Nevertheless, he went ahead, carrying out the rite on both 19 and 20 March. The results achieved on the latter day were startling, Crowley receiving a psychic message that a new epoch in man's history had come, that he was destined to be its prophet and that he was intended to act as a link between 'the solar-spiritual force' and humanity. Rose, whom Crowley was by now calling 'Ouarda the Seer' – although she knew little of occultism and cared less – gave him a further message from the gods. He was to sit down for an hour between noon and 1 pm on each of three days, 8, 9 and 10 April, and would then receive a 'direct voice' message from the gods of the new age that was dawning.

During the three days Crowley wrote down *The Book of the Law*, a daemonic prose-poem in three short chapters, much of its content written in a heavily jewelled prose strongly reminiscent of some of the writers of the 1890s:

. . . if under the night-stars in the desert thou presently burnest mine incense before me, invoking me with a pure heart, and the Serpent flame therein, thou shalt come a little to lie in my bosom. For one kiss wilt thou then be willing to give all; but whoso gives one particle of dust shall lose all in that hour. Ye shall gather goods and store of women and spices; ye shall wear rich jewels; ye shall exceed the nations of the earth in splendour and pride; but always in the love of me, and so shall ye come to my joy. . . . Pale or purple, veiled or voluptuous, I who am all pleasure and purple, and drunkenness of the innermost sense, desire you. Put on the wings, and arouse the coiled splendour within you; come unto me!

A full exegesis of *The Book of the Law* would be beyond my powers. Indeed it was beyond Crowley's for, although he wrote two lengthy commentaries on the work, he affirmed to the end of his life that certain parts of it were beyond his understanding.

Nevertheless the basic message of *The Book of the Law* can be easily summarized. Crowley is to be the prophet of a new age, 'the Aeon of Horus'. The religion of this new age will be Crowleyanity – Buddhism, Islam and Christianity, religions of the slave-gods, will all be overthrown. The basic moral principles of the new age are to be complete self-fulfilment, for 'Every man and woman is a star' – that is, each human entity is a unique individual with a right to develop in his or her own way – and 'Do what thou wilt shall be the whole of the law', for 'Thou hast no right but to do thy will' and 'The word of Sin is restriction'. Crowley was always careful to point out that 'Do what thou wilt' was not 'Do what you like'; what this injunction meant, so he said, was 'find the way of life that is compatible with your innermost desires and live it to the full'.

The Book of the Law made clear that the new religion it taught was not for everyone, but only for 'the kingly men' as distinguished from those with a slave-mentality: 'These are dead, these fellows; they feel not. We are not for the poor and sad; the lords of the earth are our kinsfolk. We have nothing with the outcast and the unfit: let them die in their misery. For they feel not. Compassion is the vice of kings: stamp down the wretched and the weak: this is the law of the strong: this is our law and the joy of the world.'

As well as teaching the new faith and its moral principles *The Book of the Law* contained certain parts that seemed meaningless ('ALGMOR3YX24 89 RPSTOVAL') and others that were vaguely prophetic. For instance: 'I am the warrior Lord of the Forties; the Eighties cower before me, and are abased. I will bring you to victory and joy: I will be at your arms in battle and ye shall delight to slay. Success is your proof; courage is your armour; go on, go on, in my strength; and ye shall not turn back for any!' Some occultists influenced by Crowley have argued that the first clause of this passage is an accurate prediction of the world and cold wars that occupied all the forties of the present century. The rest of the passage, so it is argued, prophesies another world war in the 1980s, a war from which only those who accept *The Book of the Law* will emerge triumphantly.

Who was the real author of *The Book of the Law*? Was it consciously written by Crowley himself in an attempt to foist a new-forged gospel upon the world? Or was it an emanation of some part of Crowley's unconscious mind? Or was it, as Crowley asserted, a communication from those whom the Golden Dawn called Secret Chiefs, delivered through the medium of a spiritual entity called Aiwass or Aiwaz? There seems no doubt that the first possibility must be dismissed. For it is certain that Crowley believed that the text of the work was quite literally inspired and that the new religion of Crowleyanity was destined to replace all existing religions for the next two thousand years or so.

The next possibility, that in *The Book of the Law* an aspect of Crowley's own unconscious was speaking to him, must be taken more seriously. For in spite of the fact that he argued that the book was totally different from his own style, and that he found some passages of it 'rambling and unintelligible' and others 'repugnant to reason by their absurdity' or 'abhorrent to the heart' because of their 'barbaric ferocity', there is no doubt that some of Crowley's more 'inspirational' published writings bore stylistic similarities to *The Book of the Law*. Examples of this similarity can be easily found in his *Liber VII* which abounds in such strange verses as: 'O all ye toads and cats, rejoice! Ye slimy things come hither! Dance, dance to the Lord our God.' This interpretation of the work is strengthened by the fact that it contains many sections which derive from, or are at least completely compatible with, the occult teachings of the Golden Dawn. Thus, as the depth-analyst and occultist Israel Regardie has pointed out in his fascinating book *The Eye in the Triangle*, there are 'innumerable subtle references to Qabalah and Tarot – all contents of Crowley's mind, materials derived from the Order which shaped his life'.

Crowley of course would have denied that the teachings of the Golden Dawn influenced those of *The Book of the Law*. He would simply have argued that there was a necessary compatibility between the two because both originated from the same Secret Chiefs. He always denied that it was any aspect of himself that was responsible for the book and its moral and occult teachings. It was

a message, he argued, from superhuman beings, call them gods
or Secret Chiefs, and it had been delivered to him by Aiwass,
who was none other than his personal Holy Guardian Angel. In a
letter he wrote towards the end of his life he explained that this
Angel was, so he believed, not a dissociated part of his own
personality but a spiritual entity in its own right: '. . . the Angel
is an actual Individual, with his own Universe, exactly as a man
is; or, for the matter of that, a bluebottle. He is not a mere
abstraction, a selection from, and exaltation of, one's own
favourite qualities. . . . He is something more than a man,
possibly a being who has already passed through the stage of
humanity, and his peculiarly intimate relation with his client is
that of friendship, of community, of brotherhood or fatherhood.'

Many occultists and magicians who admire Crowley and his
religion of 'Force and Fire' have argued that it is in a sense unimportant whether Aiwass was an individual being or merely an
aspect of Crowley's own mind for, in the words of Israel
Regardie, 'It makes very little difference in the long run whether
the Book was dictated by a praeterhuman intelligence named
Aiwass or whether it stemmed from the creative deeps of
Aleister Crowley. The Book was written. And he became the
mouthpiece for the *Zeitgeist*, accurately expressing the intrinsic
nature of our time as no one else has done to date'.

After the dictation of *The Book of the Law* Crowley and his wife
returned to their Scottish home. From there Crowley issued a
sort of magical encyclical to G. C. Jones and his other occult
associates announcing the reception of the book and the beginning of the new aeon. Simultaneously he wrote to Mathers
announcing that the Secret Chiefs had deposed him from his
office of visible head of the Golden Dawn and appointed him,
Crowley, in his place. To this he added the information that a new
magical system based on *The Book of the Law* had replaced that
taught in the Golden Dawn.

Not surprisingly, no answer was received. Or at least no answer
on an ordinary level. But some of Crowley's bloodhounds died,
his servants fell ill and a workman doing a job in the house
experienced an acute attack of mania in the course of which he

attacked Rose. Crowley attributed all these events to the
machination of Mathers who, he was convinced, had launched a
black magical attack against him. All Crowley's admiration for
his former chief turned to bitter hatred. In May 1904 he was
writing a memorandum on what action should be taken to
destroy Mathers: '. . . a special task, find a man who can go to
entrap Mathers. Let him read Lévi; then go.' Soon Crowley was
invoking Beelzebub and his forty-nine servitors to consecrate
talismans aimed against Mathers and his followers. Presumably
the rite was successful, for Rose, who by this time was developing
either clairvoyance or delusions, saw Beelzebub's assistants and
gave descriptions of their appearance. These were uniformly
nasty; Nimorup for example appeared as a stunted dwarf with
greenish-bronze, slobbery lips, while Holastri appeared as a
giant pink bug and Nominon as a large red jellyfish with one
luminous green spot.

Beelzebub defended Crowley and his wife successfully;
Mathers's assaults ended and Crowley rapidly lost his resumed
interest in ceremonial magic. Before he did so however he issued
a pirated edition of Mathers's version of the *Goetia* to which he
prefaced a note claiming that Mathers had 'succumbed unhappily
to the assaults of the *Four Great Princes* (acting notably under
Martial influences)' and that Mathers and his wife had had their
own souls displaced by those of two occult charlatans who called
themselves Mr and Mrs Horos and had been engaged in running
a bogus occult order in London's Gower Street. Crowley
insisted that a clairvoyant investigation had confirmed the truth
of this spiritual diagnosis: 'The investigation of a competent
Skryer', he wrote, 'into the house of our unhappy Brother,
confirmed this divination; neither our Brother nor his Hermetic
wife were there seen; but only the terrible shapes of the evil
Adepts . . . whose original bodies having been sequestered by
Justice,[4] were no longer of use to them.'[5]

For a time Crowley not only lost interest in magic but in *The
Book of the Law* and its new gospel of which he was to be the
prophet. Although he had retained a typescript of the work the
original manuscript was regarded by him as being of so little

importance that he mislaid it, accidentally rediscovering it in July 1909 when he was searching his loft for some magical paintings – curious multi-coloured, lettered squares which the initiates of the Golden Dawn referred to as 'the Elemental Watchtowers of Dr Dee'. By 1910, as we shall see, *The Book of the Law* had mastered Crowley; from then until his death in 1947 he was to conduct his occult life in accordance with its precepts.

4

Towards the Silver Star

IN 1907 CROWLEY's interest in Western magic, as distinct from oriental mysticism, once more revived. Two important events dominated the occult life of Crowley in that year. The first was the foundation of an occult fraternity – a magician, as John Symonds has remarked needs an order as a politician needs a party – which its creator called the Silver Star or more usually the AA, these initials being those of the Latin equivalent of the title of the fraternity. The second was the composition of the 'Holy Books', curious works which were regarded as being particularly important by Crowley and destined to become holy writ for the members of his new magical order.

These books were produced by a process which was neither under the control of Crowley's conscious mind, nor bore any resemblance to the way in which *The Book of the Law* had been dictated. Presumably they were the result of something very like the automatic writing which is such a familiar form of mediumship and were therefore a reflection, or a regurgitation, of the contents of Crowley's unconscious mind. It is therefore interesting to note that their form and style are reminiscent of both that of *The Book of the Law* and some prose-poems of the 1890s. He described how he felt while writing down these books:

> The perfume of Pan pervading, the taste of him utterly filling my mouth, so that the tongue breaks forth into a weird and monstrous speech.
>
> The embrace of him intense on every centre of pain and pleasure.
>
> The sixth interior sense aflame with the inmost self of Him.
>
> Myself flung down the precipice of being even to the abyss, annihilation.

An end to loneliness as to all.
Pan! Pan! Io Pan! Io Pan!

At first Crowley and G. C. Jones were the only members of
the AA, and as the latter played no active part in the life of the
order, Crowley reigned in solitary splendour. Soon however he
acquired two disciples: Captain J. F. C. Fuller, a young infantry
officer who was eventually to become a major-general, an expert
on tank warfare and a personal friend of Adolf Hitler,[1] and Victor
Neuburg, a young poet who had been brought up as an orthodox
Jew but had become an agnostic. Fuller had originally met
Crowley as a result of writing *The Star in the West* (1907), a study
of Crowley's prose and poetry which contained such purple
passages of gross adulation as:

> Crowley is more than a new born Dionysus, he is more than a Blake, a
> Rabelais or a Heine; for he stands before us as some priest of Apollo, hovering
> betwixt the misty blue of the heavens, and the more serious purple of the vast
> waters of the deep.
>
> It has taken 100,000,000 years to produce Aleister Crowley. The world has
> indeed laboured, and has at last brought forth a man.

Fuller was friendly with Neuburg, who was from 1906 to 1909
a Cambridge undergraduate, having met him at the house of
W. S. Ross, an agnostic editor who called himself 'Saladin'. In
1909, at Fuller's suggestion, Crowley visited Neuburg's Cambridge rooms and introduced himself. Neuburg found in
Crowley everything he had been looking for in life and was
immediately captivated by the latter's personality, poetry and
above all magic. Indeed it would not be going too far to say that
Neuburg fell in love with Crowley, in whose Order of the Silver
Star he immediately became a Probationer. He looked upon
Crowley as his Guru, his holy teacher, of whom he was proud to
be a chela, or pupil.

Crowley decided that Neuburg must make a ten-day 'magical
retirement', that is, follow an intensive crash-course in practical
occultism, and to that end in June 1909 took him to stay at his
Scottish home. In the morning after his arrival at Boleskine, as
Crowley's house was called, Neuburg was taken to the room

which was to be his temple. Its floor was marked out with a
magic circle within which stood an altar with incense burning
upon it. A reserve of incense was supplied, as were a magic
sword and a ceremonial robe for Neuburg to wear. The temple
was cold; for a time Neuburg walked about aimlessly, then he
paced about the magic circle chanting words which welled up
from his subconscious – something about seven gods above and
seven below. It struck him that he ought to carry out the
Golden Dawn Banishing Ritual, a simple ceremony involving the
tracing of pentagrams in the air, which Crowley had instructed
him should precede any occult working. He tried to do this with
the sword, but found that there was not enough space to do so.
Finally he sat down in a yogic posture, reciting aloud the mantra
(mystical phrase) '*Aum sat tat aum*'; after a time he fell into a
trance, experiencing visions of sea and sky, and was still in this
state when called down to lunch.

As the days went by Neuburg received, or at least thought he
received, deeper and deeper illuminations. These he recorded in
his occult diary, his 'magic record', a document which conveys
with great clarity the techniques to which Crowley subjected his
pupils:

June 21, 5.2 am

Performed 'Bornless One' Ritual about 10 pm. At midnight, Banishing
Ritual.[2]

At about 1.30 am my Guru entered and gave me certain advice. At about
2.25 I performed 'Bornless One' and Banishing Rituals, afterwards rising on the
planes.

By 'rising on the planes', he meant a technique of astral
projection – that is getting the consciousness free of the physical
body and using it to explore the astral world – which Crowley had
taken from the Golden Dawn. The method involved imagining
a second, or astral, body situated some distance away from the
physical body, transferring one's consciousness to it, the most
difficult part of the operation, and then rising on the planes,
that is, imagining one's new body rising at right angles to the
physical earth until it reached the wondrous sights and sounds
of the astral world, with its angelic beings and its strange land-

scapes. Put in occult terminology the whole process sounds like a piece of esoteric gobbledygook to the non-occultist. As Dr Israel Regardie has pointed out however rising on the planes can also be expressed in psychological terms as an example of what Jung called 'creative fantasy' and regarded as an excellent mode of attaining self-awareness.

Neuburg's record goes on to describe his adventures in the astral world:

> I travelled up swiftly and easily again meeting 'Gabriel'. . . . He was clad in white with green spots upon his wings; upon his head was a Maltese Cross.
>
> After some time I slept by the fire, awakening at about 4.25. I suffered two emissions of semen (possibly one only; I am not quite sure) with somatic dreams.

To this record Neuburg added his explanation of why he had had these involuntary sexual climaxes – it was some combination of sleeping close to the fire with lack of food and exercise. In fact it seems more likely that he found both the practise of magical rites and the presence of Crowley sexually stimulating; later as we shall see the two magicians were to enjoy a homosexual relationship.

Neuburg's record continues:

> I again performed the 'Bornless One' Ritual about 4.30. I left the Chamber just after 5 am.
>
> It is now 5.10; I am tired out and after performing the Banishing Ritual I shall go to bed.

After meticulously recording such details as what he had for breakfast Neuburg went back into the temple at 9.30 am. 'Midday. Almost immediately on reaching the Chamber did I perform the Preliminary Invocation. I then meditated on myself for an hour, sometimes reading *Thelema*.' By *Thelema* Neuburg meant either *The Book of the Law* or much less likely one of the 'Holy Books' mentioned at the beginning of this chapter. Neuburg's record went on:

> Just after 11 am I performed the Banishing Ritual, the Preliminary Ritual, burnt incense, recited *Aum Mani Padme Hum*, and rose upon the planes. I went very far indeed. Early I met my Angel. I slew him. I then rose through many

planes; eventually I was detained by my Mother, a huge brown woman, my Father, a little green man, a voluptuous woman, and an hermaphrodite. They sought one by one to detain me. I passed them all.

At length I reached a coffin labelled

RESURGAM

OF THE TENTH SPHERE

I was now forcibly drawn into this, but escaped into a whirlpool of light, wherein I was utterly absorbed. Rapidly I sank back, reaching my body at about 11.25.

Then did I meditate and read *Thelema*. . . .

After this Neuburg read 'a certain book of Magic' he had with him, meditated and had lunch. Afterwards Crowley joined him in the temple where they talked 'of Magic and other matters'. At 4.40 pm Neuburg again experimented with astral projection, this time with alarming results:

I rose on the planes, reaching rapidly the white light. I struggled through to the top where I was crucified by two angels. I threw the angels off with the Pentagram, then I floated about in space helplessly, attached to the Cross. This also I got rid of by the Pentagram.

I reached soon after a fountain or whirlpool of red light; struggling through this, I was confronted by a Red Giant against whom I was powerless, though I attacked him furiously by every means in my power. All my weapons and words were useless against him. He cut me to pieces and chased me back to my body, effectually preventing me from rising by falling upon me every time I strove to rise.

I had rather great difficulty in arranging myself in my body after my return, failing once or twice in the effort. At length however, I accomplished the feat successfully.

If Neuburg was unable to cope with the 'Red Giant', and the dissociation of consciousness presumably indicated by his difficulty in arranging himself in his body, Crowley felt that he knew the way to handle beings of this order and wrote a footnote to Neuburg's record: 'Concerning Red Giants. I will teach thee the sign and god-forms necessary.' These signs and god-forms took the form of two magical gestures derived from the Golden Dawn, the 'Sign of Horus' and the 'Sign of Harpocrates'; the first involved leaning forward while stretching out the arms, the second the placing of the left forefinger on the lip.

In the evening Neuburg slept until 10.30 pm when Crowley awoke him, dowsed his head with cold water and instructed him how to deal with Red Giants. Almost immediately Neuburg commenced an experiment in rising on the planes:

> I rose at once, slaying the Red Giant with the Harpocrates formula; then I slew a Black Giant. I then became a green triangle (apex upwards) in a violet crown or circle; then a blazing comet flaring in the hair of a God; then a flaming star. After this I became absorbed in and identified with white light. This experience was accompanied by extreme ecstasy.
>
> I now found myself at the Court of Horus (he was jet-black), who gave me two tablets inscribed INRI and TARO respectively. I now found that I had no hands: they were severed at the wrists. Horus sent me out to gaze at the clear blue heavens, wherein were myriads of stars. He pointed upwards; I could not mount any higher though I tried (or someone tried for me) to attach the sword and the *ankh* to my feet.

From 11.15 pm to 12.30 am Crowley gave magical instruction to Neuburg. Presumably this was on the subject of astral projection, for as soon as the instruction was over Neuburg made another attempt at this after Crowley had carried out the preliminary rites on his behalf.

> June 22. 1.28 am I have again risen on the planes, the preliminaries being performed by Most Excellent Guru. I rose to a great height, far beyond the Court of Horus. I began rising at about 12.50. I had many adventures, passing by crowds of beings, most of whom gave me passage on my presenting my Chief's card, as it were, though many of them ignored me altogether, turning their backs upon me. Three incidents stand out prominently.
>
> I reached a fair garden where there was an enormous, white-clad angel, who gave the impression of Gabriel. He spoke to me, wishing me to leave my sword and *ankh*. I refused, and he suffered me to depart with them; all I can remember of his speech is, 'Thine is the destiny of the Magi'.
>
> Afterwards I passed through strata, as it were, of the four elements, later reaching a kind of green globe, around which I floated in a little boat with a fair woman; at or about this time I was in a slight state of ecstasy. I would here remark in parenthesis that my physical feet became very painful during this rising, probably because I was in my Japanese yoga posture for an hour or more, I think, inclusive of the time in which my Guru was invoking, etc.

By 'my Japanese yoga posture' Neuburg meant that he was kneeling while sitting back on his heels. The magical record continues: 'Eventually, after many minor adventures – passing through funnels, voids and so on – I reached a hawk-shaped creature who cut off my hands and feet. I fell back, and had the greatest difficulty in returning. I performed the Harpocrates formula, and lay prostrate on the floor for several minutes, being apparently unable to rise.' Worried by this Neuburg summoned Crowley, who urged him to repeat the Sign of Harpocrates. This he did, this time with satisfactory results.

Performing rising on the planes on the next day his vision began at the place where his hands and feet had been cut off on the previous day. He made his way to a temple – curiously enough he remarked that he had known it 'all his life' – where a maiden first sacrificed him upon an altar and then raised him to life again by uttering certain magical formulae over his body. He had many other adventures on this astral journey, one of which well illustrates his ambisexuality: 'I was tempted by a little black boy drawing water from a stream, and a fair woman. I succumbed – O virtuous one! – to the temptations of neither.'

At about ten in the evening a curious episode took place, an incident which seems to have been an indication that, under the guise of a teacher-pupil relationship and quite probably unconsciously, the two magicians were living out a sado-masochistic fantasy. 'My Guru', wrote Neuburg, 'was dissatisfied, upbraiding me bitterly for being among the Qlipoth.' The Qlipoth, literally 'harlots', are the evil and adverse spheres of the kabalistic symbol known as the 'Tree of Life'. Crowley did more than upbraid him – he gave him 'thirty-two strokes with a gorse-switch which drew blood'. According to Neuburg the carrying out of this 'ceremony' afforded his teacher obvious satisfaction. Neuburg reacted by laughing, a response which Crowley thought, probably correctly, indicated a certain masochism.

Other sado-masochistic events took place. One night, for example Crowley came to Neuburg's room and beat him on the buttocks with stinging nettles. On another occasion Crowley resorted to verbal sadism, making anti-semitic remarks and sneering at Neuburg's Jewishness. This made more impact than the physical violence:

> My worthy Guru is unnecessarily rude and brutal. I know not why. Probably he does not know himself. He is apparently brutal merely to amuse himself and pass the time away.
>
> Anyhow, I won't stick it any more.
>
> It seems to me that unnecessary and brutal rudeness is a prerogative of a cad of the lowest type. It is the very limit of meanness to grouse at a man because of his race. The 'argument' is, I admit, unanswerable to the accused; it is also inexcusable in the accuser. It is ungenerous also to abuse one's position as a Guru: it is like striking an inferior who will be ruined if he retaliates. Were it not for my Vow, I would not stay longer under my Guru's roof. I will not have my family and race perpetually insulted.

It is tempting, particularly if one is a person who has some admiration for Crowley as an occult teacher, to explain the offensive remarks he made to Neuburg merely as an attempt to use brutal methods to get a strong psychic reaction and not an indication of a deep-rooted anti-semitism. There is evidence however that Crowley quite often jeered at Jews for the crime of being Jewish. He once claimed that the Jew often possesses the bad qualities for which he is supposedly disliked, and in 1937 he wrote a scurrilous letter, reeking of cheap anti-semitism, about Israel Regardie. To be fair to Crowley it must be admitted that there was a good deal of anti-semitism in Victorian and Edwardian England – one thinks of the writing of Belloc and Chesterton – and that Crowley could not completely escape being a man of his own time. All things considered however one is forced to accept the conclusion that Crowley was, as Neuburg said, being 'caddish' when he subjected his pupil to racial abuse.

On day eight of his ten-day retirement Neuburg passed through that dark phase which some mystics have called 'spiritual dryness'. He came to the conclusion that all existence was un-interrupted misery. He could see no end to this unhappiness for, as a believer in reincarnation – during his retirement he believed that he had recovered some memories of previous lives including one of being burned at the stake – he believed that his soul would go on for all eternity; unlike Crowley he could not accept the idea that one day his central self would dissolve into the blissful ocean of nirvana.

Crowley was impressed with this gloom and doom, seeing it as a foreshadowing of the initiation of the Exempt Adept, the person freed from the wheel of birth and death. This reaction from his Guru pleased Neuburg, who ended his ten-day record on an optimistic note. It is unlikely that Neuburg's cheerfulness lasted for long for his teacher followed up the end of the ten-day retirement with another sadistic episode; for ten nights Neuburg had to sleep naked on a bed made up of the prickly branches of furze. Apart from the pain inflicted by these, the cold was intense, and Neuburg's biographer, Jean Overton Fuller, has suggested that it was these ten days of misery which implanted the seeds of the tuberculosis that was to kill him thirty years later.

Neuburg's record[3] tells us a good deal about both Crowley and himself apart from the fact that the latter had a pleasant style. Firstly it is clear that both men had strongly sado-masochistic elements in their make-up – even in the brutal discipline inflicted by Zen Buddhist masters on their pupils there is nothing to compare with the incidents when Crowley beat his pupil with gorse and nettles. Secondly it is apparent that Neuburg had both an enormous respect for Crowley as a teacher and was in love with him; on no other hypotheses can one explain either Neuburg remaining in a house where he was continually subjected to anti-semitic remarks or his agreement to spend ten nights naked on a bed of gorse. Finally Neuburg's success in rising on the planes and his remarkable astral visions make it clear that either like Blake he possessed that form of eidetic vision which enabled him to 'see' anything he thought of, or – as perhaps an occultist would say – he had 'the soul of a natural magician'.

After Neuburg's ten days of sleeping on gorse he and Crowley made their way to London. Here Neuburg's task was to help his teacher in preparing the second number of the *Equinox*, a bulky twice-yearly magazine of which Crowley had brought out the first issue in the preceding March.

While Neuburg was staying with Crowley he met the latter's

wife, Rose. She was, he later confided to his friend Hayter Preston, 'sunken in drink, a virtual dipsomaniac'. Neuburg's judgement was correct. Rose had been drinking heavily for two or three years; in five months of 1907 she had run up a bill for 159 bottles of whisky with one supplier alone. Even if Crowley had been an ideal husband no marriage could have survived happily for very long on this basis: clearly Rose had become a thoroughly unsatisfactory wife. On the other hand Crowley, with his perpetual wanderings off for months at a time and his dealings with Secret Chiefs, had always been an unsatisfactory, one might say impossible, husband.

In 1909 the marriage came to its inevitable end when Rose divorced Crowley – on evidence supplied by him – for adultery. Fortunately the two were considered to be domiciled in Scotland and thus eligible for a divorce under the laws of that country, for at the time the law of England did not allow for divorce on the grounds of the husband's adultery.

After her divorce Rose continued to drink heavily and, in September 1911, was certified as insane by reason of alcoholic dementia. 'Dried out' in the mental hospital to which she was confined she made a good recovery, was released and married a Dr Gormley – a pious Catholic whose moral scruples about marrying a divorced woman were overcome by the discovery that the Church considered Rose's marriage to Crowley null and void because the latter had been baptised according to an incomplete, and therefore defective, formula. After a time, however, heavy drinking on Rose's part made this marriage, like the one to Crowley, thoroughly unhappy. Eventually she died of alcoholism and the fatty degeneration of the liver so often associated with it.

5

Choronzon

THE *Equinox*, No. 2, containing much poetry, occult lore and the first instalment of an occult biography of Crowley written by J. F. C. Fuller, and quite as full of admiration for its subject as his *The Star in the West*, appeared on 21 September 1909. Neuburg had virtually edited this issue and after his work upon it was finished he and Crowley set off for a holiday in North Africa, arriving in Algiers on 17 November. They took a tram to Arba and from there walked south through the desert to Aumale. There in a primitive hotel Crowley heard a voice urging him 'to call Me'; it was the same voice which had dictated *The Book of the Law*.

With him Crowley had some notebooks dealing with a curious magical system called, variously, 'Enochian magic', 'Angelic magic' and 'the magic of the Thirty Aires'. Enochian magic is a strange subject, bearing not much resemblance to any other aspect of what has been called by occultists 'the Western esoteric tradition'. It originated with Dr Dee, Queen Elizabeth's astrologer and his clairvoyant Edward Kelley. The latter had gazed into a 'shew-stone' – which in this connection seems to have meant a polished black mirror rather than a crystal ball – and seen a number of spirits who had dictated various messages to him. Some of these messages were clear enough; Dee and Kelley were urged for example to enjoy one another's wives. Others were more obscure, delivered in splendid Elizabethan English and having a good deal of resemblance to sixteenth-century translations of some Old Testament prophets: 'I am the daughter of

Fortitude, and ravished every hour, from my youth. For, behold, I am Understanding, and Science dwelleth in me; the heavens oppress me, they covet and desire me with infinite appetite: few or none that are earthly have embraced me, for I am shadowed with the Circle of the Stone. . . .'

Most mysterious of all were nineteen 'Keyes' or 'Calls' – that is invocations – given in an unknown language, usually called Enochian. Some occultists have claimed that this unknown tongue was known in fifteenth-century Florence, others that it was the speech of lost Atlantis; no one however has been able to find definite traces of it before Dee and Kelley. In the Golden Dawn great importance was attached to Enochian and it was believed that eighteen of the Calls were designed to invoke the Angels of various magic squares while the purpose of the last was to invoke one or other of thirty Aires, these being considered by Mathers and his disciples as new dimensions of consciousness.[1] Strangely enough, while all the Adepti of the Golden Dawn were taught about the thirty Aires and the Call which supposedly removed the minds of their users to these Aires, no one ever seems to have practised the technique save Crowley[2] who in Mexico in 1900 had invoked the two outermost Aires – the thirtieth and twenty-ninth – with some success. His psyche had entered a vast crystal cube in the form of the god Harpocrates and this cube had been surrounded by a sphere guarded by four black-robed Archangels.

One of the notebooks Crowley had with him in North Africa contained the nineteenth Call, that is, the one that gained entrance to the thirty Aires: '*Madriaax Ds Praf* [the name of the Aire] *Chis Micaobz Saanir Caosgo Od Fisis Babzizras Iaida! Nonca Gohulim: Micma Adoian Mad, Iaod Bliorb, Soba Ooaona Chis Luciftias Piripsol. Ds Abraassa Noncf Netaaib Caosgi. . . .*' In the translation supplied by Dee and Kelley[3] this reads: '*The Heavens which dwell in* [the name of the Aire] *Are Mighty in the Parts of the Earth And execute the Judgment of the highest! Unto you it is said: Behold the Face of your God, The Beginnings of Comfort, Whose Eyes are the Brightness of the Heavens, Which Provided You for the Government of Earth. . . .*'

Presumably taking the presence of the nineteenth Call in his rucksack as something more than fortuitous – perhaps as a message from the gods – Crowley decided to begin where he had left off in Mexico nine years before and make a clairvoyant examination of the remaining twenty-eight Aires, starting at the last numbered and working backwards to the first. The method he chose for making this examination was simple enough and was as follows: with him he had a vermilion-painted Calvary Cross – that is, the type of cross familiarly encountered in Christian churches – with a large topaz set in it at the meeting place of the vertical and horizontal bar. This stone was engraved with an equal-armed cross charged with a rose of forty-nine petals.[4] He would find a quiet place, hold the cross in his hand and make the Call. If all went well his consciousness would immediately enter a new dimension; what he saw there and the psychological sensations he experienced he would describe aloud (for his physical body was unaffected by the alterations in consciousness) and Neuburg would write down this description. Usually one Aire was called each day but this was not always so; thus on 28 November 1909 both the twenty-third and twenty-second Aires were called.

Most of the visions perceived by Crowley were apocalyptic in nature, but they were, so Crowley thought, more than merely apocalyptic, rather they were indications of a great initiation to come. Take for example the nineteenth Aire. The emphasis of this was on death – but Crowley interpreted this death as the ego-extinction of nirvana:

Now at last cometh forth the Angel of the Aethyr [an alternative name for an Aire] who is like the Angel of the fourteenth key of Rota [this means the tarot trump numbered fourteen] with beautiful blue wings, blue robes, the sun in her girdle like a brooch, and the two crescents of the moon shapen into sandals for her feet. . . .

She comes and kisses me on the mouth, and says: Blessed art thou who have beheld Sebek my Lord in his glory. Many are the champions of life, but all are unhorsed by the lance of death. Many are the children of the light, but their eyes shall be put out by the Mother of Darkness. . . . I am the veiled one that sitteth between the pillars veiled with a shining veil [an allusion to the tarot trump called the High Priestess] and on my lap is the open Book of the mysteries of the ineffable Light. I am the aspiration unto the higher; I am the love of the unknown; I am the blind ache within the heart of man. I am the minister of the sacrament of pain. . . . I am the Priestess of the Silver Star [the esoteric Golden Dawn name for the High Priestess tarot trump].

And she catches me up to her as a mother catches her babe, and holds me up in her left arm, and sets my lips to her breast. And upon her breast is written: *Rosa Mundi est Lilium Coeli*[5] [the Rose of the World is the Lily of Heaven].

Crowley interpreted the appearance of this Angel as a promise that this being would be his personal guide through a coming initiation. In the following Aire, the Angel ceremonially prepared him for this initiation while in the seventeenth he was given, so he said, a profound understanding of the occult doctrine of equilibrium which made him realize that all movement and change is a falling away from perfection and that for further magical progress he must destroy his ego-personality. The following Aire, the sixteenth, explained how this should be done; he must become one with the infinite. In the fifteenth Aire he spiritually underwent a ritual initiation in the course of which he was formally promoted to the grade of Master of the Temple. This was a giant step; Crowley was now himself one of the Secret Chiefs from whom the knowledge and techniques of the Golden Dawn and other occult societies were derived. He was still only in name a Master of the Temple however; the new grade could only become a full reality when he had obtained access to the further Aires.

Crowley found great difficulty in entering the fourteenth Aire, called at Mount Dal'leh Addin between 2.50 pm and 3.15 pm on 3 December. He tore aside veil after veil of blackness while a great voice tolled: 'There is no light or knowledge or beauty or stability in the Kingdom of the Grave, whither thou goest. All that thou wast hath he eaten up, and all that thou art is his pasture until tomorrow. And all thou shalt be is nothing. Thou who wouldst enter the domain of the Great One of the Night of Time [the esoteric Golden Dawn name for the tarot trump numbered 21], this burden thou must take up.'[6]

In spite of all Crowley's efforts he could not tear away the veils that hampered him and reach the heart of the fourteenth

Aire. He and Neuburg had begun their descent from the mount when Crowley was seized with an impulse to carry out a ritual homosexual act with his fellow magician and dedicate it to the god Pan. They went back to the top of the mount, arranged large stones in a magic circle, which they protected with 'words of power' written in the sand, and erected a rough stone altar. On this, Crowley said, he sacrificed himself in a way which consumed every particle of his ego – in other words he deliberately humiliated himself by being Neuburg's passive partner in an act of buggery. This almost casual act of sex done in honour of Pan produced a change in Crowley's way of thinking; he had felt for a long time that all sexual acts were harmless to the occultist, that they did not hamper his or her relationship with the gods, but from now on he believed that sex could be positively helpful, that it could become a sacrament, a rite performed to the glory of the gods.

That evening at 9.50 pm the sex act of the afternoon produced 'a great wonder'; Crowley returned to the Aire and again the blackness surrounded him, but this time the Angel muttered the magical word that admitted him to the company of the Masters of the Temple. He saw before him what seemed to be a circle of rocks, which he suddenly realized to be veiled Masters sitting absolutely still and silent. Then the Angel spoke to him:

Behold where thine Angel hath led thee! Thou didst ask fame, power and pleasure, health and wealth and love, and length and strength of days . . . and lo! thou art become as one of These. Bowed are their backs, whereon resteth the Universe. Veiled are their faces, that have beheld the glory ineffable.

These adepts seem like pyramids. . . . Verily is the Pyramid a Temple of Initiation. Verily also is it a tomb. Thinkest thou that there is life within the Masters of the Temple? Verily, there is no life in them.

Israel Regardie, the American psychiatrist and expert on the modern occult revival has drawn attention[7] to the shattering effect of this revelation – that in becoming a Master of the Temple he had to die as far as his ordinary personality was concerned – upon Crowley. Ever since he had first written to Waite he had desired to be admitted to the Secret Sanctuary of the Saints, ever since he had undergone the Neophyte initiation he had desired to be one of the Secret Chiefs. Now in the fourteenth Aire he was confronted with the same basic idea, but a different interpretation of it. The Secret Sanctuary was a school, a school in which the pupils had had their egos destroyed and in which the teacher was Death; he had been admitted to that school, or so he firmly believed, and 'the credentials of admission were the evidence of his own decease', the uniting of his spirit with the ocean of infinity.

In the thirteenth, twelfth and eleventh Aires a new series of concepts were presented to Crowley – or, if one chooses to make a psychological interpretation of what was happening to him when he called the Aires – welled up from his unconscious mind. One of these concepts was the nature of the task of the Master of the Temple. This was to tend a secret garden in which all the flowers should be cultivated in accordance with their inner nature – this seems to mean that a Master should give his teaching to all, not distinguishing between one and another and not worrying which of his flowers shall become a 'magical son' – another Secret Chief.

The most important of the concepts communicated in these Aires was concerned with the symbolism, drawn from the New Testament Revelation of st John the Divine, of the Lady Babylon (spelt Babalon by Crowley for numerological reasons) and the Beast whereon she rides. This Christian symbolism tends to reduce the clarity of the message which was basically concerned with the Shakti-Shiva doctrine of some schools of Hindu mysticism. This doctrine is not easy to express in Western terms but putting it as simply as possible it conceives of a mindless universal energy, personified as the goddess Shakti, locked in sexual embrace with the god Shiva, intelligence and spirit. From the eternal orgasm of the two, from their explosion into one ecstasy, all manifestation, every single factor in the universe, is formed.

Babalon, the Scarlet Woman who rides upon the Beast, may at times manifest herself in a particular woman, but in her highest aspect she is Sakti, infinite energy and the mistress of the Masters of the Temple and all that is of the nature of intelligence.

'This is the Mystery of Babalon,' said Crowley's mystic voice, 'the Mother of Abominations, and this is the mystery of her adulteries, for she hath yielded up herself to everything that liveth, and hath become a partaker in its mystery. And because she has made herself the servant of each, therefore is she become the mistress of all. . . .'

In the eleventh Aire Crowley received the intimation that although he had unconsciously crossed the Abyss – the psychological barrier between ordinary men and the Secret Chiefs – he must now, in the tenth Aire, cross it consciously. To this end he and Neuburg prepared for a ceremonial evocation to Choronzon, the 'mighty devil' of the Abyss. This was done on 6 December at Bou Saada, where they walked from the town until they found an isolated valley floored with fine sand. A large circle of rocks was constructed, around it were drawn protective Names of Power, and outside was drawn a large triangle. This last was designed to be the place in which Choronzon, 'first and deadliest of all the powers of evil', was to manifest himself, and around it further protective 'names of power' were traced in the sand. At the points of the triangle Crowley sacrificed three pigeons so that the elemental force derived from their blood would provide a material basis for Choronzon to manifest himself – perhaps one should say 'itself' for according to Crowley the important thing about this demon is that it is made up of complete negation; in essence it has no personality, for that is a positive thing.

Neuburg sat within the circle, carrying a magical dagger for protection, and a notebook and writing instruments so that he could make a record of whatever Choronzon did and said. Then, before Crowley called the Aire, Neuburg swore an oath:

I . . . a Probationer of the AA, solemnly promise upon my magical honour and swear by Adonai the Angel that guardeth me, that I will defend this magic Circle of Art with thoughts and words and deeds. I promise to threaten with the dagger and command back into the triangle the spirit incontinent if he should try to escape from it; and to strike with the dagger at anything that may seek to enter this Circle, were it in appearance the body of the Seer himself [Crowley]. And I will be exceedingly wary, armed against force and cunning;

and I will preserve with my life the inviolability of this Circle. Amen. And I
summon my Holy Guardian Angel to witness my oath, the which if I break,
may I perish, forsaken of Him. Amen and Amen.

But where was Crowley while Neuburg was swearing his oath,
and where was Crowley to be during the evocation if not in the
protective circle with his companion? The text of the record
appears mysterious on this point, merely saying that Crowley
'shall retire to a secret place, where is neither sight nor hearing,
and sit within his black robe, secretly invoking the Aethyr'.
Elsewhere however it is quite specific:

Now, then, the Seer [Crowley] being entered within the triangle, let him
take the Victims [the pigeons] and cut their throats, pouring the blood within
the Triangle, and being most heedful that not one drop fall without the Triangle;
or else Choronzon shall be able to manifest in the universe. And when the sand
hath sucked up the blood of the victims, let him recite the call of the Aethyr
apart secretly as aforesaid. Then will the Vision be revealed, and the Voice
heard.

In other words Crowley was to be the first magician in occult
history to keep his body in the mystic triangle and offer it for an
evil spirit to manifest itself through. During this process Crowley
was to be in full trance, his everyday consciousness in 'a secret
place' and unaware of the doings of Choronzon.

After Crowley had called the Aire Neuburg heard a voice cry
out 'Zazas, Zasas, Nasatanda Zasas'.[8] This voice, which according
to Neuburg simulated Crowley's own voice, went on to utter
various blasphemies. Then Neuburg began to see things. He
beheld in the triangle a woman's body resembling that of a
prostitute he had known in Paris. She tried to seduce him, but
he, deciding that it was Choronzon who had adopted this form
in the hope of getting within the protective circle, resisted. The
woman – or the demon – then changed its shape, apologized and
made an appeal to Neuburg's pride by offering to lay her head
beneath his foot in token of submission. Neuburg resisted this
blandishment also. Choronzon turned into an old man, then into
a snake, then into the form of Crowley, who begged for water,
a request which Neuburg refused.

Neuburg then went on to the occult offensive, conjuring Choronzon in the name of the Most High to declare his nature. The devil was unaffected by this, replying that he spat 'upon the name of the Most High. . . . I fear not the power of the Penta-gram, for I am Master of the Triangle. . . . I shall say words . . . and thou wilt write them down, thinking them to be great secrets of magic power, and they will only be my jesting with thee'.

Neuburg then invoked Aiwass, the entity which had supposedly dictated *The Book of the Law* and which both magicians believed to be Crowley's Holy Guardian Angel. Choronzon cried out that he knew the name of this Angel 'and all thy dealings with him are but a cloak for thy filthy sorceries'. Neuburg replied that his knowledge was greater than that of the demon, that he feared him not, and that he ordered him to make a clear statement of his nature. Choronzon then gave his name as 'Dispersion' and claimed that he could not be bested in argument. He followed this with much blasphemy, delivered at a great rate. While Neuburg attempted to write all this down the demon cunningly threw sand over the magic circle until its protective outline became blurred. This being done Choronzon, taking the form of a naked man, jumped into the circle and threw Neuburg to the ground. They fought in the sand, the demon making frantic efforts to tear out Neuburg's throat with his teeth, until the latter was able to drive him back into the triangle and repair the circle with his magic dagger.

For some time Neuburg and the devil went on arguing, the latter threatening all the tortures of hell, the former denouncing Choronzon as a liar. Then the demon vanished, leaving Crowley alone in the triangle to trace the word BABALON in the sand as an indication that the rite was ended. Together the two magicians lit a purificatory fire and obliterated the circle and the triangle.

What really happened at the evocation of Choronzon? The common-sense explanation must be that all the forms of Choronzon were aspects of Crowley, that Neuburg argued and fought with a man possessed. Neuburg always remained convinced that he had literally wrestled with a demon, but he never said whether that demon was in Crowley's body or had a form of its own. This brings us to another possibility, one that has found favour with some occultists. It is that Crowley acted as a physical medium, giving off 'ectoplasm' – that is, astral raw material capable of being formed into a dense shape – that further ectoplasm was given out by the spilled blood of the sacrificed pigeons and that from these two sources Choronzon shaped a semi-material body which was capable of the physical actions of throwing sand, wrestling with Neuburg and so on. The final possibility is that none of the supposed physical events actually took place, that the ritual excitement dissociated some aspects of Neuburg's consciousness and caused him to fight thin air.

Whatever the truth of the matter may have been both magicians were well satisfied with their achievement; they were convinced that Crowley had conquered Choronzon, demon of Dispersion, and was now a full Master of the Temple, a veritable Secret Chief in the full meaning of the words. The remaining nine Aires were totally in contrast to the sinister content of the tenth. In the words of Dr Israel Regardie, they were 'lyrical paeans of joy and gladness', commemorations of the magical victory that had been won by 'crossing the Abyss and by subduing its sole inhabitant, the Demon Choronzon'.

On the last day of 1909 the magicians, their Enochian experiments concluded, set sail from Algiers to Southampton. Whatever happened in the course of these experiments, whether or not the surviving records of them are or are not to be relied upon as accounts of objective happenings, there is no doubt that they exerted a pronounced subjective effect upon Crowley. From now on he regarded himself above all as a teacher, a prophet whose one task was to convert the world to the doctrines expressed in *The Book of the Law*.

6

The Rites of Eleusis

AFTER THEIR RETURN from Algeria Crowley and Neuburg busied themselves with the preparation of the *Equinox*, No. 3, due for publication in the following March. This was planned to be the most important issue yet, containing for all to see the most secret of the Golden Dawn's rituals, that for the initiation of the Minor Adept. Mathers, who had been warned of what was to come by an advance announcement, scraped up enough funds to apply for an injunction to forbid publication on the grounds that he owned the copyright of the ritual in question. A temporary injunction was granted and on appeal to Mr Justice Bucknill was made permanent. Crowley was furious; it was more than a coincidence that Bucknill was a leading freemason, he asserted, arguing that the judge had made his decision on the basis that all secret rituals should remain secret for evermore. Crowley took his case to the Appeal Court, consecrated a talisman 'to gain the favour of a judge' – and won his case, the *Equinox* appearing late but intact.

After the magazine had been published Crowley, one of his mistresses, a half-Maori violinist named Leila Waddell, Neuburg and several other people vaguely interested in the occult joined a house party at the Dorset home of Commander Marston, formerly a serving officer of the Royal Navy. Marston was one of the more eccentric of Crowley's friends, his particular interest being the rhythm of the tom-tom and its supposed effects on the emotions of those listening to it. He claimed for example to have carried out some 'classical and conclusive' experiments on the

effect of the tom-tom on the psychology of married English
women. These had at first been productive of a vague unrest,
which gradually assumed a sexual form, then finally led to
'shameless masturbation or indecent advances'.

Ritual magic was also of interest to Commander Marston and,
with his agreement, it was decided to attempt to evoke Bartzabel,
the spirit of Mars, with a ritual written by Crowley.[1] Neuburg
would sit in the triangle and would himself, with the aid of
others, persuade Bartzabel to occupy his body and use his mouth
to prophesy and answer questions. This was duly done, with
Neuburg improvising a free-form dance intended to bring down
the spirit into him. Bartzabel duly took possession of Neuburg's
body, and proceeded to answer questions. Commander Marston
was still enough of a fighting man to be interested in military
matters, so he asked Neuburg-Bartzabel about the possibility of
an outbreak of war in Europe. Neuburg replied that within five
years there would be two conflicts; the storm-centre of the first
would be Turkey and that of the second would be the German
Empire. The eventual result of these wars would be the destruction of the Turkish and German Empires. Curiously enough both
these prophecies were destined to be fulfilled to the letter; the
Balkan War of 1912 and the World War of 1914–18 destroying
the two empires whose demise Bartzabel had foreseen.

The audience at the ritual had found that Neuburg's dancing,
which had been accompanied by Leila Waddell's violin playing,
provided a powerful stimulant to their jaded artistic and emotional
palates. Why not, it was suggested, give semi-public perform-
ances at which the audience would pay a substantial fee to see
Neuburg, Waddell and perhaps some others, invoke the gods?
Crowley took up the idea with enthusiasm and prepared seven
rites.[2] Each would involve Neuburg 'dancing down' a particular
god while Leila Waddell played and Crowley recited explanatory
poetry – mostly his own verse but supplemented by a certain
amount of Swinburne.

In the early summer costumes were prepared, rehearsals
carried out, and tickets sold for the rites which would be carried
out at Crowley's London flat, 124 Victoria Street. The rites were

exhibited in August 1910 to what was to prove a largely appreci-
ative audience; to some extent their goodwill may have resulted
from a 'loving cup' administered to them before each of the
ceremonies. This contained fruit juices, alcohol, 'alkaloids of
opium' – presumably either morphine or more likely heroin –
and a substance which Crowley referred to as 'the elixir introduced by me to Europe'. This last was probably an infusion of
mescal buttons, which Crowley had first encountered in Mexico.
The whole brew was somewhat unpleasant to the taste, and was
described by one member of the audience as somewhat resembling rotten apples.

Ethel Archer, a young poetess whose verse was published in
the *Equinox*, has left a description of how the rites affected her,
a young woman who had only the vaguest interest in the occult.
On arrival at Crowley's flat she and her husband were taken into
the sitting-room which was in semi-darkness, the heavy curtains
having been drawn to keep out the light of the setting sun and
the only illumination coming from a swinging silver lamp. They,
with the rest of the potential audience, sat on cushions scattered
around the circumference of the room, all its usual furniture
having been removed. Neuburg passed them the 'loving cup'
and then they lost sight of him, his function of steward being
taken over by Crowley's friend Dr E. T. Jensen. When next they
saw Neuburg he was dressed in the white robe of a Probationer
of the AA and was engaged in a wild informal dance, something
like that of a whirling dervish, to the music of Leila Waddell.
Meanwhile Crowley recited poetry. The dance reached its high
point – the descent of the god – and Neuburg collapsed on to the
floor where he lay unconscious for several minutes. The effect
on the audience was to make them feel 'pepped up and lively';
in the case of Ethel Archer and her husband this feeling persisted
for a week or so. Interestingly enough they attributed this to the
liquid they had drunk rather than to a magical effect of the
ceremony.

Some representatives of the Press had been invited to the
ceremonies and an extraordinarily favourable review of them –
one almost suspects that it was written by a friend of Crowley

– appeared in the *Sketch* of 28 August 1910. This review gives a fairly full account of what took place:

. . . Frater Omnia Vincam [Neuburg] was commanded to dance 'the dance of Syrinx and Pan in honour of our lady Artemis'. A young poet, whose verse is often read [Neuburg], then astonished by a graceful and beautiful dance, which he continued until he fell exhausted in the middle of the room where, by the way, he lay until the end. Crowley then made supplication to the goddess in a beautiful and unpublished poem. A dead silence ensued. After a long pause, the figure enthroned [Leila Waddell] took a violin and played – played with passion and feeling, like a master. We were thrilled to our very bones. Once again the figure took the violin and played . . . with such an intense feeling that in very deed most of us experienced that ecstasy which Crowley so earnestly seeks. Then came a prolonged and intense silence, after which the Master of the Ceremonies dismissed us in these words: 'By the power in me vested, I declare the Temple closed'.

So ended a really beautiful ceremony. . . . I do not pretend to understand the ritual that runs like a thread of magic through these meetings of the A.A. I do not even know what the A.A. is. But I do know the whole ceremony was impressive, artistic and produced in those present such a feeling as Crowley must have had when he wrote –

> 'So shalt thou conquer space, and lastly climb,
> The walls of time:
> And by the golden path the great have trod
> Reach up to God'

Pleased by the reaction of the Press and their audience, Crowley and Neuburg decided to give a more public performance of the rites. To this end they recruited another dancer, a young girl from the Royal Academy of Dramatic Art named Joan Hayes, and hired Caxton Hall for seven consecutive Wednesday evenings in October and November. The admission to these was 5 guineas for the series. This time the Press was less favourable, and a curious scandal-sheet called the *Looking Glass* produced an unpleasant report which was to lead to a libel action in which a good deal of mud was spattered over what reputation Crowley enjoyed.

After depositing our hat and coat with an attendant [wrote the reporter of the *Looking Glass*] we were conducted by our guide to a door, at which stood a rather dirty looking person attired in a sort of imitation Eastern robe, with a drawn sword in his hand, who, after inspecting our cards, admitted us to a dimly lighted room heavy with incense. Across this room low stools were placed in rows, and when we arrived a good many of these were already occupied by various men and women, for the most part in evening dress.

At the extreme end of the room was a heavy curtain, and in front of this sat a huddled-up figure in draperies, beating a kind of monotonous tom-tom.

When we had all been admitted the doors were shut, and the light, which had always been exceedingly dim, was completely extinguished save for a slight flicker on the 'altar'. Then after a while more ghostly figures appeared on the stage, and a person in a red hood, supported on each side by a blue-chinned gentleman in a sort of Turkish bath costume, commenced to read some gibberish to which the attendants made response at intervals.

Our guide informed us that this was known as the banishing rite of the pentagram.

More Turkish bath attendants then appeared, and executed a kind of Morris dance round the stage. Then the gentleman in the red cloak, supported by brothers Aquarius and Capricornus – the aforesaid blue-chinned gentlemen – made fervent appeals to the Mother of Heaven to hear them, and after a little while a not unprepossessing lady appeared, informed them that she was the Mother of Heaven, and asked if she could do anything for them. . . . They beg her to summon the Master, as they wish to learn from him if there is any God, or if they are free to behave as they please. The Mother of Heaven thereupon takes up a violin and plays not unskilfully for about ten minutes, during which time the room is again plunged in complete darkness. The playing is succeeded by a loud hammering, in which all the robed figures on the stage join, and after a din sufficient to wake the Seven Sleepers the lights are turned up a little and a figure appears from a recess and asks what they want. They beseech him to let them know whether there is really a God, as, if not, they will amuse themselves without any fear of the consequences. 'The Master' promises to give the matter his best attention, and, after producing a flame from the floor by the simple expedient of opening a trap-door, he retires with the Mother of Heaven for 'meditation', during which time darkness again supervenes. After a considerable period he returns, flings aside a curtain on the stage, and declares that the space behind it is empty, and that there is no God. He then exhorts his followers to do as they like and make the most of this life.

The article went on to suggest that some sexual irregularity took place in the semi-darkness and dropped dark hints about the significance of a harmless photograph of the rite which showed

Leila Waddell kneeling on Crowley's chest. More revelations were promised for future issues. Two further attacks followed, and it is clear that at least some of the information was derived from MacGregor Mathers. It was said for instance that Crowley had lived with 'the rascally sham Buddhist monk Allan Bennett' – Bennett had by this time become a Buddhist monk in Burma, had visited England to spread the doctrines of his faith and consequently won a certain amount of notoriety – and that the two had engaged in 'unmentionable immoralities'. There was also a mention of G. C. Jones which was taken by some to imply that he, a happily married man with several children, had engaged in homosexual activities with Crowley and Bennett.

Captain Fuller, still a strong admirer of Crowley, urged him to issue a writ for libel – as a serving officer it must have made life difficult for him to be known as a close friend of an occultist who committed 'unmentionable immoralities'. Crowley refused, much to Fuller's annoyance, saying that he believed in the doctrine of non-resistance to evil. Jones however decided to fight and issued a writ claiming that the words used were defamatory in their implication that he was a homosexual, and claiming a considerable sum in damages. The *Looking Glass* defence was that the words used by its reporter did not have the meaning Jones attached to them, that the article certainly made no claim that Jones was a homosexual and that in any case anyone as closely associated with Crowley as Jones had no worthwhile reputation to lose. This last claim of the defence turned the action, which took place in April 1911, into something very like a trial of Crowley's morals, even though he was not formally involved in the case to the extent of even being a witness. Mathers and various of his associates appeared to give evidence of Crowley's turpitude. Thus Dr Berridge, a homoeopathic physician who was an initiate of the Golden Dawn and headed a London temple loyal to Mathers, gave evidence reported in a newspaper as follows:

Dr. Berridge: 'On one occasion when Crowley was over here as an envoy on official matters concerning the Order, I had an opportunity of speaking alone with him, and I said to him: "Do you know what they accuse you of?" – meaning the members of the Order. I will not express it too plainly as I see there are ladies in the Court.'

Mr. Justice Scrutton: 'Any ladies who may be in this Court probably are beyond any scruples of that sort.'

Dr. Berridge: 'Well, I said: "They accuse you of unnatural vice", and he made a very peculiar answer: he neither admitted nor denied it '

This sort of thing did a great deal of harm to the reputation of Crowley and also to Jones, as his close friend. Equally damning were some printed Latin marginal notes in the 1906 edition of Crowley's essay '*Ambrosii Magi Hortus Rosarum*'. These, which were produced in court, read: '*Pater Iubet Scientiam Scribe*', '*Culpa Urbium Nota Terrae femina Rapta Inspirate gaudium*', '*Adest Rosa Secreta Eros*' and '*Quid Umbratur In Mari*'. The initial letters of these Latin words form words which, while unlikely to shock anyone greatly at the present day, were regarded by the judge and jury which tried Jones's libel action as being particularly indecent. Crowley pretended that the words formed by the Latin letters were coincidental and pointed out that Scrutton, the name of the judge, was an anagram of 'cunts rot'; it seems most unlikely that anyone save Crowley himself was impressed by this argument.

Eventually the jury gave its decision, finding that the words used did mean that Jones engaged in homosexual activities and that this was true in substance and in fact. This adverse verdict caused a slowing down of recruitment to the AA – few occultists naturally enough were anxious to be tarred with the same brush as Crowley – and the departure of Captain Fuller, who not only left Crowley's order but ended his personal friendship with its leader. Fifty years later Fuller claimed that he took this action as a protest at Crowley 'letting down Jones by not going into the box as a witness'. This seems an unlikely explanation, for if Crowley *had* been a witness counsel representing the *Looking Glass* could have cross-examined him on his private life and it is most improbable that his answers could have done Jones anything but harm. On the whole Crowley's account of Fuller's departure seems more believable. According to this Fuller felt both his personal reputation and his military career would suffer if he remained publicly connected with the AA, but offered to continue as long as his membership remained a secret and Crowley did not mention his name. On Crowley's refusal to agree with this curious but understandable proposition Fuller abandoned the AA, Crowley and magic itself.

Six months after the trial Crowley met Mary d'Esté Sturges, a half-Irish, half-Italian woman who was to be his companion in a new occult adventure.

7

Book Four

IN HIS *Confessions* Crowley refers to 'an obscure prig', a 'brainless and conceited youth', named Monet-Knott. In fact the reference is to Hener Skene, a great friend of the dancer Isadora Duncan and a pianist of some merit. Skene was presumably unaware of Crowley's low opinion of him, for when the two men had accidentally met on the evening of 11 October 1911 Crowley had been invited by Skene to come along to the Savoy with him and meet Isadora Duncan. When they arrived at the dancer's suite they found in progress a rowdy party held in celebration of the birthday of Mary d'Esté Sturges, a close friend of Isadora Duncan.[1]

The personality of Mary d'Esté Sturges made an immediate impact on Crowley. He felt that she possessed a 'terrific magnetism', and he was so overcome by this that he sat on the floor at her feet 'exchanging electricity with her'. He met her again two days later and expressed his passion for her. A month or so later, after a whirlwind courtship, the two set off for Switzerland with the intention of spending a skating holiday in St Moritz. They broke their journey at Zürich, booking in at the National Hotel on 21 November. Here, finding life dull, they both got extremely drunk. It is likely that they also took drugs – probably mescal with its capacity for producing highly coloured visual hallucinations – for at around midnight Mary d'Esté Sturges began to see visions.

First of all appeared an old man dressed in white with a white beard and carrying a wand, and soon joined by four others robed

in the same way. Suddenly the robes of these five white clad
figures turned red; this is interesting because abrupt colour
changes are an attribute of mescal visions. At first Crowley took
little note of his companion's description of her visions, attrib-
uting them to hysteria, but suddenly she said, 'Here is a book for
Frater Perdurabo'. Crowley was astonished at this, for as far as
he knew she had no prior knowledge that this was one of his
magical names. He was even more surprised when she said that
the book was named *Aba* and that its number was four, for this
statement revealed a knowledge of gematria, the aspect of the
Kabalah which is concerned with turning words into numbers
and vice versa.[2]

The ancient one gave his name as Ab-ul-Diz and Crowley,
speaking to this astral wizard through his companion, enquired
'What about 78?' – at the time Crowley believed that this was
kabalistically the number of the being who had dictated *The Book
of the Law* to him. The being replied that he, Ab-ul-Diz, was 78
and went on to give Crowley's kabalistic number as 1400; not a
very satisfying statement to Crowley as by Kabalah this is one of
the numbers of chaos. Crowley felt that his attempts to discover
the real identity of the Ab-ul-Diz and to decide whether his
communications should or should not be accepted as messages
from the gods, had been fruitless. Nevertheless he was pleased
when Ab-ul-Diz said that he would return in a week's time and
speak more clearly.

They moved to the Palace Hotel, St Moritz, where Crowley
spent much of the week's waiting time explaining and giving
details of his occult career to his companion; he wanted to avoid
complications as to what she might or might not have previously
known. He planned to use ceremonial as a prelude to his next
meeting – or rather Mary's next meeting – with Ab-ul-Diz and
he was pleased to find that he had exactly the right magical
implements with him. These were a scarlet robe, his magic bell
and ring, the 'shew-stone' set in a cross which he had used when
calling the Enochian Aires with Neuburg two years previously,
and most important of all his serpent-girded magic wand with a
star-sapphire set in its tip. It impressed him that he had brought

these things with him and he decided that it was no mere coincidence but that he had been guided by the gods. He found it equally significant that Mary had with her a blue *abbai*, an Arab gown, almost totally resembling one his wife had owned at the time when he had received *The Book of the Law*.

At 11 pm on the appointed date the two were ready for their appointment with Ab-ul-Diz. They had turned the sitting-room of their suite into a makeshift temple. Most of its furniture had been pushed into a corner and cut off from sight by a screen; on an eight-sided table in the middle of the room were Crowley's magical implements and a censer smoking with the incense of Abramelin,[3] while behind it was an oblong table on which were placed a clock and a lamp, as symbols of time and space, and writing materials to enable Crowley to write down his questions and the answers received through his companion's visions and the words she heard with her psychic hearing. Mary had been suitably prepared for her entrancement with drink and sex – by this time Crowley accepted that these were ideal preparations for astral vision – and probably drugs also.[4] These appear to have fulfilled their purpose for promptly at eleven the wizard Ab-ul-Diz made his appearance. He announced that his function was to arrange for Crowley to be given a book and that the actual giver of this book would be Mary.

A series of bewildering questions and answers followed. Crowley for example asked if Ab-ul-Diz knew the word MAKHASHANAH – a mystic word he had received two years before when he had called the twenty-seventh Enochian Aire. In reply Ab-ul-Diz, so Mary reported, merely wrote the word in golden letters and placed after it a black cross. Occasionally one of the answers received made more sense. Thus when Crowley asked whether MacGregor Mathers was 'one of us' – the phrase lacked its present day meaning – the wizard replied, 'No, no longer', an answer which satisfied all Crowley's prejudices about Mathers who so Crowley thought was now controlled by demons.

Eventually Mary complained of an alien presence, a being who appeared to be interfering with her perceptions of Ab-ul-Diz. Simultaneously Crowley became conscious of elementals – the

tricksy spirits of Earth, Air, Fire and Water – dodging about the
room. Crowley knew immediately what to do; he got Mary to
banish the unwelcome entities by thinking of the number 541.
This, by Greek gematria, is the number of Priapus, the ithy-
phallic god whom Crowley regarded as being peculiarly holy.
For almost an hour more questions were asked and more seemingly
wrong or meaningless answers were given. Finally Mary complained of tiredness and after making a further appointment with
Ab-ul-Diz for a meeting in a week's time Crowley closed the
temple.

The next session duly took place. The answers received to
questions were quite as futile as on the previous occasions but
the wizard did inform Mary that her magical name was Virakam.
A further astral appointment was made – in spite of the thoroughly
disappointing nature of the visions so far Crowley hoped that in
due course something of importance would come through from
the astral plane. At this next vision Virakam – from now on we
may as well refer to her by her magical motto – had even more
difficulty in reducing the jumbled images that raced through her
mind into some sort of order. Crowley was by now thoroughly
sick of Switzerland and asked if they should go on to France or
Italy. In answer Virakam saw a triple candlestick which Crowley,
for reasons not clear to me, decided was an indication that they
should go to Italy.

On later days more astral visions by Virakam took place.
While the symbolism of these was confused, to say the least, and
while Crowley considered Virakam to be a thoroughly unsatisfactory seer, he eventually came to the conclusion that Ab-ul-Diz
was instructing him and Virakam to go to Italy and there write a
book on magic and mysticism to be called *Book Four*. Crowley and
Virakam travelled to Milan, where they had a conversation with
Ab-ul-Diz who said he would not reappear and gave his final
instructions. They were to go beyond Rome, find a villa, and
there write *Book Four* together. For the first time Crowley
received a message from Ab-ul-Diz which just flashed into his
consciousness – they would recognize the right place for the
dictation of the book by the presence of two Persian nut trees.

Eventually, near Naples, they found the Villa Caldarazzo, which was not only marked by the expected nut trees, but the letters of which, when transliterated into Hebrew, and by gematria, added up to 418, according to Crowley the 'Magical Formula of the Aeon'. Crowley found the psychic atmosphere of the villa exactly suitable to what he was planning. This was that he should dictate a four-part work, dealing with mysticism, magic and *The Book of the Law*, to Virakam, who would transcribe it and, whenever she found anything obscure in Crowley's words, would get him to dictate further explanatory material.

Part I, supposedly dealing with mysticism in general, but in fact largely confined to yoga, was published in 1913 at a price of 'four groats' (1s 4d). In this Crowley clearly achieved what he set out to do; even at the present day there is no better elementary account, written in ordinary, understandable, everyday language, of the aims and processes of yoga than this. Part II, *Magick* – for the first time Crowley adopted this archaic spelling to distinguish his own brand of magic from all others – was also brought out in 1913. Its price was 'four tanners' (2s). This was by no means as helpful or as clear a book as Part I. For, although it gave clear descriptions of magical implements and how they should be made, it gave no real indication of *why* anyone should go to the trouble of making them. Similarly it failed to give any indication of the theories of the universe which underlie ceremonial magic (see chapter 1 of this book), nor did it manage in any way to convey what magic in general and 'magick' in particular was all about. To the occultist who had already gone through the rites of the Golden Dawn, or had studied all the issues of the *Equinox* that had appeared by 1913, the book may have been meaningful; to the ordinary reader the book could have conveyed very little.

Nevertheless the book was no ordinary one and it is still worth reading at the present day if only for 'An Interlude', a marvellously funny interpretation of the occult significance of nursery rhymes.[5] Far more extraordinary than 'An Interlude' however was an incident which concluded its dictation – nothing less than Crowley's transfiguration! What happened has been described by Virakam:

Nearly midnight. At this moment we stopped dictating and began to converse. Then Fra. P. [Crowley] said: 'Oh, if only I could dictate a book like the *Tao Teh King*!' Then he closed his eyes as if meditating. Just before I had noticed a change in his face, most extraordinary, as if he were no longer the same person; in fact, in the ten minutes we were talking, he seemed to be any number of different people. I especially noticed the pupils of his eyes were so enlarged that the entire eye seemed black. (I tremble so and I have such a quaking feeling inside, simply in thinking of last night, that I can't form letters.) Then, quite slowly, the entire room filled with a thick yellow light (deep golden, but not brilliant. I mean not dazzling, but soft). Fra. P. [Crowley] looked like a person I have never seen but seemed to know quite well – his face, clothes and all were of this same yellow. I was so disturbed that I looked up to the ceiling to see what caused this light, but could only see the candles. Then the chair on which he sat seemed to rise; it was like a throne, and he seemed to be either dead or sleeping, but it was certainly no longer Fra. P. This frightened me, and I tried to understand by looking round the room; when I looked back the chair was raised, and he was still the same. I realized I was alone; and thinking he was dead or gone – or some other terrible thing – I lost consciousness.

Only the first two parts of the book, and not the four intended, were concluded, for quarrels, heavy drinking and Virakam's over-hasty marriage to a Turk whom she had known for only a short time led to the break-up of both her sexual and magical relationships with Crowley.[6]

Meanwhile Crowley's magical order – the AA – was attracting a surprisingly large number of members; by 1913 according to John Symonds there were eighty-eight of these including Nina Hammett, an artist whom Crowley was eventually to sue for libel, and Cheiro, the society palmist, who was in arrears with his subscription. Besides his more orthodox magical activities in the AA Crowley, by now desperately short of money, seems to have been putting on private, theatrical and pseudo-satanic occult shows for those willing to pay for the privilege. Elliot O'Donnell has left an amusing description of one of the more innocent of these:

Arranged in a semicircle round the room there were rows of chairs for the audience, and between the chairs and the wall at the back of them there were placed, at regular intervals, busts, which we were informed were those of Pan, Lucifer, and other mystic beings of questionable reputation. A kind of altar occupied the empty space in the centre of the room, and behind it, set against the wall, in front of which were no busts and no chairs, stood three tall, wooden structures. . . .

When everyone was seated Mr. Aleister Crowley, arrayed in quasi-sacerdotal vestments, read extracts from a book which he told us was the Book of Death. After this we listened for a time to some rather doleful music. When that ceased, from the first (counting from left to right) of the wooden boxes arranged against the wall emerged a lady, clad in a filmy green robe and carrying a harp. She played on her harp for some minutes in front of the altar, and then tripped noiselessly back to her box, whilst another damsel, clad in the same sort of filmy garment though of some other hue, and carrying a harp, emerged from the second box. She, too, for a few minutes played on her harp in front of the altar, and then retired to her box, whilst yet another . . . damsel entertained us for some minutes in the same manner as her predecessors and then retired, and upon her retirement there followed a brief interval, during which the lights went lower and lower. Then, when the room was almost ominously dark, Mr. Aleister Crowley strode out from behind a curtain, and advancing in approved theatrical fashion to the altar, invoked certain gods of a none too respectable order. Having done this, he raised his voice to a shrill scream, exclaiming: 'Now I will cut my chest'.

Almost simultaneously with this announcement, something bright flashed through the air and a short, sharp, crinkly sound was heard, a sound which was followed immediately by horrified murmurs from most of the ladies present, and by a whisper from one of my friends, consisting if I heard aright, of some vague allusion to isinglass, parchment, and potato chips.

After a dramatic pause, sufficient to enable the ladies to recover from their fright, Mr. Crowley said, 'I will now dip a burning wafer in my blood'.

He passed something, I could not see what, through the flame of a candle, and then held it close to his bare chest, thereby eliciting more cries of horror from the ladies. Then after another dramatic pause, he informed us that he was going to pay his respects to the busts around the room . . . he paid his respects very briefly . . . and, after making a few passes in the air with a dagger – or . . . after making a few vicious jabs in the air with a bread-knife; but no matter whether dagger or bread-knife, jabs or passes, the effect was sufficiently alarming to call forth a chorus of 'Ohs' – he announced that the ceremonies for the time being were at an end.

Later on, we understood, rites of an even more enthralling nature were performed in private. . . .[7]

It all sounds fairly innocent – indeed, the wooden boxes from which the harpists emerged must have seemed charming – but

at 'the rites of an even more enthralling nature' much stronger
meat was on offer and a journalist's description of them has
survived:

I found myself in a large, high-ceilinged studio the atmosphere of which was
coloured a deep blue by the reek of a peculiar smelling incense. In the first room
stood row on row of books bound in black and marked on their backs with
queer, malformed crosses wrought in silver. The second room was fitted with
divans and literally carpeted with multitudes of cushions tossed here and yon.
In the third and largest room stood a tall, perpendicular canopy under which
the high priest [Crowley] sat during the celebration of black mass. Directly in
front of it . . . stood the altar, a black pedestal on top of which was affixed a
golden circle. Across the latter lay a golden serpent, as if arrested in the act
of crawling. I heard someone behind a curtain playing a weird Chinese-like air
on some sort of stringed instrument. . . .

One by one the worshippers entered. They were mostly women of aristocratic
type. Their delicate fingers adorned with costly rings, their rustling silks, the
indefinable elegance of their carriage, attested their station in life. . . . Everybody wore a little black domino which concealed the upper part of the face,
making identification impossible. Hung with black velvet curtains, the place
presented a decidedly sepulchral aspect. The complexions of the women seemed
as white as wax. There was fitful light furnished by a single candlestick having
seven branches. Suddenly this went out and the place was filled with subter-
ranean noises. . . . Then came the slow, monotonous chant of the high priest:

'There is no good. Evil is good. Blessed be the Principle of Evil. All hail,
Prince of the World, to whom even God Himself has given dominion'. . . .
Men and women danced about, leaping and swaying to the whining of infernal
and discordant music. They sang obscene words set to hymn tunes and gibbered
unintelligible jargon. Women tore their bodices; some partially disrobed. One
fair worshipper, seizing upon the high priest's dagger wounded herself in the
breasts. At this all seemed to go madder than ever. . . .[8]

By 1914, when this description was written, Crowley was to
some extent losing interest in the type of ceremonial magic
which his AA had taken from the Golden Dawn; another and
perhaps more sinister type of occult practice was beginning to
occupy his attention.

8

Western Tantrism

IT WILL BE remembered that MacGregor Mathers had on two occasions appeared in a law court to give evidence against Crowley. Both on the first occasion, when he unsuccessfully attempted to get an injunction to prevent the publication of the *Equinox*, No. 3 (March 1910), and on the second, when he gave evidence for the defence in *Jones v. the Looking Glass*, he publicly claimed that he was Chief of the Rosicrucian Order. This claim infuriated a number of occult cranks, each of whom claimed that he and he alone was the Head of the Rosicrucians and, as Crowley was clearly Mathers's opponent, these supposed leaders showered occult and pseudo-masonic dignities upon him. So numerous were these that Crowley claimed that if he attempted to wear at the same time all the medals, chains and badges which had been conferred upon him he would have been quite unable to walk.

Among the orders to which Crowley was admitted at this time was a German one called the *Ordo Templi Orientis*, the 'Order of Eastern Templars', usually referred to by its initials as the OTO. At first Crowley thought of the OTO as no more than another of the many spurious masonic fraternities which flourished in pre-1914 Europe, and on this basis he became a member of it, probably feeling that it was amusing to add yet one more supposed masonic qualification to those he already possessed. In fact however the OTO was something very much more interesting than a masonic brotherhood; it was a fraternity teaching to its highest-grade initiates a Western form of tantrism, that mysticism which seeks to transform sexual orgasm into a mode of attaining the Divine Union.

The exact beginnings of the OTO are almost as mysterious as those of the Golden Dawn. But it seems likely that its origins are to be found in the oriental travels of Karl Kellner, a wealthy German iron-founder and high-grade freemason, who claimed to have learned 'sexual magic' from three adepts in this art, two Arab and one Hindu. If these adepts existed outside Kellner's imagination – and this is by no means certain – it is likely that the Indian was a Bengali tantric, a member of one of the sects who strives for union with the Great Mother Goddess by means of sexual practices, and that the Arabs were initiates of some highly unorthodox Sufi fraternity.

Kellner is supposed to have founded the OTO in 1895, but if so it must have been a very small and secretive organization, for nothing is known of it until 1904, when flattering references both to it and to Kellner began to appear in an obscure German masonic periodical called *Oriflamme*. Such references were some-times accompanied by hintings about a 'great secret' of which the OTO was the custodian. These were specific enough for the individual reader to conclude that they somehow concerned the sexual act and by 1912 the editors of *Oriflamme* felt secure enough to frankly announce that: 'Our Order possesses the KEY which opens up all Masonic and Hermetic secrets, namely, the teaching of sexual magic, and this teaching explains, without exception, all the secrets of Freemasonry and all systems of religion.'

Seven years before this avowal was published Kellner had died and been succeeded as head of the OTO by a man named Theodor Reuss. Reuss was a very odd character indeed. He was a paid agent of the German secret service, and sometimes posed as an ardent devotee of Marxist socialism. As the latter, with the object of spying on the surviving children of Karl Marx, he had infiltrated the infant British socialist movement – strongly influenced by exiled Germans at that time, in the 1890s. It is pleasant to know that Marx's daughter Eleanor took an immediate dislike to him; she particularly objected to a vulgar song he had sung at a social meeting of the Socialist League, suspected him of being a spy and got him expelled from the organization.

Under Reuss the OTO enjoyed a certain modest success giving charters – although not necessarily passing on its sexual secrets – to occult brotherhoods in France, Denmark, Switzerland, the USA and Austria. It was divided into nine degrees, of which the first six were masonic in nature. In the seventh degree the initiate began to be taught the theory of sex magic and in the eighth and ninth degrees respectively he or she – for the order included women as well as men in its membership – was expected to practise auto- and heterosexual magic.

What were – or rather are, for several splinters from the OTO still survive – the secrets of the sex magic taught by Reuss? A large number of manuscripts outlining the nature of these secrets have been written and, although these are often expressed in a symbolic language derived from alchemy, they are very easily interpreted. Thus the code phrase for the penis is the *athanor*, that for the semen is the *blood of the red lion*, or the *Serpent*, while the vagina is referred to as the *retort* or the *cucurbite*. The organically complex mixture of liquids which lubricate the female organ are the *menstruum of the gluten* and the mixture of these with the male discharge is the *first matter* or, when it has been impregnated with magic power, the *Elixir*.

Those who used (and still use) the techniques of this sexual alchemy claimed that success in any occult operation, from the invocation of a god to the finding of hidden treasure, could be obtained by its use. If for example they wanted to 'charge a talisman' – that is to imbue with magic power a mascot intended to secure a particular purpose – they engaged in an auto- or heterosexual act while throughout the performance concentrating on the talisman and its purpose. Afterwards the mascot was anointed with semen or, if the act had been carried out heterosexually, the Elixir. Those who have employed talismans charged in this way have asserted their effectuality. I have for example met a former follower of Crowley – the man Jean Overton Fuller referred to in her biography of Neuburg as 'ex-disciple' – who owned a talisman 'to find a treasure' which had been consecrated in this way by Crowley. Ex-disciple used it as a magic charm to find rare occult books, seemingly with great success.

A variation of this talismanic magic was used to ensure that a letter written for a particular purpose was effective in attaining that same purpose. In this case a magic symbol appropriate to the matter concerned – for instance the sigil of Saturn if the matter concerned an inheritance – was traced on the envelope in either semen or the *Elixir*. To invoke a god into themselves, that is, to strengthen and set into flaming activity all the subjective psychological factors symbolized by a particular deity, the practitioners of sex magic mentally concentrated on the form of the god throughout intercourse, building up a creative visualization of his or her form and imagining that it had a life of its own. At orgasm they attempted to transfer their own consciousness to that of the image they had built up, blending the personalities of the god and themselves into one.[1]

At some time – according to Crowley in the year 1912 – Reuss called on Crowley at his London flat and accused him of revealing the innermost secrets of the ninth degree of the OTO. Crowley was not a man averse to revealing secrets – after all he had revealed all those of Mathers and the Golden Dawn – but he was astonished at this charge, for the simple reason that he had never been admitted to this degree and could therefore hardly be privy to its secrets. Crowley pointed this out to Reuss who then produced a copy of Crowley's *The Book of Lies*, a series of occult mystical free verse. Silently Reuss opened the volume at page 46, 'The Ritual of the Star Sapphire', and pointed out its opening words: 'Let the Adept be armed with his *Magick Rood* and provided with his Mystic Rose.' Crowley, in an intuitive flash, realized the sexual nature of the magic of the OTO.

For two hours the Adepts talked, Reuss expounding sexual alchemy, Crowley the revelations of *The Book of the Law* and its compatibility with the OTO. He would have found no difficulty in finding passages of the book to support this thesis. For example the phallic significance of: 'I am the Snake that giveth Knowledge and Delight and bright glory, and stir the hearts of men with drunkenness. To worship me take wine and strange drugs. . . .

O man! lust, enjoy all things of sense and rapture: fear not that any God shall deny thee for this.' Eventually Crowley and Reuss agreed that the former should head a new, British section of the OTO, to be called *Mysteria Mystica Maxima*. Subsequently Crowley visited Berlin, received copies of the OTO instructional manuscripts and received the title of 'Supreme and Holy King of Ireland, Iona and all the Britains within the Sanctuary of the Gnosis'.

There is one thing that is odd about this account, which is based on Crowley's written and spoken reminiscences, and that is that *The Book of Lies*, which Reuss allegedly produced in 1912, was not according to its title page published until 1913. Either the two Adepts were as Crowley seemed to imply in his *Confessions* caught in a slip in time, or it was some other of Crowley's writings which contained that which could be interpreted as a revelation of the workings of the OTO's ninth degree or most likely of all *The Book of Lies* bears an incorrect publication date.

After his return from Berlin Crowley at first made only a few casual experiments with sex magic; but he issued a manifesto of the *Mysteria Mystica Maxima* which seems to indicate that he was prepared to initiate more or less anyone who could come up with the fees demanded. It promises that those who enter it will

1. . . . have not only access to, but instruction in, the whole body of hidden knowledge preserved in the Sanctuary from the beginning of its manifestation. In the lower grades the final secrets are hinted, and conveyed in symbol, beneath veil, and through sacrament. . . .

2. They become partakers of the current of Universal Life in Liberty, Beauty, Harmony, and Love which flames within the heart of the O.T.O., and the Light of that august fraternity insensibly illuminates them ever more and more as they approach its central Sun. .

3. They meet those persons most complemental to their own nature. . . .

4. They obtain the right to sojourn in the secret houses of the O.T.O., permanently or for a greater or lesser period of the year. . . .

5. The Knowledge of the Preparation and Use of the Universal Medicine [another alchemical code phrase for the mingled male and female secretions] is restricted to members of the IX^0; but it may be administered to members of the VIII^0 and VII^0 in special circumstances. . . .

6. In the V^0 all members are pledged to bring immediate and perfect relief to

all distress of mind, body or estate, in which they may find any of their fellows of that degree. The Order thus affords a perfect system of insurance. . . .

7. Members of the IX^0 become part proprietors of the Estates and Goods of the Order. . . .

8. The order gives practical assistance in life to worthy members of even lower degrees, so that, even if originally poor, they become well able to afford the comparatively high fees of the VII^0, VIII^0 and IX^0.

On exaltation to the IV^0 each Companion may file an account of his circumstances, and state in what direction he requires help.

It seems unlikely that in reality any person who joined the *Mysteria Mystica Maxima* found it either a source of 'immediate and perfect relief' for their financial problems or even a 'perfect system of insurance'. On the other hand the manifesto was accurate enough when it referred to the fees charged as being 'comparatively high'; to ascend to the IX^0 would have cost the would-be initiate a total of £103.10s in entry fees – a very considerable sum for the period – and he or she would then have been expected to pay an annual subscription of 33 guineas.

At the beginning of 1914 Crowley carried out the series of sexo-magical operations which those who follow him refer to as The Paris Workings.[2] These had the primary object of invoking the gods Jupiter and Mercury and the secondary one of getting these same gods to supply Crowley and Neuburg with money, and were homosexual in type, Neuburg playing the active part. It is likely that Crowley decided to use this method, not practised in the original OTO, firstly because it appealed to elements in his own psychological make-up, secondly because of the 'casual act of sex' which almost four years before had been homosexual in nature and had produced 'a great wonder', Crowley's attainment of the grade of Master of the Temple, and lastly because Crowley always wanted to experiment with any and every type of occult technique.

The magical workings began on 31 December 1913 with Crowley 'receiving the sacrament from a certain priest A.B.' – a curious phrase which in this context means that Crowley had had a homosexual connection with 'A.B.' – and painting a pentacle, that is a magical, symbolic design of the god Mercury.

At 11.30 pm the two began the working proper by Neuburg
dancing the Banishing Ritual of the Pentagram following which
they invoked Thoth-Hermes, the Graeco-Egyptian equivalent of
Mercury by Crowley's The Building of the Pyramid, Ritual
DCLXXI.[3] This ceremony included sado-masochistic elements,
Crowley scourging Neuburg on the buttocks, cutting a cross
over his heart and binding a chain round his forehead. The
invocation was concluded by midnight and an act of buggery took
place, Crowley being the passive partner, during which the two
magicians chanted:

> Jungitur in vati vates, rex inclyte rhabdou
> Hermes tu venias, verba nefanda ferens.
> (Magician is joined with magician; Hermes King of
> the Rod, appear, bringing the unspeakable word.)

This Latin hexameter had been composed for Crowley by his
friend Walter Duranty, foreign correspondent of the *New York
Times*, who lived until 1957 and was probably the 'priest A.B.'
from whom Crowley had 'received the sacrament'.

The buggery did not result in a sexual climax on Neuburg's
part; either because as the record seems to claim Mercury was in
a mischievous mood and made Neuburg over-excited or much
more probably because he was not excited enough by Crowley's
charms. Nevertheless it was considered that the rite had been
partially successful, for to Crowley's psychic vision the room
appeared full of snake-wreathed staffs of Mercury with the snakes
alive and moving, while Neuburg felt himself partially possessed
by the spirit of the god.

On 1 January Crowley modelled from yellow wax what was
referred to as an 'image of Mercury' but took the form of an
erect penis; presumably this was a piece of sympathetic magic
designed to ensure that in the operations to come Neuburg would
not again be troubled by impotence. The second working was
begun at 11.20 pm on the same day. This time Neuburg reached
orgasm and was fully possessed by the god; in a sense he had
become the god and as such Crowley questioned him to get magical
advice. Crowley for example asked how Mercury could be better

invoked and the entranced Neuburg replied: 'Use a gold
pentagram, placing the same in a prominent position; drink
yellow wine and eat fish before the ceremony. Let the clock be
removed.' The god also gave advice on how Jupiter should be
summoned: 'Scarlet and silver should be worn, and the crown
by o.s.v. [the initials of one of Crowley's magical mottoes]. L.T.
['*Lampada tradam*', the magical motto of Neuburg][4] is to wear
the scarlet robe. Violets are to be strewn and trodden with bare
feet.'

Crowley enquired of Mercury when he could expect to receive
occult promotion from the grade he claimed at the time, that of
Master of the Temple, to the next grade, that of Magus. Mercury
gave a mysterious reply: 'L.P.L. is 50 and P is 6.' To this, years
later Crowley was to comment that the time elapsed between his
becoming a Master of the Temple on 3 December 1909 and his
attainment of the grade of Magus on 12 October 1915 was six
years less fifty days. There was something wrong with Crowley's
mathematics; the actual period was six years less fifty-two days.

The third working commenced at midnight on 3 January. The
ritual ended at about 1 o'clock and Crowley became possessed
of the god. As such Neuburg records him as giving a long
inspired verbal instruction on the subject of the relationship
between himself (as the god) and semen:

Every drop of semen which Hermes sheds is a world. The technical term for
this semen is KRATOS. . . . People upon the worlds are like maggots upon an
apple, all forms of life bred by the worlds are in the nature of parasites. Pure
worlds are flaming globes, each a conscious being. . . .

Ma is the name of the god who seduced the Phallus away from the Yoni;
hence the physical universe. All worlds are excreta, they represent wasted
semen. Therefore all is blasphemy. This explains why man made God in his own
image.

In the same monologue Mercury was identified with Christ, a
theological statement which Crowley found quite new to him
although as Jean Overton Fuller has pointed out it can be found
in the writings of Madame Blavatsky.

Mercury went on to suggest that he should be invoked on the
following day not by ritual but by geomancy – a form of divination

in which judgement is made from the marks made by stabbing a pointed stick into a box of earth. For the four days following this Jupiter should be homosexually invoked. Mercury then stated that it was important that the two magicians should have banquets and should 'overcome shame generally'. The method which the god urged to carry out the last suggestion was not recorded but it seems likely that it was proposed that Crowley should take part in an act of buggery before some of his friends. This it would appear was actually done at the house of Crowley's mistress Jane Cheron, his partner in the act being Walter Duranty.

Finally Mercury instructed that the working in progress should be concluded with another homosexual act but as both men were by now very tired this was done 'in symbolic form only'. This act of disobedience annoyed the god, or so the magicians believed, for it was to this that they attributed a heavy cold which Crowley developed on the next day. At lunchtime on 5 January they made good the omission; Crowley became entranced and, as the god, spoke at great length, his most notable piece of advice being that: 'Respectability is the greatest of all blinds. The general key in reading ancient documents of a magical nature is to suspect the worse.' This advice of course served to strengthen the tendency which Crowley had acquired from Reuss to interpret alchemical manuscripts from a sexual point of view.

The temple was formally closed and the magicians sat talking. Suddenly Neuburg became possessed. He said that they were unleashing an enormous magical force, that international complications were to be feared and that 'those who adopt this rite will either succeed completely or fail utterly. There is no middle path for it is impossible to escape the ring of Divine Karma created.' As soon as the god had left Neuburg's body Crowley became entranced, being – as the two later considered – obsessed by an evil spirit posing as Mercury. This entity informed them that the supreme act of sexual magic involved the rape, ritual murder and dissection into nine pieces of the body of a young girl. The resulting chunks of flesh were to be offered as sacrifices to the immortal gods; the head to Juno, the right shoulder to Jupiter

and the left to Saturn, the right buttock to Mars and the left to
Venus, the arms to Priapus and the legs to Pan. It is only fair to
Crowley and Neuburg to emphasize that they both believed that
the obsessing entity's advice smacked of black magic and should
therefore be disregarded. Neuburg again became possessed and
uttered a number of predictions – that he himself would get
married in the following June for example. All these prophecies
were to prove false.

In the evening of the same day what was officially regarded as
the fourth working took place, the events of lunchtime being
regarded as a continuation of the third working. This was an
invocation of Jupiter with Crowley playing the male part,
probably because Neuburg was sexually exhausted. The verse
chanted, again composed by Duranty, was:

> Haud secus ac puerum spumanti semini vates
> Lustrat, dum gaudens accipit alter acquas;
> Sparge, precor, servus, hominum rex atque deorum;
> Juppiter omnipotens, aurea dona, tuis.
> (As the magician washes the boy with foaming semen,
> While the other in his joy receives the waters,
> So do thou, Almighty Jupiter, King of men and gods,
> Shower thy slaves with thine own gold.)

The temple was closed at 10.30 pm, after which the two sat
talking. At about 1 o'clock in the morning Neuburg had a vision
of Jupiter and received a cryptic Latin message meaning: 'The
road is today. The names of the Holiest in happiness have the
road. God gives a sign in the road.'

It would be exacting too much of the readers of this book to
give details of all the other twenty homosexual rites, the last
taking place on 12 February, which made up the Paris Working,
but it is worth giving brief details of the eleventh and thirteenth
rites as they exhibited much of occult interest. The former
working, which took place on Wednesday, 21 January, and was
an invocation of Jupiter in his Egyptian form of Ammon-Ra,
was notable for the wonders of psychic vision which accompanied
it – thus Ammon-Ra was himself seen while a cone of white
astral light whirled above the wax model of a penis which was

upon the altar. Neuburg became entranced and obtained from
Jupiter a message, expressed in the magical language developed
by the Elizabethan occultists Dee and Kelley, informing him that
the old gods wanted to regain their ancient rule over the earth
and had chosen him and Crowley as 'fiery arrows' to be shot
against the 'slave-gods'. This message of course was identical
with that of *The Book of the Law*.

At the conclusion of the thirteenth rite, which took place on
26 January, both magicians remembered, or at any rate thought
they remembered, a previous life in which their souls had been
incarnated in ancient Crete. Crowley had been a female temple-
dancer named Aia; Neuburg had been a candidate for initiation
named Mardocles. The latter had been subjected to an ordeal;
he had to watch Aia performing an erotic dance and either remain
completely cool and unmoved by her charms or rape her. If he
failed to do either he was to be castrated by a barbaric instrument
resembling a huge candle-snuffer. Mardocles was sexually aroused
by Aia's dancing but out of pity for the girl failed to violate her.
In spite of this he escaped the usual penalty, for he was a favourite
of the High Priest. Nevertheless both Mardocles and Aia were
sold into slavery to a household where their main task was to
'amuse the family by various copulations'.

This recovery of a past incarnation inspired Crowley to
philosophical musings on the relationship between Neuburg and
himself: 'I am always', he said, 'unlucky for you, you know;
you always have to sacrifice everything for my love. You don't
want to in the least; that is because we both have hold of the
wrong end of the stick. If only I could leave you and you could
love me. It would be lucky. But that apparently has never
happened. Mutual indifference and mutual passion, and so on.'
This is a revealing comment, indicating that Crowley still loved
Neuburg but that the latter's 'Crowleyitis' – the sick passion
which can be deduced from Neuburg's record of his 1909
magical retirement in Scotland – had passed away.

The final rite of the series took place on 12 February. This was
'calm and deep, the very aroma of earth in spring'. According to
Crowley the Paris Working was highly successful. Its aim had

been to get Neuburg the gift of Jupiter, that is, money, and he duly received some, probably from his Aunt Ti, who was unfailingly generous to him. But unfortunately for Crowley Neuburg became 'Jupiter the Bestower, and had unworthy guests' – this seems to mean that he gave money to others than Crowley. On the whole however Crowley was satisfied; he felt that the sex magic techniques of the OTO had given quicker and better results than the pure ritual methods he had learned in the Golden Dawn and he made up his mind to make extensive experiments with them.

9

The Departure and Later Life of Neuburg

THE PARIS WORKING was to prove the last occult operation Crowley and Neuburg were to undertake together. The latter rushed back to London at the end of the homosexual rites in which he had taken part and for some time avoided Crowley, making it apparent to disinterested observers that he preferred the company of almost anyone else to that of the man whom officially he still regarded as his 'Holy Guru'.

In May Crowley sought out Neuburg – the first time he had had cause to do so, for previously the latter had followed him about like a pet dog – and Crowley had a violent argument with Hayter Preston, a close friend of Neuburg's family, who strongly disapproved of the association between their relative and Crowley and were in near-despair at the considerable amounts of Neuburg family money that had ended up in Crowley's pocket. Neuburg was invited to spend the summer with Olivia Haddon, a woman formerly associated with some of Crowley's magical activities who had rented three cottages at Branscombe in Devon.

Here Neuburg had many long conversations on occult matters with Vittoria Cremers, a one-time admirer of Crowley who now habitually referred to him as 'that impostor' and 'that charlatan'. She seems to have strengthened Neuburg's half-formed resolve to break with Crowley and at some time between 23 September and 24 October 1914 he plucked up his courage, visited Crowley and told him of his determination to leave the AA and to have nothing more to do with the man with whom, to use his own phrase, he had 'been right down in the deeps of horror, and upon the heights'. Crowley ritually cursed him as a traitor.

There is a common belief that Crowley's disciples usually ended their magical careers by suicide or incarceration in a mental hospital. As Neuburg was intimately associated with Crowley and his occult practices for five years – indeed it would not be going too far to say that throughout the entire period of Crowley's life no man had such a lengthy or close occult connection with him as Neuburg – his later career is not without interest. Immediately after Crowley had cursed him Neuburg became mentally ill – unable to concentrate, to write or to conduct his life in an ordered manner, and having what was referred to at the time as 'a nervous breakdown'. He was treated for this by E. T. Jensen, the physician who had officiated at the Rites of Eleusis and had edited some of Crowley's writings. Jensen, who had also broken off his friendship with Crowley, was one of the earliest English admirers of Freud and it seems likely that he treated Neuburg by some sort of psychoanalysis. Whether this was so, or whether he used the traditional bromides of English medicine or employed some combination of the two, there is no doubt that he won his patient's gratitude; the late C. R. Cammell had a drawing of Neuburg by Howard Sommerville inscribed on the back: 'To my sweet Leech, Ernest Thomas Jensen, Esquire, M.D. From his defaulting poet-patient, Victor B. Neuburg, XIII:XII:MCMXVI.'[1]

In the following year Neuburg was conscripted into the army as a private in the Army Service Corps and sent to France, arriving at Le Havre on 20 September. He was the most unmilitary of soldiers, developing a limp which forced him to carry a walking stick as well as a rifle, and having to be kept on the lightest of light duties. His biographer Jean Overton Fuller has brought to light a description of him by his Sergeant-Major: 'He was only kept together by string and sealing wax. He could never shave without cutting himself and so he always looked like Death from a Thousand Cuts. He had no manual dexterity. His movements were not synchronized. His hands and feet worked from two different dynamos. He was the walking mockery of the entire Army system and everything it was meant to be.'[2]

By the autumn of 1919 Neuburg was out of the army and living at Vine Cottage – the property of his aunt – in the Sussex village of Steyning. It was here, when he and a friend were looking over a railway bridge, that he made an extraordinary remark about Ione de Forest, the professional dancer who had been hired to take part in the Rites of Eleusis. 'Crowley', said Neuburg, 'murdered Ione de Forest.' In the ordinary sense of the words Neuburg was talking rubbish; 'Ione de Forest' had died by her own hand at the beginning of August 1912. On the other hand the statement does much to explain Neuburg's change in attitude from love to hate towards Crowley.

'Ione de Forest' was the stage name adopted by Joan Hayes, a former student of the Royal Academy of Dramatic Art with a somewhat humble background – her father kept a lodging-house in the Brixton Road and her fees at RADA had been paid by a local businessman, perhaps a bookmaker or a grocer.[3] She had taken part in the Rites of Eleusis without having any prior interest in or knowledge of the occult in general or magic in particular. She had simply answered an advertisement in the *Stage* and from there gone on to dance as various goddesses under Crowley's direction. Neuburg was fascinated by her from the first and felt an affection for her which so it would seem Crowley disapproved of on the grounds that she was a 'Circe' who might bewitch Neuburg away from the magical path. He was much relieved therefore when in December 1911 Joan Hayes married not Neuburg but an old friend of his named Wilfred Merton.

Six months after the marriage however Joan left her husband and took up residence in a Chelsea studio. At the same time, or perhaps slightly before, she became Neuburg's mistress and the two took a cottage in Essex which they used at weekends; Crowley was furious. Two months later she shot herself. No clear reason for this act of self-murder became apparent at the inquest – but Neuburg was convinced that Crowley had put a spell on her, as a 'Circe'. And perhaps he had, for there is a revealing passage in Crowley's *Magick in Theory and Practice* in which he stated that he had once 'found it necessary to slay a

Circe who was bewitching brethren. He merely walked to the door of her room and drew an astral T ('traditore') and the symbol of Saturn with an astral dagger. Within 48 hours she shot herself'.

Crowley added a curious moral apologia for this alleged psychic murder; he claimed that the woman in question 'was not human, the sheath of a Star, but an advanced planetary demon whose rash ambition had captured a body beyond its capacity to conduct'. If indeed the 'advanced planetary demon' was Joan Hayes it is easy enough to understand why Neuburg's love and admiration for his teacher turned to hate. Nor is there anything surprising in the fact that it was eighteen months after Joan's death before Neuburg broke with Crowley; such psychological wounds as that which he had suffered often fester unseen for months or even years before they finally burst.

At Steyning Neuburg established a small private press, the Vine Press, whose productions, most of them Neuburg's own poetry, were characterized by the curious type-fount used. This had an unusually wide letter W and a linked double OO. Financially the press was not a success – Neuburg's poetry was much admired by some critics, Katherine Mansfield for example, but never attracted more than a few dozen readers.

Nevertheless in November 1921 Neuburg married Kathleen Goddard, an old mistress from pre-war days. It might be thought that this marriage was an indication that he had psychologically recovered from the effects of his relationship with Crowley, that the glamorous lure of magic had lost its appeal for him, but this was not so. He had only married Kathleen because she wanted to have a child but was not prepared to do so outside the marriage bond. Spiritually and psychologically he lacked life force. Hayter Preston, who knew him well, has described his condition at that time: 'Victor, at Steyning, was a dead man; he gave up magic and spent the whole of the rest of his life feeling he was not doing what he was meant to be doing.'[4] In March 1924 Neuburg's wife gave birth to a son; three months later she took a lover. Neuburg, full of the conventionally 'progressive' views of his time, not only made no objection to this but actually went to the lengths of seeing the pair off when they went away for weekends.

The shadow of Crowley occasionally fell blackly across Neuburg's path. In 1926 for example he was delighted to have some poems accepted for *Argosy*; they never appeared, for the managing director of the firm informed the editor that Neuburg was blacklisted as an associate of Crowley. Neuburg was more fortunate with the *Bookman's Journal*, which in the same year published 'The Green Ladie', a ballad which according to some critics Dryden could have written:

> Oh come with me strolling
> The white clouds are rolling,
> The sky's blue is pale and the chaffinches sing:
> The sun is full shining,
> It's time for divining
> The birth of the year from the heart of the Spring.

This poem came to the attention of C. R. Cammell, a Scottish poet, critic and student of occultism – later he was to be, with Lewis Spence, co-editor of the occult journal *Atlantis Quarterly* – who carried on a lengthy correspondence with him although they did not have a personal meeting until 1930. It was not until 1933, when he was reading Crowley's *Equinox* in an Edinburgh library, that Cammell discovered that Crowley and Neuburg had been acquainted. It tells us a good deal about the depth of the psychological wound which had been inflicted upon Neuburg by Crowley and his magic that he had been on terms of intimate friendship with a fellow poet for seven years without once revealing that he had even heard of Aleister Crowley. Cammell however was not afraid to raise the subject with his friend.

Once I had discovered [wrote Cammell] Victor's connection with Crowley I tackled him about it. He avowed the friendship, the magical experiments. Did the magic really work, I asked him. Only too well, he replied. He would, he swore, never meet A[leister] C[rowley] again; but he would talk of him. He admitted that Crowley was a great poet – 'the greatest of the age' – this from such a poet as Neuburg, himself one of the few immortals of our time, as I am convinced he is, and long estranged from and embittered against Crowley, is an important testimony.[5]

During his years at Steyning Neuburg's main place of recreation was the Sanctuary, a sort of open colony for anarchists, Bohemians and anyone who wanted to live on the land and grow vegetables, which was owned by Vera Pragnell, a disciple of Edward Carpenter. Here a curious incident occurred which may perhaps throw some light on the psychological effect which Crowley had on Neuburg during their years of association. It arose out of a conversation between Neuburg and Vera Pragnell on the way in which some beings resemble animals in appearance. Vera Pragnell referred to an individual she knew who looked like a horse and Neuburg told her that she herself was round and cuddly 'like a bear crossed with a dove'. Suddenly the conversation took a more sinister turn; what happened is told in a page from Vera Pragnell's diary:

'And you – you are awfully goat-like' I began, when I noticed he stiffened and under his sallowness he seemed to go deathly white.

'Darling Vicky,' I said, throwing my arms round him. 'I love goats, don't you?'

'No – no, not really.'

'But why are you so upset?'

He sat down and buried his face in his hands. After ages he muttered, 'I *was* one. A goat was my curse.'

Within minutes he was fooling again. 'Forget it.' But it was weird; one just couldn't forget.[6]

In other words Crowley had brought to the fore in Neuburg a ruttish, lustful side to his personality, the evil and averse side of the god Pan.[7]

As well as his visits to the Sanctuary Neuburg had the occasional pleasure of calls from those who were either old friends or admirers of his poetry who wanted to meet him. Among the latter were Tallulah Bankhead, Gertrude Stein and Lord Alfred Douglas, who had the door slammed in his face by Neuburg's wife. An old friend who called at fairly frequent intervals was Philip Heseltine – Peter Warlock the composer – whose anthology of drinking songs, *The Merry Go Down*, allegedly compiled by one 'Rab Noolas' ('Saloon Bar' backwards), had been issued by Neuburg's Vine Press. Interestingly enough Heseltine was himself a practitioner of ritual magic[8] – presumably this was the reason for him choosing the name Warlock as his musical pseudonym – so it is clear that Neuburg's revulsion from occultism was confined to the Crowleyan version of it.

At some time in the summer of 1930 Neuburg met at the Sanctuary a woman who had a real admiration for him. This was balm to Neuburg's soul, for his wife now treated him with utter contempt, and within a year he was living with this woman in North London. This had a stimulating effect upon him and he threw himself into a number of activities in a way he had not done since his break from Crowley. He was for example one of the founders and the first secretary of the pioneer criminological organization which started life as the Association for the Scientific Treatment of Criminals and ultimately became the Institute for the Study and Treatment of Delinquency. Far more important, since it had a real influence on some aspects of the development of English twentieth-century poetry, was his appointment in 1933 as poetry editor of the *Sunday Referee*. Each week he held a poetry competition and, although naturally enough the standard of the weekly winner was often low, Neuburg made some important poetic discoveries including Pamela Hansford Johnson, Jean Overton Fuller and most notable of all Dylan Thomas.

The first poem which Thomas submitted to Neuburg's competition – one beginning 'That sanity be kept . . .' – was published as a weekly prize-winner on 3 September 1933 and was described by Neuburg as 'the best modernist poem I have yet received'. Another, and today very well-known, poem by Thomas – 'The force that through the green fuse drives the flower' – was the prize-winner for the following 29 October. Neuburg was most enthusiastic about this, describing it as 'cosmic in outlook . . . a large poem greatly expressed'. Further Thomas poems were published on 7 January 1934 – 'Love me not as the dreaming nurses' – and 11 February – 'A process in the weather of the heart'.[9] So impressed was Neuburg with Thomas's verse that he wanted to bring out a small book of it under the patronage of the *Sunday Referee*. But the editor of the paper was suspicious; it hardly seemed possible to him that a boy of eighteen could have written work of such profundity and he considered it likely that Neuburg was the victim of some elaborate practical joke played by one or more intellectuals. To settle the matter Thomas was invited to London, where a party was given in his honour and he managed to convince the *Sunday Referee* of the authenticity of his poems. Later in the same year *18 Poems* by Dylan Thomas was published jointly by the *Sunday Referee* and the Parton Press, the former paying sixty per cent, the latter forty per cent, of the costs of production. The book was favourably received, sold moderately well, and from this small beginning Dylan Thomas was able to carve out a considerable literary reputation for himself.

By now Neuburg was printing in the *Sunday Referee* many poets who were eventually to become well known in one or another literary field. Besides Thomas, Pamela Hansford Johnson and Jean Overton Fuller, those whom he printed, mostly for the first time, included Ewart Milne, Francis Berry, Idris Davies, Ruthven Todd, Julian Symons, David Gascoyne and Laurie Lee.

Curiously enough at around this time Crowley published an article called 'My Search for the Absolute' in the *Sunday Referee*. He insisted that this article was the first of a series which he had been contracted to write; the editor of the paper as strongly insisted that it was intended to be a single article and not the beginning of a series. A legal action followed, which Crowley lost. Years later, when the *Sunday Referee* ceased publication, Crowley sent its former editor a postcard reading, 'So you didn't win after all'.

It is likely that this near contact with Crowley upset Neuburg but all things considered it was probably the happiest period of his life; he had a job, he got great pleasure from associating with the young poets with whom that job brought him into contact, he was living with a woman of whom he was fond, and who was fond of him, and he had almost recovered from the psychological wounds inflicted on him during his years with Crowley. He died of tuberculosis on 31 May 1940.

10

Sexual Wisdom

THE PARIS WORKING with Neuburg had been, so Crowley considered, thoroughly successful. But *why*, he asked himself, had it been successful? What was the rationale of the magic of the OTO? The answers he arrived at are essential knowledge if one desires to understand Crowley's life between 1914 and his death in 1947. He had already attempted to answer these questions in an essay entitled 'Energized Enthusiasm' published in the *Equinox*, No. 9 (March 1913). This essay marked an important stage in Crowley's intellectual development and took as its starting-point two basic assumptions:

(1) That any form of sexual activity was good in itself. This view was taken to what the sexual liberals of the time would have considered extreme lengths; thus he wrote that he agreed with 'the Head Master of Eton that paederastic passions do no harm', adding that he thought them 'the only redeeming feature of sexual life at public schools'.

(2) That there was some close connection between sexuality and genius. He wrote that 'the divine consciousness which is reflected and refracted in the works of Genius feeds upon a certain secretion . . . analogous to semen but not identical with it'. This point of view bears a certain relationship to certain tantric teachings according to which *ojas*, a subtle essence derived from but not identical with *bindhu*, semen, fills the lower centres of the tantric adept, rises through subtle passages, unknown to ordinary science, to the top of the spine and once

there, goes through a transformation which results in the physical body being flooded with a divine essence.

Having decided that genius had a link with sexuality, particularly male sexuality – Crowley argued that few women displayed genius and those who did had an element of hermaphroditism in their psycho-physical make-up – Crowley went on to ask firstly how genius could be created in an individual and secondly how once created, it could be brought into productive action. His answer was very simple: Bacchus, Aphrodite and Apollo – that is, wine, women and song – should be invoked. Crowley gave considerable thought as to how exactly this should be done.

The invocation of Bacchus was simple enough; wine and other alcoholic drinks were freely available. Their only possible disadvantage was that they might make some people drunk, not a state usually compatible with the sudden achievement of genius. The best thing, he decided, would be to have a cup-bearer who was a magical adept and would carefully avoid giving drink to anyone who showed the least sign of drunkenness. Or perhaps, mused Crowley, it was better to avoid alcohol altogether and instead to invoke Bacchus by 'the elixir introduced by me to Europe' – an infusion in fruit juices of the hallucinogenic cactus mescaline.

The invocation of Apollo – that is, some form or other of music – presented more difficulties, for so few musical instruments were really suitable for the purpose. The harmonium for example could not be used because it was 'horrible' (presumably Crowley associated it with the religious exercises of Protestant Christianity). On the whole, he decided, the best instruments for the purpose were the organ, the violin and the tom-tom, the old favourite of his friend Commander Marston.

Most difficult of all was the problem of 'invoking Aphrodite', that is, achieving a state of sexual excitement, without becoming merely lascivious. Crowley did not give his answer to this problem, for after posing the question he broke off his essay – presumably because there were fairly strict limits on what he could safely say in an openly published form – and concluded with a very discreet description of a sexo-magical rite.

After his experiments with Neuburg he felt that he was now a real expert on sexual magic, whether auto-, hetero-, or homo-, and he wrote a series of instructions for the seventh, eighth and ninth degrees of the OTO in which he gave his considered opinion and advice on the subject. Most of these instructions were translated into German and published by Reuss shortly before the outbreak of the 1914–18 war. It is only recently however that they have been published in English.[1] These documents are worthy of some description, comment and criticism, for from 1914 to his death in 1947 they provided, with *The Book of the Law*, the solid core of theory on which Crowley based all his magical activities.

Of the Nature of the Gods, an instruction for initiates of the seventh degree of the OTO, gives little practical instruction in sexual magic but largely confines itself to Crowleyan theology. It is taught that in the macrocosm, that is the 'great world' or universe, there is only one true god and that is the sun. 'Not only', says this instruction, 'is the Earth but a chilled spark of the Sun, a dropped petal of the Rose of Heaven, but the source of all Light and Life upon the planet is that same Sun. Not only is He creator, but sustainer, and it is He also that destroyeth in due season, and redeemeth when the time is come.'[2] For Crowley then the sun was the supreme deity. On earth however he is represented by the phallus, the male sexual organ, which is 'the viceregent of the Sun', 'the sole giver of life'. All the universal gods – that is deities such as the gods and goddesses of the moon, of fire, of mountains and of trees – are, it is asserted, but personifications of the penis. Thus the fire-deity is an image of the sun 'and a fable of the Phallus'; the tree is 'but the flowering of the Phallus', while the moon-deity is an image of the vagina 'only worshipped with Sol in aspect as an extension of the Phallus'.

After making these specific theological assertions the instruction goes on to denounce all orthodox religion, particularly Christianity: '. . . the Christs of the Latin, Lutheran and Anglican Churches alike are but the machine-gods of all fraud and oppression. . . .' The OTO initiate is urged to fight against these

and other 'machine-gods': '. . . war constantly upon all tyranny
and superstition, and mostly against such bigotries as "orthodox"
Christianity as interpreted in its material sense, old wives' tales
and foolish fables, the immoral doctrines of original sin and
vicarious atonement, and the most hideous eschatology in the
history of false religion. Nor can much less be averred against
all other orthodoxies, with their fables equally absurd, their
postulates equally immoral.'[3]

Having declared that all orthodox religions are rubbish, and
that the sole true gods are the sun and his 'viceregent' the penis,
the instruction goes on to give directions for the worship of the
latter: 'Let every Knight [that is, OTO initiate], appoint a privy
Chapel . . . having an ever-burning lamp as an image of the Sun
to give light to a Phallus carved or moulded in gold, silver,
platinum or bronze by the fine art of the sculptor. And let the
Knight keep oft times vigil before it . . . in such wise that the
Image becomes consecrated by his will. Thus shall it be a store-
house of strength, and a focus or magnet drawing to itself all
subtle forces, and radiating benediction.'[4] What was considered
by Crowley to be 'a deeper worship' of the penis was also
recommended. This instructed the 'Knight' firstly to imagine a
sacred phallus to be present in some part of his own body, then
to 'worship and cherish that image with unwearying care' and
finally to consecrate himself with oaths to 'the service of the
Lord' (that is, the penis).

Of the Secret Marriages of Gods with Men, an instruction intended
for members of the eighth degree of the OTO, gives both theoretical teaching and instruction in an occult technique which can
only be called magical masturbation. What first strikes the reader
of the present day however is not the theory given or the
practice taught but an extraordinary passage which seems to give
serious acceptance to one of the darker legends of Eastern
European anti-semitism – the myth of Jewish blood sacrifice of
Gentiles: 'It is said that there is a sect of the Jewish Brethren
called Chassidim whose practice is the sacrifice of a man. Thus
preferably a child, but also an adult, is taken from among the
Gentiles, and ceremonially slain so that not a drop of blood is lost,

lest the spirit of the victim, taking refuge in that drop, escape the Exorcist. This blood is then consumed as a sacrament, or employed for talismanic purposes. . . .'

It has been argued by apologists for Crowley that this passage does not really mean what it seems to mean, that the 'It is said' at the beginning implies that he was merely using the old story of Jewish blood-sacrifice as a peg on which to hang some occult theorizing. Unfortunately for this explanation however there is a passage in the introduction to *Sepher Sephiroth*, a kabalistic dictionary published in No. 8 of the *Equinox*, which makes it quite clear that Crowley really believed that the Jews of Eastern Europe practised ritual murder. The passage reads as follows:

That the 'Old Testament' is mainly the history of the struggle of the phallic Jehovah against the rest of the Elohim, and that his sacrifices were of blood, and human blood at that, is indisputable.

Human sacrifices are today still practised by the Jews of Eastern Europe, as is set forth at length by the late Sir Richard Burton in the MS. which the wealthy Jews of England have compassed heaven and earth to suppress, and evidenced by the ever-recurring Pogroms against which so senseless an outcry is made by those who live among those degenerate Jews who are at least not cannibals.[5]

From this passage it is very clear that Neuburg was completely justified when he called Crowley an anti-semite.

As well as referring to blood sacrifices supposedly conducted by Jews, and making an apology for the pogroms that disgraced Czarist Russia, Crowley in the same document made admiring reference to the supposed orgies of the mediaeval witches' sabbath:

In the black hours of the earth, when the Christian superstition with fell blight withered most malignantly the peoples of Europe, when our own Holy Order was dispersed . . . there were yet found certain to hold Truth in their hearts. . . . And these at certain seasons went at night by ways open or hidden to heaths and mountains, and there dancing together, and with strange suppers and spells diverse, did call forth Him whom the enemy called ignorantly Satan, and was in truth the Great God Pan. . . . And each when first inducted to the revel was made partner of the Incarnate One by the Consummation of the Rite of Marriage.[6]

The hard, sexual core of this instruction is contained in two short sections entitled respectively *Of Great Marriages* and *Of Lesser Marriages*; these outline the practice of magical masturbation. The 'greater marriage' it is instructed should be carried out as follows:

> On every occasion before sleep let the Adept figure his goddess before him, wooing her ardently in imagination. . . . Therefore, with or without an assistant, let him purge himself fully and freely [that is, let him masturbate to orgasm] at the end of restraint trained and ordered unto exhaustion, concentrating ever ardently upon the Body of the Great Goddess, and let the Offering [the semen] be preserved in her consecrated temple or in a talisman especially prepared for this practice . . . it is to be noted in all this that both God and the Soul are male or female as convenience requires. See, for a curious example, the mystic treatise called the *Bagh-i-Muattur*.[7]

It is worth noting that the *Bagh-i-Muattur*, a spoof 'translation' from the Persian published by Crowley in 1910, is not a 'mystic treatise' in the ordinary sense of the words. It is in fact a verse-treatise on homosexuality and Crowley gave it an obscene dedication to 'Those Persons whose Unbending Uprightness, Penetration, Retentiveness, Capacity for Hard Work, Over-flowing Ability, and Inside Knowledge have so much enlarged the Fundamental Basis of my Philosophy'.

Of Lesser Marriages gives instruction on how the OTO initiate should obtain 'familiar spirits' – that is elementals (spirits of Earth, Air, Fire and Water) who will invisibly serve the magician and help him obtain the things he desires. The adept is first given various warnings; he must not fall from the love of the Great Goddess into affection for these lower creatures, but must be to them a master; he must not have more than four familiar spirits and he must regulate their service, laying down at what hours each should work for him; he must treat them firmly but kindly being on guard against their tricks.

The actual techniques laid down for obtaining familiar spirits are simple enough; they are to be called 'by the Keys of Enoch . . . and let there be after the Calls an evocation by the Wand and let the Marrow of the Wand be preserved within the pyramids. . . .' By 'the Keys of Enoch' is meant the strange invocations of the

ABOVE LEFT Crowley when a schoolboy

ABOVE RIGHT MacGregor Mathers, head of the Order of the Golden Dawn

RIGHT Crowley with his wife Rose Kelly and child in 1910

ABOVE LEFT A drawing of Crowley
Augustus John

ABOVE RIGHT Crowley demonstra
the yogic technique of breath cont
(pranayama)

LEFT Victor Neuburg

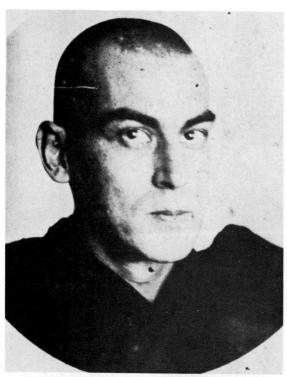

ABOVE Alan Bennett

RIGHT Leila Waddell playing her
violin for the mysteries of Eleusis

LEFT Lea Hirsig in front of Crowley's portrait of her

BELOW The Abbey of Thele with the great rock of Cefal towering in the background

ABOVE LEFT Crowley and Lea Hirsig
with the children outside the
Abbey of Thelema

ABOVE RIGHT Jane Wolfe and Lea
Hirsig outside the Abbey of Thelema

LEFT Raoul Loveday

LEFT Betty May,
Loveday's wife

BELOW The Sanct
Sanctorum –
Crowley's templ
the Abbey of
Thelema

LEFT Crowley drawn by Augustus John two years before his death in 1947

BELOW LEFT Crowley's drawing of his second wife Maria de Miramar

BELOW RIGHT Crowley – a self portrait

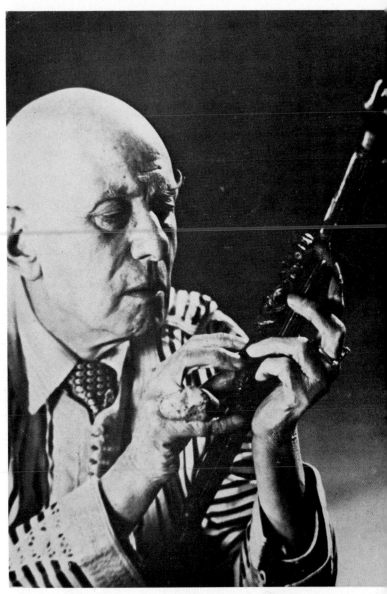

Crowley holding his magic wand

sixteenth-century magicians Dee and Kelley (see p. 51), by the 'Wand' is meant the penis of the magician, the 'pyramids' are talismans drawn on parchment in the shape of truncated pyramids, while 'the Marrow of the Wand' means the male sexual secretion. In other words, the magician is instructed to take one of the pyramidical talismans of the Enochian system of Dee and Kelley, recite an invocation to its ruling spirit and then, concentrating the imagination upon that same spirit, masturbate over the talisman.

The thirteenth section of *Of the Secret Marriages* is of some interest; in it Crowley warns the initiated adepts of the OTO that they cannot approach sex in the fairly casual way of ordinary men and women:

> To you . . . if you have dared to use this force of the Holy Phallus, is its abuse fatal and deadly.
>
> To the man of earth it matters but little if he suffer nocturnal pollution, or indulge in wantonness; to you that are Adepts it is ruin absolute.
>
> For all that Force which passeth from under your control, unless so directed and fortified by your Will that it is but a loyal soldier unto death, is as artillery abandoned that is seized upon by the enemy and turned against you. . . . Be wary therefore, for obsession, bodily wasting and disease, madness and even murder upon you may be inflicted by the engines that ye, having forged for the service of mankind and for the glory of the Lord, leave to the malignancy of the demon that he may turn them to your own destruction. [8]

Liber Agapé is Crowley's definitive treatise on sexual magic. However, while it gives fairly full details of the techniques to be adopted by OTO adepts, these instructions are often couched in a pseudo-archaic and symbolic language which makes it difficult for the ordinary reader to understand their exact nature. While the treatise is largely concerned with heterosexual magic, a guarded, but favourable, reference to the type of homosexual magic he had practised with Neuburg is made in the section of the work entitled *Tractate of the Great Thing Hidden in the Palace of the King*:

> . . . albeit Man is active and Woman passive, yet Man is Peace and Woman Power. . . .
>
> There is therefore one magick act that leadeth unto life [that is, normal sexual relations between man and woman] another that abutteth upon death

[that is, abnormal sexual relations]. And the first unlimiteth and the second returneth unto itself. Yet therefore is the last perfect, a true rite of the Highest, too exalted even for the vulgar even of our holy and illuminated brethren.

And in its profanation it cometh forth from the demon and is manifested in all uncleanness. . . . Yet is it, albeit limited and unable to proceed from life to life, the highest of all means of Grace, for as wine is to water so is it unto the others in its exaltation of the soul of man; and whoso mastereth the same, even he is found worthy of rule. This was the secret . . . of our brother Richard Wagner . . . and of so many others, whose fame is eternal without our Order as within. . . . To this aspire ye above all things; for the True Light abideth therein yet more intensely than in the Other. For he that reverseth the whirlings of matter is greater than he that worketh therein.

Crowley added, 'But of all this is not here written: this is the Book of the Pathway that leadeth unto Life' – in other words sexual magic concerned with the normal relationship between men and women.

Liber Agapé often employs both Christian symbolism – sexual intercourse for example being referred to as 'the Sacrifice of the Mass' – and alchemical terminology, the mingled male and female secretions being called 'the Elixir'. Thus supposed miracles are to be achieved by following a technique symbolically described as follows:

. . . entering the privy chapel [the woman's vagina] do thou bestow at least one hour in adoration at the altar [that is, sexual play] exalting thyself in love toward God, and extolling Him in strophe and antistrophe.

Then do thou perform the Sacrifice of the Mass [that is, achieve orgasm].

The Elixir being then prepared solemnly and in silence, do thou consume it utterly [in other words the adept should swallow the mingled male and female secretions].

It is recommended that the preparation of the Elixir – described as 'the most powerful, the most radiant thing that existeth in the whole universe' – should be accompanied by rhythmic incantation. Thus for any work (*opus*, work, was the word normally used by Crowley to describe an act of sexual magic) pertaining to the goddess Venus the following incantation should be chanted during sexual intercourse and orgasm:

> *Tu Venus orta mari venias tu filia Patris,*
> *Exaudi penis carmina blanda, precor,*
> *Ne sit culpa nates nobis futuisse viriles,*
> *Sed caleat cunnus semper amore meo.*
> (O Venus, risen from the sea, come thou daughter of the Father,
> Listen to the bland songs of the penis, I pray,
> Let it be no sin to us to have buggered the virile arse,
> But let the vagina always be hot with my love.)

Liber Agapé was so curiously and almost archly worded that Crowley wrote his own comment upon it, *De Arte Magica*,[9] in which he conveyed his own ideas 'as to its right use, with other matters germane'. Crowley was first of all concerned with the right bodily state for the preparation of the Elixir. Here he saw a certain difficulty; for without 'Ceres and Bacchus' – bread and wine – he believed that it was difficult to raise the sexual ardour but on the other hand, 'the body should be free of all gross nutriment, so that the Elixir may be sucked up eagerly, and, running nobly into every part, revivify the whole'. On the whole he decided it was best if one had a full meal not less than three hours before a sex magic operation. After this no food should be taken but one could continue if one so wished to take wine and 'subtler agents' – that is, drugs.

Crowley was also concerned with the problem of whether or not sex magical workings could be carried out at the time when a woman was menstruating and considered this in a section entitled *Of the Course of the Moon and of her Influence*. He gave an affirmative answer to this, stating that in his belief this time was preferable to all others – 'the Sacrament is more efficacious than at any other time, as is figured by our ancient Brethren the Alchemists in their preference of the Red Tincture to the White'.

In another section he made some remarks on types of sexual activity, whether or not with a woman, which did not involve the penetration of the vagina and the mingling of male and female secretions: 'Now herein is a difficulty, since in this case the Matter of the Sacrament [the mingled secretions] cannot exist, for that there is no White Eagle [female secretions] to generate

the Gluten.' In spite of this Crowley held that such a rite was
efficacious; 'it may be', he said, 'that for certain operations it is
equal or superior to that explained in Initiates of the ninth
degree.'

After dealing with such matters as the choice of an assistant in
the rites, certain theories about the nature of Lilith and other
demons expressed in kabalistic treatises, and the quality and
quantity of the Elixir, Crowley wrote a section which illuminates
his own erotic fantasies. This deals with orgasm continued to the
point of death and is entitled *Of Eroto-Comatose Lucidity*. The
rite described in this begins by 'the Candidate' engaging in a
combination of heavy eating and drinking with athletic training.
On the day appointed for his ordeal one or more sexually
experienced women follow a process of arousing and exhausting
his sexual abilities. Every means possible is to be employed to
reach these ends; he is to be given ether, alcohol and strychnine
– although cocaine must be used with 'a certain prudence' – his
penis is to be given 'frictions' of brandy and eau-de-cologne,
while a spray of capsicum in ether is to be applied to his stomach.

Eventually the person undergoing the process will either fall
into a sleep from which he cannot be woken, however much
sexual stimulation is applied, or will carry out a final performance
of the sexual act. The stimulation may then either cease, and the
man allowed to sleep, or be continued until he dies of exhaustion.
'The most favourable death', said Crowley, 'is that occurring
during the orgasm, and is called Mors Justi.' To which extraordinary suggestion Crowley added the pious hope: 'Let me die
the death of the Righteous, and let my last end be like his.'
Needless to say an ordinary, healthy man would be unable to
achieve any further sexual excitation long before he reached the
point of death. The whole passage is valueless as a piece of
practical advice, even for those who want to practise sexual
magic, but reveals a great deal about the nature of Crowley's
psychology.

From this section Crowley moved on to what he called 'certain
Hindu theories' which dealt with some tantric theories and
practices and to 'a suggested course of experiment' – a list of

desired objects for which he thought the use of sex magic should be recommended, among them the 'increase of the OTO' and 'ease of circumstances'.

In his next section Crowley dealt with fellatio, and other forms of oral-genital contact, which he referred to as 'vampirism'. This, like the section on the achievement of death through orgasm, is psychologically revealing, and from it one can draw the conclusion that Crowley believed, as ardently as any Victorian writer on sex,[10] that semen contained 'life force' and that the loss of this magical substance was to be deprecated.

> The Vampire [he said] selects the victim, stout and vigorous as may be, and with the magical intention of transferring all that strength to himself, exhausts the quarry by a suitable use of the body, most usually the mouth, without himself entering in any other way into the matter. . . . The exhaustion should be complete; if the work be skilfully executed, a few minutes should suffice to produce a state resembling, and not far removed from, coma.
>
> Experts may push this practice to the point of the death of the victim, thus not merely obtaining the physical strength, but imprisoning and enslaving the soul. The soul then serves as a familiar spirit.

After stating that 'the practice was held to be dangerous' – earlier in this section he had remarked that by some it was held to partake of the nature of black magic – Crowley went on to name some of its alleged practitioners. These included Oscar Wilde and amazingly enough MacGregor Mathers and his wife. While there is no doubt at all that Wilde took part, usually the passive part, in oral-genital sex there is not the slightest evidence that Mr and Mrs Mathers ever did so – in fact there is some reason to believe that both regarded sex as incompatible with the practice of white magic and never consummated their marriage in any manner whatsoever. One can only assume that Crowley's listing of the Matherses as 'vampires' sprang out of his hatred for them.

Crowley concluded *De Arte Magica* with a 'Thesaurus of the OTO' – a list of its occult treasures of which the first and of course most notable was its 'secret of the ninth degree'.

The final sexo-magical treatise written by Crowley at this time concerned the manufacture of the homunculus, an artificial man or woman. Belief in the possibility of manufacturing such a being is of great antiquity and is one of the most fascinating of occult legends. It was first mentioned in classical times when a Christian writer accused the arch-Gnostic Simon Magus of manufacturing one of these beings by an instrument resembling a cupping-glass, taking the spirit of a dead boy and changing it successively to air, water, blood and flesh. The sixteenth-century alchemist, physician and magician Paracelsus gave the most detailed recipe for the manufacture of the homunculus. This involved putting a man's semen in a sealed flask and burying it in warm, fermenting horse manure for forty days. Apparently a form resembling a human being but transparent would develop during this period. After its end the embryo homunculus was to be fed with human blood for forty weeks. This would result in the creation of a human child which according to Paracelsus could be 'raised and educated like any other child until it grows older and is able to look after itself'.

Crowley knew of this and other occult legends, but did not take them very seriously, and in his treatise *Of the Homunculus*[11] was concerned not with them but with a 'method of producing that which, if not a true homunculus, at least serves all proper purposes thereunto pertinent'. Before he outlined this method however he had to outline his 'theory of incarnation' – his ideas about body and soul – and the method of evocation he had applied when he got Neuburg to take part in the Rites of Eleusis.

For the first three months after the primary act of gestation, said Crowley, the foetus is simply a lump of protoplasm without any indwelling soul. It then attracts a soul for which it is a suitable vehicle. Should this not happen the result is a spontaneous abortion, a still-birth or the birth of an idiot. In this last case, claimed Crowley, the foetus has been obsessed by a non-human spirit of 'exceptional Karma' – that is, nature and tendency. If this doctrine should be accepted, Crowley argued logically enough, it is possible that a magician could (a) 'bar the gate against any human ego' and (b) 'cause the incarnation of some non-human being, such as an elemental or planetary spirit, of a nature fitted to some desired end'. Thus if one wanted to create a being exhibiting military genius the magician would get a Martian spirit to incarnate in the foetus.

Crowley went on from this exposition to outline what he claimed had happened during the Rites of Eleusis:

We have succeeded in the temporary expulsion of a weak and wandering soul, and its replacement. For example We [as head of the British o.t.o. Crowley was in the habit of applying the royal plural to himself] once supplanted the soul of a Caliban-creature, a certain deformed and filthy abortion without moral character, named Victor Neuburg, by a soul of Isis, by a soul of Mars and by a soul of Jupiter in turn, so that this quasi-human shape, not being a poet, did yet write verses goodly and great in praise of Isis; and not being a prophet yet did foretell most accurately the wars which even now [September 1914] devastate the earth; and not being generous or wealthy yet did for a season support many dependants upon his bounty.

Crowley then outlined his method of creating the homunculus – that is getting a non-human spirit to incarnate itself in a three-month foetus. The first thing was to get hold of potential parents; a father who was preferably an oto initiate with a horoscope which harmonized with the 'nature of the work', a mother also equipped with a suitable horoscope – if for example it was desired to incarnate a 'spirit of benevolence', she should have 'Jupiter rising in Pisces with good aspects of Sol, Venus, and Luna'. The two future parents should 'copulate continuously . . . in a ceremonial manner in a prepared temple, whose particular arrangement and decoration is . . . suitable to the work' until impregnation takes place. The impregnated woman should then be taken to a 'great desert' and there placed within a magic circle, outside which she should never venture. 'Let the mind of the woman be strengthened to resist all impression, except of the spirit desired. Let the incense of this spirit be burnt continually; let his colours, and his only, be displayed; and let his shapes, and his only, appear so far as may be in all things.'

As well as encouraging the desired spirit to incarnate in the foetus by the methods described above he must directly be invoked: '. . . let him be most earnestly and continually be invoked in a temple duly dedicated, the woman being placed in a great triangle, while thou from the circle dost perform daily the proper form of Evocation to Material Appearance. And let this be done twice every day, once while she is awake and once when she is asleep.' Throughout pregnancy the mother-to-be should be 'constantly educated by words and by looks and by pictures of a nature consonant' with the spirit 'so that all causes may work together for the defence and sustenance of the Spirit, and for its true development'.

All these techniques will supposedly ensure the incarnation and birth into the world of a non-human spirit of the desired nature; 'Now then thou hast a being of perfect human form, with all powers and privileges of humanity, but with the essence of a particular chosen force, and with all the knowledge and might of its sphere; and this being is thy creation and thy dependent; to it thou art Sole God and Lord, and it must serve thee.'[12] Crowley ended his treatise on the homunculus with a blessing cast in thoroughly suitable form for a document dealing with sexual magic: 'Now the Father of All prosper ye, my Brethren that dare lay hold upon the Phallus of the All-One, and call forth its streams to irrigate your fields.'

The type of magical techniques which Crowley outlined in the treatises he wrote in 1914 are both curious and in complete contrast to the ritual – and non-sexual – magic he had learned in the Golden Dawn and practised for a period of fifteen or so years. Sex magic does however seem more in conformity with *The Book of the Law* than the Golden Dawn methods and it is not surprising that from 1914 onwards this was the type of magic which held all Crowley's attention.

11

America

ON 24 OCTOBER 1914, Crowley, armed only with £40, several masonic charters and some books on magic, sailed for America with the firm intention of making an occult conquest of the New World – this, he felt sure, was ripe for a pagan revival. He wrote to his disciple C. S. Jones, a magician who made his living as a Vancouver accountant, as follows:

> The time is just right for a natural religion. People like rites and ceremonies, and they are tired of hypothetical gods. Insist on the real benefits of the Sun, the Mother-Force, the Father-Force and so on; and show that by celebrating these benefits worthily the worshippers unite themselves more fully with the current of life. Let the religion be Joy, with but a worthy and dignified sorrow in death itself; and treat death as an ordeal, an initiation. Do not gloss over facts, but transmute them in the Athanor of your ecstasy. In short be the founder of a new and greater Pagan cult in the beautiful land which you have made your home. As you go on you can add new festivals of corn and wine, and all things useful and noble and inspiring.

Jones was an ardent admirer of Crowley. So much so that when one day his automobile mysteriously refused to go a passing friend sarcastically suggested that he should inspire the machine into activity by reading it some of Crowley's more erotic verse. 'I've tried that,' replied Jones gloomily, 'and all she does is drip oil.'

In spite of Jones's fanatical dedication to Crowley and *The Book of the Law* he was unable to initiate more than a few people into his Vancouver lodge of the OTO. Nor was Crowley much more successful in spreading his new gospel; he lectured to many small groups and made a few friends and followers but totally failed to get the mass following he wanted. Nor was he adept at earning money, being reduced to becoming a paid hack for the German propaganda machine in the USA and writing anti-British articles for the magazines the *Fatherland* and the *International*. According to Crowley himself he was in no sense a traitor to his country; actually he was doing it a service by writing propaganda of such surpassing silliness that it brought Germany into disrepute. So extraordinary were some of Crowley's pro-German articles that one is forced to accept that his claim may have been justified. Thus for example he wrote an article in which he compared the Kaiser to the saintly knight Parsifal, and another in which he grumbled about the ineffectiveness of German air-raids on London: 'A great deal of damage was done at Croydon, especially at its suburb Addiscombe, where my aunt lives. Unfortunately her house was not hit. Count Zeppelin is respectfully requested to try again. The exact address is Eton Lodge, Outram Road.'

His main occult activity was continued experimentation with sex magic, auto-, hetero- and homo-. All his activities of this sort were carefully recorded in a sexual diary he called *Rex de Arte Regia*, 'the King on the Royal Art'. Often those who participated with him in these sexual 'works' were quite unconscious of the fact that they were taking part in sexual magic. Thus frequently he resorted to prostitutes, carefully recording their names and appearances in the sex diary:[1] 'Viola. Hideous taurine doped prostitute. Helen Marshall. Irish-American prostitute. Taurus rising. Beautiful lazy type. Not actually passionate or perverse. A cheerful comfortable girl. . . . Anna Grey, prostitute. Big fat negress, very passionate.' Crowley's partners in acts of homosexual magic were even more casually acquired. Thus on one evening he had three sexual contacts with strangers in a dimly lit Turkish bath; two of these contacts buggered him, on the other he carried out an act of fellatio – Crowley almost always played the passive part in his homosexual adventures.

Besides homo- and heterosexual magic Crowley also regularly practised 'operations of the eighth degree of the OTO' – magical masturbation – usually with the object of obtaining a 'Scarlet Woman', a physical incarnation of Babalon (see p. 56) who would be his regular partner in acts of sex magic. Several of these Scarlet Women came and in due course went; probably more than one of them was repelled by the fact that Crowley insisted on having intercourse with them 'by the unspeakable vessel' (*per vas nefandum*) – that is, buggery. Two of these women, Jane Foster (Sister Hilarion) and Roddie Minor (Sister Achitha) were associated with magical events of great importance to Crowley. By the former he had a 'magical son'; this happened as follows.

In *The Book of the Law* it is stated that 'one cometh after him, whence I say not, who shall discover the Key of it All'. Crowley believed that the 'him' of this passage meant himself as prophet of the new age while the 'one cometh after him' would be some-one who would explain some or all of the unsolved kabalistic mysteries of *The Book of the Law*. From another passage in the book Crowley drew the conclusion that this person would be his 'child', but perhaps not in the ordinary sense of the word. At the autumn equinox of 1915 Crowley, who had been devoting much thought to the significance of these passages from *The Book of the Law*, carried out a number of sex magic rites with the object of begetting this child. Nine months later at the summer solstice of 1916 the 'son' was born; C. S. Jones had received the command of the Secret Chiefs to ascend to the grade of Master of the Temple – to reach the same lofty position as Crowley himself had done in 1910 – and had gone into his private temple and sworn the appropriate oath.[2] Crowley was excited by all this. It was, he thought, unprecedented in the history of magic.

Meanwhile in 1915 and 1916 Crowley himself had ceased to be a Master of the Temple; he had passed into the next grade, that of Magus. The ritual which ratified this achievement was carried out in the summer of 1916 and was, from the point of view of both orthodox Christianity and the occultism of the Golden Dawn, sheer black magic. It began with the capture of a frog which, after gold, frankincense and myrrh had been offered it, was baptised by the ordinary Christian rite as Jesus of Nazareth. Following this a day was spent worshipping the frog as

God incarnate, at the end of which period the frog was 'arrested' and charged with blasphemy and sedition in the following words:

Do What Thou Wilt Shall Be the Whole Of The Law. Lo, Jesus of Nazareth, how thou art taken in my snare. All my life long thou hast plagued me and affronted me. In thy name – with all other free souls in Christendom – I have been tortured in my boyhood; all delights have been forbidden unto me; all that I had has been taken from me, and that which is owed to me they pay not – in thy name. Now, at last, I have thee; the Slave-God is in the power of the Lord of Freedom. Thine hour is come; as I blot thee out from this earth, so surely shall the eclipse pass; and Light, Life, Love and Liberty be once more the Law of Earth. Give thou place to me, O Jesus; thine aeon is passed; the Age of Horus has arisen by the Magick of the Master the Beast that is Man; and his number is six hundred and three score and six. Love is the Law, Love under Will.

I To Mega Therion [the Great Wild Beast – Crowley's magical motto as a Magus] therefore condemn thee Jesus the Slave-God, to be mocked and spat upon and scourged and then crucified.

Following this the unfortunate frog had the sentence executed upon it and Crowley recited a revealing declaration: 'I assume unto myself and take into my service the elemental spirit of this frog, to be about me as a lying spirit, to go forth upon the earth as a guardian for me in my Work for Man; that men may speak of my piety and my gentleness and of all virtues and bring to me love and service and all material things soever where I may stand in need. And this shall be its reward, to stand beside me and hear the truth that I utter, the falsehood whereof shall deceive men.' The elemental spirit of the frog never seems to have carried out its appointed task; few, before or after his death, have spoken of Crowley's piety, gentleness and virtues. After the frog was dead – its sufferings ended by being stabbed by the Dagger of Art – Crowley cooked and ate its legs as a sacrament to confirm his 'compact with the frog' and burnt to ashes the rest of its body in order to 'consume finally the aeon of the accursed one'.

Apart from this odd, and thoroughly sadistic, rite the magical high points of Crowley's stay in America were his dealing with 'the wizard Amalantrah', an astral being who conveyed much occult wisdom to him. His first contact with Amalantrah was made on 4 January 1918 while he was sitting at his desk composing *Liber Aleph*, a treatise on *The Book of the Law*, drugs, sex magic and many other recondite matters written in the form of an extended letter to his magical son C. S. Jones. What happened was described by his Scarlet Woman, Roddie Minor (Sister Achitha) in her magical record.

> While with The Lady of Our Dreams [that is, while under the influence of opium] I had a vision of myself as a spreading candlestick with thirteen candles. Over each flame was the opening of a tube which could hold water as a fountain. These tubes met the flame in a throbbing vibration which became almost excruciating; then, suddenly, the part of the candlestick above the stem broke off and became a crown. The crown floated in the air, tilted at a slight angle; and a circle, which was a halo, came down from heaven and dropped into the crown. In the centre a wand came, and then it all hovered above the candlestick with a veil round it. The veil in some way appeared as rays of light.

Crowley was fascinated by this vision and explained to Roddie how he had previously received astral revelations through the mediumship of women, how one 'tested' figures on the astral plane, and the magical significance of the number 93 – the key number of *The Book of the Law* from the kabalistic point of view. Then Roddie had another vision of herself; this time she saw herself as thirteen naked women, lying in a row and all being caressed simultaneously. Crowley suggested that she should try to get some astral messages:

> I began [recorded Roddie] by asking for a vision containing a message. I first heard gurgling water and saw a dark farmhouse amid trees and green fields. The house and other things disappeared and a dark yoni [vagina] appeared just where the house had stood. I asked again for a message and saw an egg in which were many tiny convolutions of some flesh-like substance. The egg was placed in a frame. Around it were clouds, trees, mountains and water, called 'four elements'. A camel appeared in front of the whole picture.

She also saw a king:

> He was certainly not a king belonging to any kingdom but a king of men. . . . I asked his name and the word Ham appeared between the egg in the frame and the soldiers round the king.
>
> The king went to one side and a wizard linked his arms in the king's as they

disappeared. The wizard looked at me significantly as if he'd given me a wink. He was an old man with a grey beard, dressed in a long, black gown. He was infinitely wise. They went to a cave in the base of a low mountain on some shore. A spring of sparkling, cool water bubbled up near the mouth of the cave. I went into the cave and saw them doing something mysterious with a revolver. The wizard had the revolver. What they were going to do was a joke of some kind but the wizard looked grim. At Therion's [Crowley's] suggestion, I went up to them and said, 'I am Eve' [Eve was Crowley's pet name for Roddie Minor]. This seemed to stop everything. They both disappeared, the cave too. Very soon I saw the king sitting in a niche covered with a canopy, cut in the side of the mountain. In quite another place the wizard was sitting under a tree fanning himself. At Therion's suggestion, I went up to him and asked his name. . . . He only smiled at me and would not speak. It seemed I did not know enough for him to speak with me. For him to say anything, I should have to build a fire of sticks, which he showed me how to do. There was a baby connected in some way with my act of building the fire; it was like a ritual. Then a most beautiful lion was standing by the fire. The wizard was still holding one or two sticks. . . . I then saw a most beautiful naked boy of five or six years old, dancing and playing in the woods in front of us. Therion asked how he would look dressed, and when I saw him in conventional clothes, he looked very uncomfortable and repressed, as if he should be wearing a tiger skin. On one side, near the place where I had made the fire, was a large turtle, standing up like a penguin.

The wizard was very happy and satisfied. He sat down and reached out his hand to me, and had me sit beside him. As we watched the boy, he put his left hand around me tenderly and placed my head on the left side of his chest.

He said, 'it's all in the egg'.

To most people Roddie Minor's visions would appear to be no more than hallucinations produced by opium, lacking any real occult significance. Crowley was much impressed by them however. He was particularly struck by the vision of the egg and its association with trees and a camel. This was because in one of the final visions given to Sister Virakam by the wizard Ab-ul-Diz (see pp. 69 to 72) Crowley had been instructed to go to the desert and look for an egg. Crowley was also interested by Roddie's vision of the naked boy; this was probably, he decided, the infant Horus, a god who played an important part in the pagan theology which he had built up around *The Book of the Law*.

Six days later Roddie had more visions – once more with the

help of opium, 'The Lady of Our Dreams'. She met the wizard again and asked him for a message. She was given this in symbolic form; a large red letter A appeared, an eagle flew through it, a Red Indian came running like the wind. 'It was,' commented Roddie, 'very beautiful as a picture.' Perhaps so – but Crowley was unable to interpret the message, if it was a message, so he decided to join his Scarlet Woman on the astral plane. He therefore smoked opium until he too was in a visionary state. The two entered the astral plane, informing each other of what they saw and thus, presumably by the power of suggestion, sharing the same visions.

Therion and I [recorded Roddie] entered the Astral Plane. I was draped in a diaphanous, virile yellow green, he in a brilliant red with gold braid. In one hand he held a sceptre; there was a ring on the other hand. . . . We went to the place of the eye and saw a building upon something like a platform. There were many doors with signs of various sorts on them, such as the swastika etc. We went to a distant door at the end of a corridor. A dwarf stood to the right of it and a girl to the left. I asked the dwarf where the door led to. He did not answer but showed me a column, with a blazing top. . . . A beautiful lady came up. She was blonde and dressed in creamy white. . . . She lay upon the ground, and waved her hand, which looked like the fin of a fish, towards a village. We all went there. . . .

When we came to the village which was called Pontruel, we saw a church in a square in which there was a cone-shaped fountain. . . . The fountain opened and the king [of last week's vision] came out with some papers in his hand. . . . I asked about the message and he kept looking at the papers, but finally told us to go to the wizard. We went down by the stream and across into the woods where the wizard and the child were. They both looked a little lonely. I asked his name and he told me Amalantrah. I asked who I was, and he said, 'Part of the Tao'. I asked for the message and he put me off in all sorts of ways with small visions. Once he said, 'Go', which I took to mean, go to some place. Later he said 'Egypt'. He did not seem very friendly towards me and seemed worried at times.

Crowley was not particularly interested in all this astral imagery; he badly wanted to know the answer to two obscure occult questions. Firstly what was the actual meaning of the word Baphomet – his own magical name as head of the British

section of the OTO and also the name of the mysterious idol
which the mediaeval Knights Templar had been accused of
worshipping by obscene and blasphemous rites – and secondly its
correct spelling. This was important to him as from its Hebrew
or Greek spelling its kabalistic number, and hence its inner nature,
could be divined.

Crowley asked the wizard the correct spelling of the name
and, through Roddie, the wizard answered that it should be spelt
BAFOMETH in English letters transliterated from the Hebrew.
Crowley then asked whether the final TH should be taken as two
letters (that is, the Hebrew letters Tau and He) or as one (the
Hebrew letter Tau). The wizard replied that it should be taken as
one letter. Crowley was puzzled, for by an obscure kabalistic
calculation he was convinced that the name should have eight
letters. He asked what should be added as an eighth letter and
immediately there flashed into his mind the Hebrew letter Resh,
in the Golden Dawn's system of correspondences the letter of the
sun. Of course, argued Crowley, this meant that Baphomet was
identical with the sun-god Mithras and the name simply meant
'Father Mithras'. By gematria the spelling of Baphomet given by
Amalantrah (BAFOMEThR) added up to 729, kabalistically meaning
'the curse of Satan', and equally significant Amalantrah also added
up to 729. 'This is a great and wonderful Arcanum', noted
Crowley, 'and I doubt not will lead to many further mysteries of
the most holy Kingdom.'

Throughout the spring and part of the summer of 1918
Crowley and his Scarlet Woman regularly consulted Amalantrah.
They would commence each session with an act of sex magic,
with some particular object in mind and then Roddie would take
some drug – opium, hashish or mescal – ascend to the astral plane
and describe her visions to Crowley who would ask questions of
the astral entities she met. These questions would be answered
symbolically, and often very unsatisfactorily.

Question 'Egg is symbol of some new knowledge, isn't it?'
Answer 'Gimel Lamed.' [the Hebrew letters transliterated into English as GL]
Question 'What does that mean?'
Answer 'I don't know.'

On occasions things went wrong. Thus on 10 March, after buggering Roddie for the paradoxical objective of 'understanding the powers of the vagina', Crowley administered to her a large dose of mescal – a drug which Crowley believed pertained to the god Mercury. The astral visions commenced but were soon interrupted by Roddie becoming violently ill, an event recorded by Crowley in the following words: 'Achitha has been rolling about in agony, the god Mercury being too pure for her corrupt mind and body.'[3]

In the summer of 1918 Crowley announced to his friends and followers that he intended to go on a 'Greater Magical Retirement' – to withdraw from the world for a time, to meditate and to undergo new occult experiences. Or at least that was supposedly the motive, although W. B. Seabrook, who knew Crowley well at the time, has remarked that at the time it was 'as hot as hell' in New York and he believed that Crowley's decision arose from the fact that he simply wanted to go for a stay in the country. At the time Crowley was almost penniless and Seabrook and some friends clubbed together, bought him a tent and a canoe and provided him with some money to buy provisions. These latter, along with Crowley, his tent and his canoe, were to be transported up the Hudson River by boat.

When Seabrook and his fellow givers arrived at the boat to see Crowley off they found him embarking the supposed provisions. These they thought, looked somewhat suspicious and they insisted on inspecting them; they found that the 'provisions' consisted of fifty gallons of red paint, a thick rope and three large painters' brushes. Crowley had none of the subscribed funds left – all he had in his pocket was the ticket that would take him up the river to his destination, Oesopus Island.[4] Seabrook asked Crowley what he intended to eat during his magical retirement – knowing Crowley he found it difficult to believe that several weeks of absolute starvation was part of the programme. 'My children,' replied Crowley in his most pontifical manner, 'I am going to Oesopus Island, and I will be fed as Elijah was fed by the ravens.' Seabrook was not impressed by ravens as a potential source of food and called out to Crowley as his boat left, 'Are you coming back in a chariot of fire, or in a Black Maria?'

The island had cliffs on both sides. With his rope Crowley manufactured a sling and painted the basic slogan of his new religion – 'DO WHAT THOU WILT SHALL BE THE WHOLE OF THE LAW' – on each cliff in letters large enough to be read by the passengers and crew of passing boats. The local farmers seem to have been in some way impressed by this activity as they were by Crowley's appearance – his head was shaved except for one forelock which was kept in honour of the phallus, and on his fingers he wore strange rings, notably one with a great star-sapphire in it – and by his practice of sitting still for very long periods. These farmers, who either thought Crowley a peculiarly holy man or else a harmless lunatic, regularly brought him gifts of food – eggs, sweet-corn and milk. These supplies were supplemented by Roddie Minor who came to stay on the island for occasional weekends, bringing provisions with her.

Crowley returned to New York on 9 September, sunburned, thinner, in good health and equally good humour. Acquaintances who did not like Crowley thought his magical retirement an indication that he was 'crazy as a loon'; Seabrook on the other hand remembered that the Buddha had spent eleven years sitting quietly under a tree; Crowley's retirement, he decided, 'was crazy in the age of motor cars and airplanes . . . but was something'. On the day after his return to New York Crowley had lunch with Seabrook at the Plaza Grill; Crowley made up for any dietary hardships he had suffered during his retirement by having a splendid meal – whitebait, steak tartare and cream cake followed by a cigar and Napoleon brandy. Seabrook asked him what he had got out of his retirement 'beyond cleaning out your colon and taking weight off your belly'.

'I have gained greater power,' said Crowley.

'What kind of power?'

'Perhaps,' Crowley replied, 'I can show you.'

The two men strolled down Fifth Avenue, which was crowded. 'On a block where it thins out a bit,' said Crowley, 'I'll show you.'

The crowd looked thinner ahead of them in front of the public
library and, as they crossed 42nd Street, Crowley touched
Seabrook lightly on the elbow and put his finger on his lips.
Ahead of them was walking a tall, prosperous-looking man.
Crowley, 'silent as a cat', fell into step immediately behind this
man. Crowley synchronized his footsteps with the man in front
and Seabrook noticed that Crowley, who usually held himself
pompously erect and had a tendency to strut, had dropped his
shoulders, thrust his head a little forward like that of the man in
front and had begun to swing his arms in unison with his prey.
Now so perfect was Crowley's imitation of the man in front 'that
he was like a moving shadow or astral ghost of the other'.

As they neared the end of the block, Crowley, in taking a step
forward, let both his knees buckle under him, so that he dropped,
caught himself on his haunches, and was immediately erect
again, strolling happily forwards. The man whom Crowley had
been imitatively following fell 'as if his legs had been shot out
under him' and went sprawling on the sidewalk. Fortunately he
was unhurt. As a crowd gathered Crowley and Seabrook helped
him to his feet. He thanked them and looked for the banana peel
on which he assumed he had slipped. There was no banana peel;
the man then looked at the soles of his shoes, they were dry.
Puzzled, he brushed himself down, regained the hat which had
fallen from his head, thanked Crowley and Seabrook for their
help and continued his walk.

Seabrook found the whole incident very puzzling. The man
who had fallen could not have been a confederate of Crowley
because it was Seabrook himself who had suggested that they
walked down Fifth Avenue. A possible solution to the mystery,
he decided, was a psychological one; the man had subconsciously
heard the sound of Crowley's footsteps mingled with his own,
had come to identify Crowley's rhythm with his personal
rhythm and, when the former was violently broken, fell because
his subconscious mind *expected* to fall. Alternatively, decided
Seabrook, Crowley possessed supernormal powers and was
generating and sending out supersensory impressions.[5]

If Crowley is to be believed his retirement had more important effects than giving him the ability to make strolling gentlemen slip upon imaginary banana skins; he came, during his long trance-like meditations, to acquire the magical memory – to recollect his previous lives. There were many of these. The earliest in time, he claimed, was his incarnation as Ko Hsuen, a Chinese sage who had been a disciple of Lao Tse – the great figure of Taoism – and had written the *King Khang King*, the Chinese 'classic of purity'. During his retirement he translated this short work into English rhyme; he also made a translation of the great Taoist work the *Tao Teh King*.[6]

Almost every day Crowley remembered more past lives. In some of these he had been an occult figure of great importance. Thus he remembered that shortly before the time of the prophet Mahomet he had been present at a conference of the Secret Chiefs – 'a Council of Masters'. The question to be decided at this conference was the best way to help humanity. A small minority, of whom Crowley's past incarnation was one, were for a policy of action – the mysteries, they held, should be revealed to the mass of humanity. The majority however, particularly the 'Asiatic Masters', were totally opposed to such a policy which they held to be not so much dangerous as useless. Feeling that the minority should learn the lesson of the futility of positive action the majority abstained, letting the future Crowley and those who agreed with him put their policy of revelation into effect.

The minority appointed various Secret Chiefs to particular tasks. Mahomet, Luther, Adam Weishaupt (the eighteenth-century founder of the secret society known as the Illuminati), the man we know as Christian Rosenkreutz (the legendary founder of the Rosicrucians) and many 'servants of science' were appointed in this way. Crowley's own task was to bring eastern wisdom to Europe and introduce that continent to a purer form of paganism. As such – in other lives – he was one of the Knights Templar who worshipped the strange idol called Baphomet. Later he was incarnated as Alexander vi, the Borgia Pope, and made an attempt to destroy Christianity from within. Some of the movements founded at this Council of Masters, claimed Crowley, had succeeded, others had failed utterly. In his present incarnation –

that is, as Aleister Crowley – he had met several Masters who had failed in their task and were now engaged in 'building up their shattered forces'.

Crowley remembered, or at any rate believed he remembered, many fascinating lives. Immediately before his present life he had been the French magician Eliphas Lévi (see chapter 1). He remembered this in trance, going backwards through the life (in other words, his first memory of his life as Lévi was that of his death). Curiously enough most of the scenes remembered were unimportant. For example he remembered a small church with a square tower, a lot of dusty roads and a long walk he took when he was about seventeen years old; this walk, said Crowley, was more important than it seemed, for in the course of it he formulated his magical aspirations and swore an oath to achieve them. He also recollected taking minor orders in the Church of Rome and several scenes with the wife for whom he had abandoned that same Church.

Before he was Lévi Crowley had been the eighteenth-century occult charlatan 'Count Cagliostro', a man almost certainly born in Sicily as Giuseppe Balsamo and whose title was of his own devising. Crowley's remembrances of the events of this life were curiously at variance with the facts discovered by Cagliostro's biographers. Thus there is no doubt at all that Cagliostro died as a prisoner of the Inquisition; Crowley however remembered dying in a mountain woodland while on a journey with a gaily dressed peasant boy. Again Cagliostro's biographers have established beyond all reasonable doubt that he was born in Palermo, the son of a small tradesman. But Crowley remembered being born in a brothel in Tunis: 'As Cagliostro, I was born in a brothel, kept by my mother's mother. My mother was half-Arab, my father presumably some rich traveller. It was a gorgeous brothel. It was because of my birth that my mother was married off to the fisherman person. There is profound horror and gloom antecedent to this birth; at present it merely darkens as I seek to penetrate it.'

Before being Cagliostro Crowley had had a most unpleasant life. He had been a dark, pimply youth with hollow eyes, a haunted look, a head too big for his body and a dominating mother. He was so miserable in life that he hanged himself when he was still in his twenties. Presumably this miserable existence had been a punishment on him for his excesses in his previous life as a certain Heinrich van Dorn. This life had been wickedly futile; a tale of satanic pacts, black magic rites and 'crimes unworthy even of witches'.

In the same trance in which he remembered details of this unpleasant incarnation Crowley also remembered a life somewhere in the Balkans or South Poland. In this, he had been, while still very young, both a brilliant scholar and a wild adventurer. He had had as a mistress a notorious prostitute who closely resembled Crowley's ideal of feminine beauty – that is, she had a long aquiline nose, a thin but sensual mouth and her complexion was a deep red. At the same time that Crowley had been her lover she had been the mistress of the town's fat burgomaster; on him she let her sadistic impulses loose hiding Crowley in the next room when the burgomaster was being entertained so that he could watch the physical and mental humiliations she practised on her official lover.

The prostitute, remembered Crowley, had been a fine singer and a player of several musical instruments. Through her he met a mysterious, masked individual called 'the wicked Bishop'. Crowley and the bishop talked about magic together but before Crowley had learned much from him he had been murdered; it then became revealed that 'the wicked Bishop' was a special agent of the Pope. While still a student at a German university Crowley fought many duels on behalf of his prostitute-mistress. This caused him to be brought before the disciplinary authorities of the university. However he defended himself so brilliantly in classical Greek that the charges against him were dropped.

After his student days were ended he first became a soldier, taking part in a religious war, and then entered an order of military monks – presumably a branch of the Teutonic Knights as the other military monastic orders were not active in Eastern Europe. As 'Father Ivan' Crowley became the librarian of the monks. He was no orthodox Catholic, but practised magic.

His assistant in some of these latter activities was a Hungarian witch who lived in a forest. With her he carried out at least one ritual of a black magic type; this involved werewolves, vampires and a human sacrifice. Father Ivan's knowledge of occultism – he attained, said Crowley, the grade of Adeptus Major – enabled him virtually to control the other soldier-monks in whose companion-ship he lived. He ran the order's intelligence system and initiated all its political intrigues. He died at the age of forty-five.

The incarnation before that as Father Ivan had again been an unpleasant one. Crowley had been grossly deformed, suffering from both some form of tuberculosis and a terrible curvature of the spine, and his sex was indeterminate – he was a sort of hermaphrodite. He had died of syphilis contracted from a German knight who raped him.

Crowley had of course many other past incarnations – some, it will be remembered, had been revealed to him and Neuburg during the course of the Paris Working – but he considered those he had recollected in the course of his magical retirement on Oesopus Island to have probably been the most important.

12

Leah Hirsig

IN THE EARLY part of 1918, well before his magical retirement on Oesopus Island, Crowley had given, under the auspices
of a spiritualist medium named Christiansen, a lecture on
occultism. He did not care much for the audience, remarking in
his *Confessions* that the only one who bore a resemblance to a
human being was a person whom he ungallantly described as an
'old lady painted to resemble the cover of a popular magazine'.
The 'old lady' – who was not in fact particularly old – was a
Swiss-German named Alma Hirsig who was in later years to
become the High Priestess of a love-cult led by Pierre Bernard
('Oom the Omnipotent'). After the meeting Crowley chatted
to her for a while, being pleased to discover that she was a close
friend of Hereward Carrington, an investigator of spiritualism
whom he knew quite well. After the conversation was ended
Crowley saw Alma by accident on two or three occasions, each
time having a brief chat with her.

In the spring of 1918 Crowley was surprised when Alma
Hirsig, accompanied by her young sister Leah, called upon him.
Crowley, who was engaged in an 'important conference' with an
elderly but active German woman – probably this meant that he
was making love to her – could not invite his unexpected visitors
into his inner studio but saw them briefly in his outermost room.
He was immediately struck by the physical appearance and personal
magnetism of the young sister – she was thin, with luminous eyes
and a wedge-shaped face and 'radiated an indefinable sweetness'.
Crowley found this combination overpoweringly attractive and

began to kiss her. She responded with equal ardour and the two
continued kissing, with only occasional interruptions when they
spoke to Alma, until it was time to go.

At the time this strange interlude led to nothing but early in
January 1919, the two sisters called again to ask for advice about
finding an apartment in Greenwich Village – Leah, who was a
teacher by profession, was attending lectures in law in her spare
time and wanted to be near the university. As Crowley talked to
his two visitors, who were admiring his paintings – he had
recently taken up oil-painting and already regarded himself as an
'old master' – he casually undressed Leah, examined her body
and suggested that some time she should come and pose for him.

Eventually the two left, but on 11 January Leah again called
upon Crowley with the ostensible object of posing for a painting
by him. Once again he undressed her – but on this occasion he
also made love to her. After this Crowley asked her, 'What
shall I paint you as?' 'Paint me as a dead soul,' she replied.
Crowley only did a rough sketch of her; it was the first time he
had tried to paint the human body. He was not satisfied with the
result.

After Leah had gone Crowley could not sleep. The drawing of
Leah filled his thoughts and he felt he could not rest until he had
done something with it. Getting up, he examined the painting
and decided that if he turned it sideways, so that Leah's body was
vertical instead of horizontal, it would mean something. He
painted all night and finally produced a painting of Leah as 'the
Queen of Dead Souls'. The painting was a triptych. In the
central panel stood Leah, her face corpse-green, her body a
deathly white with grey-blue shadows; the left-hand panel
featured a bestially fat black woman, with a parrot on her
shoulder and her eyes fixed adoringly on Leah, while the right-
hand panel showed a kneeling woman in agony with her hair
tumbling about her hips. All along the base of the picture were
rows of misshapen heads. Everyone who saw the work, said
Crowley, considered it an exhibition of artistic genius.

On the day following the night on which Crowley had painted
his picture Leah called again. Crowley asked her to be his Scarlet

Woman, the earthly incarnation of Babalon, his companion in the practice of magic and in spreading the teachings of *The Book of the Law*. Happily she agreed; no doubt the prospect was a more agreeable and exciting one than remaining as a New York school-teacher. Crowley immediately consecrated her to her new position; surrounding her with a protective magic circle, carrying out the Golden Dawn's Lesser Banishing Ritual of the Pentagram, getting her to swear the oath of the Scarlet Woman and finally painting the Mark of the Beast – a cross within a circle – between her breasts.[1]

His Scarlet Woman having moved in with him, Crowley found his accommodation too limited in space, and to the great relief of the two Southern ladies who had lived beneath him, took a new studio at 63 Washington Square South. Here he was shortly afterwards interviewed by a reporter from the *Evening World*. The journalist was impressed by the luxury of the studio – it would be interesting to know how this luxury was paid for – and overwhelmed by Crowley's paintings. He wrote: 'The walls of this studio are covered with the wildest maelstrom of untamed and unrelated colors ever seen under one roof. They look like a collision between a Scandinavian sunset and a paint-as-you-please exhibit of the Independent Artists' Association. The effect is riotous, blinding – but not distressing, after one gets used to it. Mr. Crowley helps one to do that with a dash of cognac. . . .'[2]

Crowley spent most of the summer of 1919 in another magical retirement in the country; Leah was not with him, presumably she stayed on in their New York studio. This retirement was not as satisfactory as that spent on Oesopus Island in the previous year; Crowley came to the conclusion that the magical current that had sustained him throughout his five years in America was exhausted and that it was time for him to return to Europe. In December 1919 he sailed for England, leaving behind him a trail of bouncing cheques.

Meanwhile Leah made her way to Switzerland with one of her sisters. Crowley had planned to meet her there but for some un-explained reason instead telegraphed her to join him in Paris. Here on 11 January 1920, exactly one year after Leah had been painted by Crowley as Queen of Dead Souls, the two swore to establish an 'Abbey of Thelema', to found a mixed – and of course sexually free – monastic community whose brothers and sisters would practise magic and spread the doctrines of *The Book of the Law*.

During her crossing to Europe Leah had become friendly with Ninette Shumway, a French girl who had married an American. This man had died in a car crash and Ninette, who had been left with a two-year-old son, was looking for a job as a nursery governess. Leah was at the time several months pregnant by Crowley and needed someone to help look after her. 'Why not,' asked Crowley, 'invite Ninette to join us?' This was done and very soon Ninette became, like Leah, Crowley's mistress. She was bitterly jealous of Leah and could not understand how Crowley's love for her left undiminished his affection for Leah. At the end of February 1920 a daughter was born to Leah. She was given the formal names of Anne Leah but was nicknamed Poupée. Soon afterwards Ninette became pregnant.

On 1 March 1920 Crowley consulted the Chinese divination book the *I Ching*[3] to ask where he and Leah should establish their Abbey of Thelema, their 'College of the Holy Ghost'. After giving unfavourable responses to a number of suggestions the book gave a 'lucky hexagram' when Crowley asked it about the advisability of going to the village of Cefalu in Sicily. Crowley immediately made arrangements for the move. Leah left hospital with her daughter on 8 March and Crowley made arrangements for her to make a short stay in London while he and Ninette went on to Cefalu via Naples. They arrived at the latter place on 27 March and carried out an act of sex magic *per vas nefandum* with the object of a 'successful and speedy arrival at Cefalu'.

The object of this magical operation was achieved; on his very first day in Cefalu Crowley found a suitable villa for his Abbey; it was only half a mile or so from the village and its location – on a hillside, surrounded by olive trees – was a pleasant one. He was pleased with his discovery and that evening carried out an act of sex magic with Ninette of which the object was 'Salutation to the Gods and Goddesses of this place. May they grant us abund-

ance of all good things, and inspire me to the creation of Beauty'.
On 2 April they moved into the villa.[4] On 14 April Leah joined
Ninette and her lover at the villa – or, as it was known to
Crowley and his disciples, the Abbey. Jointly Crowley and Leah
signed a lease of the Abbey; Leah seems to have acquired
Crowley's love of bogus titles, for she signed the lease as
'Contessa Lea Harcourt'. Crowley himself signed as 'Sir Alastor
de Kerval'.

The Abbey was a one-storied farm building, its thick stone
walls plastered white. There were six main rooms, the chief one
in the middle of the Abbey, the other five radiating off it.
Crowley, Leah and Ninette soon had the place arranged to their
liking; the middle room was their temple, with a magic circle
containing a pentagram painted on its floor. In the midst of the
circle was an altar on which stood *The Book of the Law* with six
candles on either side of it, and various assorted occult impedi-
menta such as a bell, a sword, a cup and the Record – a sort of
log book – in which the more important incidents of the
Abbey's history were noted down. The walls of the Abbey were
painted by Crowley; some of these murals were innocent
enough, distinguished only by Crowley's curious artistry, others
were thoroughly obscene by ordinary standards, representing
various acts of sex magic. One for example showed a man being
buggered by the Great God Pan while his semen was sprinkling
over the accepting body of the Scarlet Woman who stood before
him with her arms outstretched.

Life in the Abbey was a curious mixture of complete freedom
and highly ritualized activity. Thus while the inmates of the
institution and its guests were allowed to spend time in wandering
round Sicily, rock climbing, swimming, taking drugs, having sex
with one another and generally enjoying themselves, they were
also expected to take part in various occult activities. Four times
a day they ritually hailed the sun – as Father of All – and daily
they were expected, usually in the morning, to carry out two
rites, the Kabalistic Cross and the Lesser Banishing Ritual of the
Pentagram, which Crowley had taken from the Golden Dawn (see
p. 43). On great occasions they were also expected to take part

in the celebration of the Gnostic Mass. This, which Crowley had written before the 1914–18 War, was a celebration of the gods and the doctrines of *The Book of the Law* bearing no resemblance to any Christian mass, black or white. Thus the 'Saints' of its 'Collect for the Saints' included such extraordinary figures as the syphilitic sixteenth-century robber-knight Ulrich von Hutten, Richard Wagner, Ludwig the mad king of Bavaria, and Crowley himself. Its communion was equally eccentric; each person who took it was given a whole goblet of wine and a 'Cake of Light', a sort of biscuit made of meal, honey, wine and blood of which the recipe had been supplied in *The Book of the Law*. The sources of this blood must have turned the stomachs of some of the weaker visitors to the Abbey: 'The best blood,' said *The Book of the Law*, 'is of the moon, monthly [that is, menstrual blood]; then the fresh blood of a child, or dropping from the host of heaven; then of enemies; then of the priest or of the worshippers; last of some beast, no matter what.'

Soon after the arrival of Crowley and his mistresses at the Abbey he attempted to carry out a sex magic rite with them both designed to celebrate the entry of the sun into the zodiacal sign Taurus (20 April 1920). Crowley was scandalized when, in the middle of the ceremony, a quarrel broke out between Leah and Ninette. The latter, weeping, ran out of the Abbey, wearing only a thin cloak. By this time it was both dark and raining, so Crowley went out to look for her. After an hour or so he found her and brought her back home. While he had been out Leah had got herself drunk on brandy. She greeted Ninette with a curse and immediately started a fight with her. Crowley consoled himself by smoking opium.

Crowley would have liked life to be more organized at his Abbey and drew up a curriculum of study and work for visitors:

Week One: Three days' hospitality. One day's silence. Three days' instruction. The Magical Oath, followed by four weeks' silence and work.

Week Six: One day's instruction.

Week Seven to Nine: Three weeks' silence and work.

Week Ten: One week's instruction and repose.

Weeks Eleven to Thirteen: Three weeks' silence and work.

This was no doubt ideal in theory but, as has been pointed out by John Symonds, 'none of the rambling bohemians who turned up at the Abbey from Paris, London or New York adhered to this routine'.

Crowley thought a good deal about his relationship with Leah, deciding that his magical powers had enabled him to discern the Great Goddess who dwelt within her physical body:

> Even as in me she divined and loved God, veil over veil of my man-shadow hiding Him, so I pierced through the painted ape's face, the live Death of her loose skin on her grim skeleton, and came to a Great Goddess, strange, perverse, hungry, implacable, and offered up my Soul – Godhead and manhood slain at one stroke of Her paw – upon Her Altar. So loving Her, rejoicing that she has accepted me as Her slave, Her Beast, Her victim, Her accomplice, I must love even Her mask, the painted simper, the lewd doll-monkey face, the haggard shamelessness of her flat breast. . . .[5]

At around this time Crowley took an oath of obedience to Leah as the Scarlet Woman. She, probably in response to suggestions from Crowley himself, then inflicted various humiliations on him, burning his breast with the glowing tip of a cigarette and getting him to eat her excrement.

On 23 July 1920 Jane Wolfe, a minor Hollywood star, arrived at Palermo with the object of going on to stay at the Abbey – she had been studying Crowley's writings since 1917 and was convinced that he was the Master who could cure her soul of sickness. According to Seabrook, who knew her well, the origins of this sickness were simple enough – she was suffering from 'an unrequited passion for some *homme fatale* of the speakeasy epoch, from too much bathtub gin, despondency, and a couple of other depressants which . . . included veronal'. Leah met Jane Wolfe at Palermo. The latter was shocked at the Scarlet Woman's appearance; she wore a black dress stained with grease on which dust had settled, her face was unwashed, her hair uncombed and her fingernails long and filthy. Leah took Jane to Crowley whose appearance seems to have been equally odd; he was wearing a highly coloured striped suit, had many bangles on his wrist and was carrying a cane.

The next day all three went to the Abbey. Jane Wolfe's impressions were unfavourable. 'It was,' she wrote, 'physically filthy, and as the day wore on, I became aware of the foul miasma enveloping the place; it steamed to high heaven. I could not breathe. When I got to my room that night, I collapsed. . . .' Nevertheless Jane Wolfe stayed on, being formally admitted into Crowley's AA a few days later. What happened later was far from what she had expected. On an isolated site near the Abbey Crowley set up a shepherd's shelter – a thatched lean-to. Behind it he dug a small pit, containing lime and designed to be used as a latrine. He took away all Jane's clothes and possessions, save a notebook and a pencil with which she was supposed to keep her magical record, and gave her in their place a single coarse, woollen gown with a cowl. She would have, said Crowley, the whole universe to look at and play with and she was to stay in her lean-to for a month. Nobody would make social visits to her but each night while she was asleep a small boy would bring her the next day's provisions – a bunch of grapes, a loaf and a jug of water.

Jane was horrified at the prospect of her retirement which was to be extremely uncomfortable – not even a straw bed was supplied to her; she had to sleep on the bare earth – and was at first angry and wracked by nervous despondency. Then for some days she was 'calm but bored'; so acute was this boredom that at the end of nineteen days she almost gave up the experiment. She stuck things out however and during the last ten days of her solitude felt 'perfect calm, deep joy, renewal of strength and courage'. After the end of her retirement Jane Wolfe stayed on at the Abbey for some time, studying 'principally self-control and the drawing on her inner resources and reserve force' – in other words aspects of Crowley's 'magick'. Eventually she returned to her acting career.

Halfway through October Anne Leah, the child of Crowley and Leah, died at the hospital in Palermo. Six days later Leah had a miscarriage. Even Crowley lost his usual good spirits – not only was he sad at the death of his daughter but he was suffering badly from boils. Leah became hysterical; all their troubles, she said, were caused by Ninette who was working witchcraft against them.

Crowley, after reading Ninette's 'magical record', seems to have agreed with her for, after carrying out a ceremony of exorcism, he handed Ninette an extraordinary notice:

NINETTE FRAUX [Fraux was Ninette Shumway's maiden name]. Do what thou wilt shall be the whole of the law. Initiation purges. There is excreted a stench and a pestilence. In your case two have been killed outright, and the rest made ill. There are signs that the process may lead to purification and things made safe within a short time. But we cannot risk further damage; if the hate is still in course, it had better coil back on its source. Keep your diary going carefully. Go and live in Cefalu alone; go to the hospital alone;[6] the day before you come out send up your diary, and I will reconsider things. I shall hope to see the ulcers healing. Do not answer this; simply do as I say. Love is the law, love under will.

The Beast 666

Sadly Ninette left the Abbey and the man she loved.

Towards the end of November a new guest arrived at the Abbey, a young man called Cecil Frederick Russell who had originally met Crowley in June 1918. 'I saw him,' wrote Russell in his oddly titled autobiography *Znuz is Znees*, 'at his apartment then on West 9th Street in New York City. He answered my knock with a hypnotic stare and made an appointment for lunch. I remained most of the day; we took an astral journey together. . . .' Russell had formerly been in the US Navy but had been medically discharged after, according to Crowley, injecting himself with forty grains of cocaine, many times the lethal dose, and attempting to set a piece of glass on fire by will-power.

Crowley decided that Russell ('Frater Genesthai') would make a suitable partner in sex magic. Crowley's 'magical record' recorded what happened: 'After dinner we sent for Genesthai. Circa 11 pm Opus V. Genesthai in ano meo. Alostrael [the magical name of Leah] had to masturbate Genesthai to effect erection, and her hand introduced his penis into my anus. Orgasm very strong and savage. Elixir, nearly all absorbed; Alostrael, to whom I offered it, could only get a few drops'.

In his autobiography Russell gave a very different, and rather amusing, account of what happened: 'What really happened, my dear Master Therion, in this case, your Circean enchantment didn't give me a bone-on – add that Ethyl Ether is no aphrodisiac – you were in bed between me and the Virgin (sic) Guardian of the Sangraal [Leah] who had to lean over you to do what she did and you played down in the Record – in fact more than merely to shake the hand of a stranger *faire gonfler son andouille* [to make his penis erect].' Even sexual magic then did not always fulfil the expectations of its practitioners.

Crowley spent February and March 1921 in Paris, leaving Leah and Ninette, who had been readmitted to the community, in charge of the Abbey. In Paris he met many people, some of whom expressed a wish to stay at the Abbey, but he failed to raise any fresh funds – by now he was desperately short of money. On 6 April he returned to Cefalu. Ten weeks later Mary Butts and Cecil Maitland, two writers he had met in Paris, came to stay. They were rapidly introduced to the magico-religious life of the community – indeed Cecil Maitland was given a key function in the preparation of the Cakes of Light (see p. 131). The ceremony in question was described in Crowley's 'magical record':

2.00 pm The ceremony of preparing the Cakes of Light. A young cock is to be baptised Peter Paul into the Catholic Church by C. J. A. Maitland, the son of an apostate Romish Priest, and therefore the ideal 'Black' Hierophant. Mary Butts and I are its sponsors. Peter and Paul are the founders of the Christian Church, and we want its blood to found our own church.

Alostrael then dances against the will of Mary, on my swearing to give to her the half of my Kingdom. She demands Peter Paul's head on the Disk.

I behead him, and the blood is caught in the silver 'charger' on the Disk. In this charger is the meal etc. for the Cakes of Light, ready except for the blood.

I conjure the spirit of Peter Paul to serve these Cakes to found our Church with, as we may use them.

The cock is slain in honour of Ra-Hoor-Khuit, who is invoked before the killing.

Rea-Hoor-Khuit, one of the key figures of *The Book of the Law*, is the martial aspect of the god Horus. The rite, which seems to have been loosely based on Oscar Wilde's play *Salome*, lasted over two hours and was solemnly watched by some of the local inhabitants.

Another magic ceremony which Cecil Maitland and Mary Butts witnessed was designed to be even more spectacular. It was intended that the naked Leah should copulate with a young He-goat who should be sacrificed, by having his throat cut by Crowley, at the very moment of orgasm. Unfortunately the goat refused to perform. Nevertheless it was still sacrificed, the blood jetting over Leah's white back. Leah was rather taken aback that things had not followed their planned course. Dripping blood, she turned to Mary Butts and asked her what she should do now. 'I'd have a bath if I were you,' replied Mary. Cecil Maitland and Mary Butts left the Abbey on 16 September. They believed that their stay had permanently injured their health; certainly both had become addicted to heroin.

From Crowley's point of view the occult high point of 1921 had been his attainment of the magical grade of Ipsissimus. This made him equal to God – in a sense he had become God – and his achievement was solemnly recorded in his *Magical Record*:

I am by insight and initiation an Ipsissimus; I'll face the phantom of myself, and tell it so to its teeth. I will invoke Insanity itself; but having thought the Truth, I will not flinch from fixing it in word and deed, whatever come of it.

9.34 pm As God goes, I go.

10.05 pm I am back at my desk having done the deed, before the Scarlet Woman as my witness. I swore to keep silence, so long as I live, about the fact of my attainment. (The Scarlet Woman is not thus bound, of course.)

Crowley spent the first few months of 1922 in France trying, with only partial success to cure himself of heroin addiction. In May, his face powdered and rouged, wearing full Highland dress, he and Leah went to London.

13

The End of the Abbey

WHEN THEY ARRIVED in England Crowley and Leah were extremely short of money; between them they had only £10. The only way in which Crowley was qualified to earn money was by writing, so he called on his old friend Austin Harrison, editor of the *English Review*. Harrison bought several articles from him and in June published a Crowley article, 'The Great Drug Delusion', which was allegedly written by 'a New York Specialist'. In the following month three more articles were published. 'Shelley' by 'Prometheus', 'The Jewish Problem Re-stated' by 'a Gentile' and 'The Drug Panic' by 'a London Physician'. In August another Crowley article, 'The Crisis in Freemasonry' by 'a Past Grand Master', was published. By the time this last appeared however Crowley and Harrison had quarrelled over money. If he wanted to survive Crowley had to find more work quickly.

At the time he was more than a little obsessed with the subjects of drugs and drug taking, of which he knew a great deal by personal experience, and he approached the publisher Grant Richards with a suggestion that he should be given a contract to write a novel about the traffic in drugs. Richards declined the proposed work but, on the strength of a short synopsis which Crowley had supplied, suggested that he try either Hutchinson or William Collins. Collins's adviser, J. D. Beresford, who knew Crowley slightly, accepted the book, paying its author a £60 advance – a generous amount for the time.

Whatever Crowley's other faults he was not afraid of hard

work; he began dictating his novel, which he had decided to call
The Diary of a Drug Fiend, on 4 June; by 1 July it was completed.
On the day he delivered his completed manuscript he also
supplied Collins with a synopsis of his proposed autobiography.
This synopsis was favourably received and a contract signed,
Crowley being given an advance of £120. In November Crowley's
novel was published. The reviews tended to be neither hostile
nor altogether admiring. *The Times Literary Supplement* for
example remarked that 'the book teems both with an amazing
fertility of incidents and ideas; and with an amazingly rich crop of
rhetoric . . . ecstasies, despairs, and, above all, verbiage'.

Crowley had taken the trouble to insert a note advertising his
Abbey at the end of his book: 'The Abbey of Thelema . . . is a
real place. It and its customs and members . . . are accurately
described. The training there given is suited to all conditions of
spiritual distress, and for the discovery and development of the
"True Will" of any person. Those interested are invited to
communicate with the author of this book.' A few neurotics
took advantage of this open invitation:

. . . I have one obsession. I have a positive mania to be the slave of practically
any good-looking youth who crosses my path. . . . I . . . have no desire for
sexual intercourse of any kind, though I feel quite sure that if any man (for
whom I had any affection) wanted to abuse me I should not refuse his request.
The dominant desire is just to serve, with a morbid wish to be whipped by any
youth who captivates my fancy. This mania has been with me for twenty years,
but it has only been indulged on two separate occasions. . . . I feel that I am a
square peg in a round hole – the only dominant desire I possess is the will to
serve others. Trusting that your Order may be able to help me find my 'Will',
I remain . . .[1]

Crowley wrote a helpful reply. 'Come to me,' he said, 'that I
may trample you underfoot and press out wine for the Lord
Dionysus.'

One man who read *The Diary of a Drug Fiend* without being
inspired to visit Crowley's Abbey, or to have Crowley help him
find his 'True Will', was James Douglas, the literary editor of
the *Sunday Express*, who on 19 November launched a bitter attack
on the book in his widely read column, under the heading 'A

Book For Burning': 'Some time ago when our highbrows, or, as
they are pleased to call themselves, our intelligentsia, were all
praising James Joyce's *Ulysses*, I ventured to put it in the pillory
as the pinnacle and apex of lubricity and obscenity. But the praise
of our highbrows has made it possible for a respectable publisher
to hurl into the British home a novel which is modelled upon that
scandalous outrage.'

It is almost needless to say that Douglas's judgement was faulty
to the point of idiocy; Crowley's novel was neither inspired by
nor in any way resembled Joyce's *Ulysses*. Douglas continued his
attack:

I have therefore determined . . . to do my best to secure the immediate
extirpation of *The Diary of a Drug Fiend*. . . . It is a novel describing the orgies
of vice practised by a group of moral degenerates who stimulate their degraded
lusts by doses of cocaine and heroin. Although there is an attempt to pretend
that the book is merely a study of the depravation caused by cocaine, in reality
it is an ecstatic eulogy of the drug and of its effects upon the body and mind. A
cocaine trafficker would welcome it as a recruiting agent which would bring him
thousands of new victims. . . .

On the following Sunday, 26 November 1922, the *Sunday
Express* followed up its review with a front page story headlined,
'COMPLETE EXPOSURE OF "DRUG FIEND" AUTHOR. Black Record
Of Aleister Crowley. Preying On The Debased. His Abbey.
Profligacy and Vice in Sicily.' By this time Crowley had returned
to his Abbey. He read the articles with disquiet and wrote a letter
to Lord Beaverbrook, proprietor of the *Sunday Express*, asking for
'fair play and an independent enquiry'. But worse attacks were to
follow; these arose out of the death of Raoul Loveday, a young
magician who had been Crowley's favourite pupil.

Loveday, who had been an Oxford undergraduate and had got
a First, had first met Crowley in the summer of 1922. He had
already been studying the *Equinox* and other magical writings for
two years or so and as soon as he had met Crowley the two men
had, with the aid of ether, gone on an astral journey together.
Betty May, a model who had married Loveday while he was still
an undergraduate, was bitterly opposed to Crowley's influence on

her husband and tried without success to wean him away from his preoccupation with magic. On 26 November 1922 Loveday and his wife arrived at Crowley's Abbey. Betty May was not impressed; she complained of the food, the dirt and Crowley's manners. Her husband on the other hand, found everything to his satisfaction from the time when he first saw the words 'Do what thou wilt shall be the whole of the law' painted on the door of the Abbey:

The door [he wrote] led into the 'Temple', a large square room out of which the other five rooms open. We noticed at once a Pompeian censer of bronze and a six-sided altar standing in the centre of a magick circle that was painted on the tiled floor. Very tired after the journey, we went to bed almost at once, to be awakened at dawn by the beating of a tom-tom and the chanting of the watchword of the Abbey. Soon we had joined the others outside on the olive-green hill, where all stretched out arms to the Sun. . . . I cannot easily express my feeling of exaltation as I stood there inhaling the sweet morning air through which the song went up to a sun, golden, shining. . . .

The rest of the morning, like others, was spent in shopping and cooking and typing by the women and chiefly in writing by the two men [Crowley and Loveday].

The keen air had made me tremendously hungry for the midday meal of meat, fruit and sharp Sicilian wine. . . . We spent our first afternoon in a way to which I would introduce all those who think the inmates of these Abbeys of Thelema spend their time in loafing and unwholesome amusement; for it was passed in climbing the great Rock [above Cefalu]. . . . High tea on our ravenous return; then came the ritual of the Pentagram.

This consisted of intoning with vibrant intensity at the four cardinal points the traditionally holy names of God and his archangels. . . . The rite was followed by the reading (which was taken in turn) of the 'Gnostic Collects'. They are invocations of the Higher. The idea is to exalt the mind by poetic appeal to the Forces of Nature; such as that to the Moon, which was hymned in these words: 'Lady of Night that turning ever about us art now visible and now invisible in Thy season, be thou favourable to hunters and lovers, and to all men that toil upon the earth, and to all mariners upon the sea.'

Talk and chess and a little mandolin-strumming followed, and at about nine o'clock we all went to bed, to read or sleep at choice. . . .

The rest of the week passed in a like manner. It was the sheer physical healthiness and enjoyment of it all that struck us most. It was so different to what friends with bated breath had told us to expect before we left London.

And now England seems too far off for us to shudder at the idea of ever having to return. We have found wisdom.[2]

In the Abbey Loveday occupied the post of 'High Priest' or 'Chief Magician', an office formerly held by Russell, who had quarrelled with Crowley and had gone back to the United States, via Australia. Some rites, one involving the sacrifice of a cat, were described by Betty May in *Tiger Woman*, her autobiography:

The ceremony opened with the solemn entrance of the Mystic [Crowley] clad in the gorgeous robes of a Grand Master of the order of Freemasons. After he had seated himself on the throne before the brazier with charcoal fire, around which hung the sacrificial knives and swords, the other members of the cult took their places on the triangular stools at the points of the star. They were dressed as a rule in robes like those in which I first saw Leah, with the cowls drawn over their faces, and only their eyes visible through the narrow eye-slits. Clouds of incense hung about the room everywhere. When all were assembled, the Mystic rose from his seat, and taking one of the swords from the side of the brazier, held it pointing towards the altar while he intoned an invocation in a language with which I was not familiar. From hearing it every day, however, the sounds remain fixed in my memory.

> '*Artay I was Malcooth – Vegabular,*
> *Vegadura, ee-ar-la – ah moon.*'[3]

The last was the high-pitched note in contrast with the rest of the chant. Following this he walked over to Raoul, rested the point of his sword on his forehead, and uttered a further rigmarole, finishing up with a loud shriek of 'Adonis', which was the name by which my husband was known in the abbey. Then he went through the identical performance in front of Leah, except that to begin with he stood silently in front of her for a full minute, breathing deeply the while – breathing in the soul of his priestess, as Raoul explained it to me afterwards.

These preliminary invocations done, the Mystic proceed to execute a variety of ecstatic dances. This was both impressive and ludicrous. He lashed himself into an absolute frenzy, brandishing his sword, and dancing about and leaping in the magic circle. His eyes blazed. The words he chanted had a compelling monotonous and exotic rhythm, and his eyes were alight with fanatical enthusiasm. Every Friday night there was a special invocation to Pan. . . .

Betty May gave a good description of the rite at which the cat was sacrificed:

. . . everybody took their accustomed position, except that for this occasion Raoul, as he was to be the executioner, changed places with the Mystic. The cat was brought out and placed, still in the sack, on the altar. The opening of the rite was the same as the Pentagram. . . . The air was thick with incense. Raoul recited the invocation and walked with upraised sword towards Leah and the others and placed its point on their brows while he uttered the usual formula. I sat outside the magic circle and watched the gruesome performance.

Presently, when much of the ceremony had been gone through, I saw Raoul take a kukri from its place by the brazier and approach the altar, on which was the squirming sack. He untied it, drew forth the struggling and terrified Mischette by the scruff of the neck, and held her with his left hand at arm's length above his head. In his right he held the kukri with its point toward the brazier. The Mystic stilled Mischette's struggles by applying a dab of ether to her nose. All was now ready for the sacrificial invocation, which Raoul had written specially for the occasion, and which he now had to recite in the fatiguing posture that I have described. . . .

As he approached the point where the killing was to take place Leah stepped down from her triangular stool, and taking a bowl from the altar, held it underneath Mischette to catch the blood, none of which is supposed to be lost. At last the moment arrived. I saw him lift back the kukri, and then closed my eyes till it should be over . . . he laid the carcase on the altar. This done, his resources were exhausted, and the Mystic had to take over the conducting of the ceremony.

Having concluded the invocation, he took the bowl containing the blood, uttered some consecratory formula over it and handed it to Leah, who was standing by. Together they approached Raoul. The Mystic then flung the cowl back from Raoul's face, and dipping a finger in the blood, traced the sign of the Pentagram on his white glistening forehead, and so to all the others, himself last. . . .

The Mystic took a small silver cup, into which he scooped some of the blood from the bowl and handed it to my husband, who drained it to the dregs.

Shortly after this ceremony both Crowley and Loveday became ill. Crowley, who fancied himself as an amateur physician, thought that they were suffering from something called Mediterranean fever, the local medical man diagnosed an infection of the liver and spleen, while Betty May thought that her husband – who was by far the sicker man of the two – had been poisoned by a combination of the cat's blood he had drunk and the many drugs supplied to him by Crowley.

On 13 February 1923 Crowley recorded in his 'magical record'
that he felt a current of magical force, 'heavy black and silent',
threatening the Abbey. The next day Loveday's health was much
worse. Dr Maggio, the local physician, diagnosed acute enteritis.
Two days later Loveday died, the immediate cause of death being
paralysis of the heart. The next day his body was given an occult
funeral under the disapproving gaze of three local monks.
Crowley was clad in magic robes and draped with occult insignia;
round his head he wore a gold fillet on which was inscribed the
name of the archangel Uriel, on his breast was his scarlet cross
with its topaz centre and on his fingers were bizarre rings. Over
the coffin Crowley read from *The Book of the Law* and from his
mystery play *The Ship*, which had been published in the tenth
issue of the *Equinox*. It was a funeral which Loveday himself,
who had abandoned a promising career for Crowley's magick,
would have wanted. The ceremony over, Crowley returned to
the Abbey and collapsed on his bed. His temperature rose to
102°, and remained at this crisis point for three weeks. Then it
rose to 104°, Crowley broke into a violent sweat and it returned
to normal. A month after the funeral he got up for the first
time.

Meanwhile Betty May had obtained her return fare to England
from the British consul at Palermo, had gone back to London and
had called on the *Sunday Express*. What she told the journalist who
interviewed her is made clear from the headlines which appeared
on 25 February: 'New Sinister Revelations Of Aleister Crowley.
Varsity Lad's Death. Enticed to "Abbey". Dreadful Ordeal Of
A Young Wife. Crowley's Plans.' The story was followed up in
the following week's issue: 'Young Wife's Story of Crowley's
Abbey. Scenes Of Horror. Drugs Magic and Vile Practices.' The
scurrilous weekly magazine *John Bull* joined in the attack,
actually going as far as to accuse Crowley of practising cannibalism
when in Kashmir: 'The natives of these parts . . . assert that he
really had the power of cowing and killing wild beasts by some
magical means. On one solitary mountain-climbing expedition it
is actually affirmed that running short of provisions, he killed
two of his native carriers and *cut them up for food*! This incredible

piece of cannibalism is cynically authenticated by "The Beast" himself. . . .'

By this time the presence of Crowley and his Abbey on Italian soil, and the consequent bad publicity, was beginning to annoy Mussolini and his Fascist government. Towards the end of April Crowley was called to the local police station and told that, under an order of expulsion issued by the minister of the interior, he and his followers must leave Italy.

'All of us?' asked Crowley.

'Yes.'

'May I see the order?'

It was shown to him and he pointed out that it referred only to himself. Reluctantly the official agreed that Crowley was right. On 1 May 1923 Crowley left his Abbey for the last time, proceeding via Palermo to Tunis. For a time some of his disciples stayed on at Cefalu. Eventually they too left. The brief but eventful existence of the Abbey of Thelema had ended.

14

Wanderings of a Magician

AFTER HIS EXPULSION from Sicily Crowley was for many months in Tunis, staying at a cheap hotel, spending most of the time dozing, chatting, playing chess and generally loafing about, and becoming more psychologically and physically reliant on drugs than was already the case. He himself was unable to decide exactly why he took as many drug doses as he did; he was particularly puzzled by his reliance on cocaine, which is a drug of psychological rather than physical, addiction. He wrote in his 'magical record':

Why is it that one takes cocaine (but no other drug) gluttonously, dose upon dose, neither feeling the need for it, nor hoping to get any good from it? I have found that every time. Three doses, intelligently taken, secure all one wants. Yet, if the stuff is at hand, it is almost impossible not to go on. One resists successfully (perhaps) for a few nights, then slides into a 'go as you please' race without rhyme or reason. One even goes on while actually cursing oneself for one's folly. (The one light spot is that so far sudden and complete suppression has been as easy as if cocaine were cabbage!) Folly! not only fear but the horse sense of not wasting a cherished and possibly irreplaceable stock. Why take thirty doses (or is it sixty? I haven't a ghost of a guess.) to get into a state neither pleasant nor in any other way desirable, but fraught with uneasiness, self-contempt, alarm, discomfort and irritation at the ever-present thought of 'Hell! Now I have to endure the reaction' while well aware that with three one can get all one wants without one single drawback.

During this and the succeeding period, Crowley entrusted the task of mending his reputation to one of his disciples named Norman Mudd, a former professor of mathematics – Crowley believed he would be able to make a mathematical expression of the doctrines of *The Book of the Law* – who had thrown up his university chair to follow Crowley. Mudd worked hard at his task, writing a Crowley apologia called *An Open Letter to Lord Beaverbrook* and sending pro-Crowley letters to any periodicals that he thought might publish them. One such letter was published in the Oxford magazine *Isis* on 14 November 1923:

. . . I have known Aleister Crowley for over thirteen years. He is admittedly one of the most remarkable poets and writers of the present day.

I have studied his scientific memoranda with great care, and I am satisfied that they would lead to discoveries which will furnish mankind with a new instrument of knowledge and a new method of research.

I have examined the accusations made against him by certain newspapers of a certain class, and find them without exception baseless falsehoods. I know that his ideals are noble, his honour stainless, and his life devoted wholly to the service of mankind. Having given his entire fortune to his work, he has been unable to refute publicly the calumnies of his assailants. He has found no men among those who know him, sufficiently prominent, powerful and courageous to come forward and vindicate him before the world.

The honour of England is concerned that her greatest poet should not perish under the malice or neglect of his fellow countrymen. . . .[1]

Crowley himself was not as impressed with his own nobility, stainless honour and devotion to the service of mankind as was Mudd; 'I may be a Black Magician,' he wrote in his diary, 'but I'm a bloody great one.'

In October 1923 Crowley decided to shelve some of the odder plans made by him during his stay in Tunis – such as walking to Cairo with J. F. C. Fuller in order to steal something from the Cairo Museum, or writing to Leon Trotsky to suggest that he should be put in charge of a materialist movement charged with the task of destroying Christianity. Instead he would restore himself to health and energy by going on a magical retirement.

He, Leah and a black youth who had become his servant and a partner in his sex magic activities, went by car to Nefta, where they hired a camel and set off into the desert. Owing to the heat they slept by day and walked through the night. Crowley carried

out acts of sex magic with his servant and smoked what he sometimes referred to as 'the grass of the Arabians' – hashish. They
had intended to stay in the desert for a full month, but Leah
became sick and after only three days they returned to the oasis
at Nefta. There on the night of 1 November, Crowley had a
supernormal experience which greatly intrigued him. He had just
completed an act of sex magic with his servant and was reaching
for his scarlet robe when he saw a red glow, visible only to
himself, resembling 'fresh blood on a bull's shoulder in bright
sunlight'. Was it, Crowley wondered, a manifestation of an
elemental which had been created by the act of sex magic? Or, a
more exciting prospect, was it 'a deliberate token of the
presence of one of the Secret Chiefs?'

After some days at Nefta Crowley fell sick and became so weak
that he could not continue to carry on his sex magic activities.
For a time Leah substituted for him but, after a while, the servant
fell sick from some (according to Crowley) occult cause:
'15 November 1.00 am Mohammed ben Brahim is quite seriously
ill: in particular, he has lost the hearing of one ear. He was
warned not to touch my Magick Bell; he did so (of course) and
gets it in the neck accordingly.'

Leah and Crowley, by now almost continuously quarrelling,
returned to Tunis. At the end of the year he left with just enough
money to get him to Nice where he had arranged to meet his old
friend Frank Harris, the journalist and author of the pornographic autobiography *My Life and Loves*. Harris had a plan; he,
who was almost penniless, and Crowley, who had no money at
all, should somehow or other raise the funds to buy the Paris-
based *Evening Telegram*, a paper which he believed to be making a
profit of 120,000 francs a year. Crowley agreed that this would
certainly solve all their problems and, after borrowing 500 francs
from Harris, made his way to Paris, there to stay at a hotel in the
Rue de Vavin to whose proprietor he already owed 2000 francs.

Both Harris and Crowley seem to have had a touching faith in
the other's ability to raise the funds required to buy the *Evening
Telegram*. 'My dear Crowley,' wrote Harris, '. . . I am keeping
things simmering as I told you. . . . Get what you can on your

side and we'll all stand together. If you can get say 300,000 francs
and I get the similar sum we'll make the capital of the paper a
couple of million francs, and then see how much we shall want
to carry on year by year. In five we ought to be able to double
the money we put in. . . .' Crowley replied with an unhelpful
exposition of *The Book of the Law* which well illustrated the magic-
religious point of view at which he had now arrived:

> Rotten as I am in a thousand ways I have been chosen by the 'Gods' –
> 'Masters' – 'Secret Chiefs' – 'Guardians of Mankind' – what you will, the idea
> is the same – to bring to Earth the Formula of the New Aeon, the basic Word
> in which Mankind will work for the next 2000 years or so – the word 'Do what
> thou wilt' with all the implications given in *The Book of the Law* (dictated to me
> by an unseen personage in Cairo twenty years ago).
>
> I have been faithless in many ways: I have tried in particular to combine my
> mission with living the regular life of an English Gentleman. And the Gods
> won't allow it. They have checkmated my plans with ever-increasing severity,
> until I have been bludgeoned, stabbed, and starved into doing their work
> wholeheartedly the way they want it done. . . .
>
> You must take my Mission seriously, and lend all your energies – which will
> then be renewed, like the eagle's – to establishing the law of Thelema.
>
> To put it very crudely, Industrial-Capitalism is heading for the cataract. The
> only alternative yet is Bolshevism, which won't do either.
>
> Now, the Law of Thelema offers a third way. These last years I have been
> training various people to act as a Brain for the human race. I have a number of
> people of some importance interested already and the idea of my lawsuit
> [against the Beaverbrook press] is to give me the opportunity of proclaiming
> this Law in such a way that it will attract all those who are ready to cut the
> painter, and come out from the raving herd, and assume Kingship to rule the
> disorganized and bewildered mob.
>
> I assure you that the world is ready for this move. Even the 'successful' are
> sick to the heart of the hollowness of everything. My lawsuit will supply the
> necessary publicity; my opening and closing speeches will be *prophetic*, the
> Forth-Speaking of the Word of the Lord. . . .

But neither then, nor in the future, did Crowley acquire the
funds required to launch a libel action against the *Sunday Express*.
   An epoch in Crowley's life had come to an end and with it, as
was inevitable, Leah's attraction for him declined. In September
1924 he removed her from her office of Scarlet Woman and

appointed a new one – an American woman called Dorothy Olsen. When winter came the two went off for a holiday to North Africa. They went from Tunis to Sfax and thence to Nefta, the place where Crowley had seen his elemental – or Secret Chief – after an act of sex magic. At Nefta they took camels and set off across that part of the Sahara known as the Great Eastern Desert. Here they encountered both a 'magical attack of flies' and an Arab chieftain who realized that Crowley was one of the Secret Chiefs and held a mighty feast in his honour. Eventually they reached Touggourt and from there took the train to Biskra.

While Crowley was in North Africa various events were taking place in Germany which were to be of importance to him. In 1922 Theodor Reuss – Frater Merlinus – had a stroke and resigned from his position as head of the OTO. It was he, it will be recalled, who had first admitted Crowley into the order and appointed him, as 'Baphomet', to be chief of its British section, and Crowley was his chosen successor as 'OHO' – 'Outer Head of the Order' – the Inner Head of the Order was, it is to be presumed, some discarnate Secret Chief. Most of the German OTO initiates were however doubtful about having an Englishman as their chief and for some time a German occultist named Tränker ('Frater Recnartus') was acting head of the organization. Tränker was also the head of a small federation of occult bodies called *Pansophia*; this owned a publishing house of the same name. Suddenly, and for no apparent reason, Tränker had a vision; he saw Crowley as the leader of a group of Secret Chiefs – it could only mean one thing, that Crowley should become head of the OTO. He invited Crowley to a conference to be held in Germany in the summer of 1925. His fare would be paid by Karl Germer (Frater Saturnus), a comparatively wealthy member of *Pansophia*.

Meanwhile in the spring of 1925 Crowley and Dorothy Olsen were again in Tunis. The latter was suffering from the sort of mental upheaval that seems to have been an occupational disease of Scarlet Women. 'A single drink of rum,' says Crowley's 'magical record' for 24 April 1925, '. . . was enough to induce in Dorothy Olsen an attack of acute mania. Lying in bed, close

cuddled . . . with a spate of the filthiest, incoherent abuse of me
and everybody connected with me. There had been a good deal of
irritation and snappiness during the afternoon and evening, with
one or two beginnings of the regular ravings; but no one took
any notice, and they subsided.'

Before Crowley went to the German conference in the summer
he sent a copy of The Book of the Law ahead of him. This was
hastily translated; the German OTO initiates were unimpressed.
Some of them were positively shocked. Thus one of them, a
certain Herr Grau, wrote:

Unhappily, too late I have been acquainted with the contents of *Liber Legis*
[The Book of the Law], a book branded with the triple KEOU. I thus to my
horror got a real glimpse of the future reconstruction, as planned by the A.A.,
of a primitive world order which suggests that blackest days of Atlantis. If
these ideas had been clearly in my knowledge at the time, Sir Crowley may rest
assured that I would not have put myself so certainly before the chariot of the
A.A. and been invited the 'boot' for services rendered in good faith. . . .

Even Herr Tränker was at first shocked by The Book of the Law,
denouncing it as a work of sinister, demoniac possession.
Shortly afterwards, however he had another revelation which
enabled him to appreciate the merits of even the most un-
pleasantly worded portions of the work, to call it a 'glorious
manifestation' and to say that its message could be summed up in
one word – civilization. In spite of this Tränker was unwilling to
resign the headship of Pansophia to Crowley. The latter took
great exception to this and a dislike to Tränker whom he
denounced by saying that 'every action of Tränker becomes
intelligible only on the hypothesis that he is a perfectly unscrup-
ulous and cunning peasant who is exploiting odds and ends of
recondite knowledge with intent to defraud'. Inevitably the
conference broke up in confusion and only a few weeks later
Tränker was applying to the legal authorities to have Crowley
expelled from Germany.[2]

Following this the so-called 'German Rosicrucian Movement'
– that is Pansophia and the OTO – split into three groups differ-
entiated from one another by their attitudes towards Crowley.

The first and it would seem the smallest of these groups abandoned any attempt to work with Crowley and his disciples and retired into occult obscurity. Tränker himself was the most notable occultist who followed this tendency. The second group formed the *Fraternitas Saturni* ('the Brotherhood of Saturn') under the leadership of Eugen Grosche, a man known to his followers as the Master Gregorius. This group refused to regard Crowley as a Secret Chief, to whom total obedience was due, but regarded him as an important teacher. The Saturnian brethren kept in touch with Crowley and developed his sex magic in eccentric directions. They believed for example that initiates should vary their coital positions according to the zodiacal settings of the planets and set this doctrine forth in an internal document headed 'Secret! Secret! Astrological Aspects as a Secret Symbolism for Coital Positions':

The ancient mystery schools [claimed the document] frequently used as part of the initiation rites of their disciples religious practices and ceremonies which, more or less openly, glorified sexual relations between men and women and used these as a basis for their cult.

This secret symbolism and specialised knowledge was, of course, deliberately withheld from the lower grades and the uninitiated. . . .

It is obvious to anyone schooled in magic that originally all magical ceremonies had a purely cosmic basis because the initiated priesthood used as a foundation for their cults the planetary prime oscillations of certain aspects in their influence on the psyche and physical organs of mankind.

As the sexual act brings about the release of the tension of the mutually negative and positive forces of the partners (above all if the act is executed as a consciously magical act) the knowledgeable, initiated individual will naturally be able to create favourable conditions for the practical application of the teaching and thus achieve total harmonisation and peak polarisation of the senses.

The fertilisation of the woman is not the aim of such sexual acts as these, for they are of a purely religious nature or are used to create so-called psychogones which are easily aroused by such sexual intoxication. Thus the position of the body becomes an important part of this religio-magical practice.

Gestures, movements, body rhythms and posture . . . are . . . structurally important factors in all magical ceremonies. . . . Therefore it is quite understandable that certain positions during intercourse are an important prerequisite for the achievement of certain magical aims.

It is the teaching of astrology . . . that the squares between those planets [that is, when one planet viewed from earth is at an angle of 90° to another planet] especially important in the sexual sphere (i.e. Venus, Mars, Neptune, and the Moon) are particularly vital and advantageous. All these squares are of a purely daemonic character and are known to be the gateways to the psyche of mankind; this is particularly so if such squares are already present in the basic horoscope of the individual in question. A person experienced in magic can therefore use with success and without difficulty important aspects whether they be formed by transits of positions in the natal horoscope or actually present in the zodiac at the time of copulation.[3]

. . . in squares of Venus and Mars sexual intercourse should be carried out in a sitting position, the exact nature of which should vary with the strength of the planets in the sign of the zodiac where they are situated. If Venus is stronger the female partner should be on top, if Mars is stronger the male should be on top. In a square of the Moon and Mars either the woman (= the Moon) or the man (= Mars) may be underneath or on top. A square Moon and Moon is said to be the most suitable for lesbian sexuality, a square of Mars and Mars for male homosexuality. Where Neptune is part of the square it is advised to use drugs in order that both partners may achieve a simultaneous state of intoxication. If there is opposition [an angle of 180°] between the above-mentioned planets, no sexual act should be carried out, and only preliminary preparations should be made, i.e. states of erotic tension may be induced. All conjunctions are to be used in a similar way to squares because a conjunction means a concentration of forces. . . .

When intended for a purely magical purpose these acts must be undertaken only as a magical ceremony under the strictest observation of all magical precautions. Defensive symbols must be employed together with protective fumes such as incense. . . .[4]

The third section into which the German Rosicrucian Movement split was made up of a small number of occult groups and individuals who totally accepted Crowley and his claims to magical supremacy. These were led by Martha Küntzel (Sister Ich Will Es), an ageing Theosophist who had exchanged her devotion to Madame Blavatsky for an equal devotion to Crowley, and Karl Germer, in many ways the most interesting of Crowley's German disciples.

Germer, born on 22 January 1885, was by no means un-intelligent. As a young man he had attended various German

universities and spent six terms at the Sorbonne. In 1914 he had
been on a visit to Russia when the First World War broke out.
He managed to escape that country and returned to his fatherland
where almost immediately he was drafted into the army – like
many educated Germans he was an officer of the reserve. He had
a good war record and won both the first- and second-class Iron
Cross for 'special services', possibly intelligence work. At the
beginning of the 1920s he had been appointed to a management
position in the Barth-Verlag, a Münich publishing house, and had
been responsible for the publication of seven short works by
Crowley (of which one, *Der Meister Therion: Eine biographische
Nachricht* has not been published elsewhere) in 1925. Between
1925 and 1935 Germer worked and lived with Crowley, supporting him financially but returning to Germany, from time
to time to superintend the activities of the Thelema-Verlag, a
small Crowleyan publishing company established by himself and
Martha Küntzel.

Some time after the German conference Crowley got rid of
Dorothy Olsen as his Scarlet Woman; her neuroses had become
too much for him and in any case she seems to have had little
native magical ability. A whole host of Scarlet Women came and
quite as rapidly went, usually with a curse from Crowley. Take
for example Margaret Binetti whom he met towards the end of
1926 and to whom he actually became engaged; Crowley got rid
of her on 6 February 1927 'by burning the talisman of Jupiter
which protected her. Her callous heartlessness and hypocritical
falsity doom her to a dire end.'

By 1929 Crowley was deeply involved with a Scarlet Woman
named Maria Theresa Ferrari de Miramar, whom he called 'High
Priestess of Voodoo' because of her considerable magical powers.
Under her influence, wrote Crowley, he had 'been able to start
serious magick with ritual precautions. The climax of the first
ceremony was marked, as it should be, by the sudden arising of a
violent wind; and subsequent ceremonies have been equally
notable. I think the results are already beginning to appear; and,
bar accidents, something important should break out during the
week'. The High Priestess of Voodoo was even more impressed

with Crowley's powers – to the point of madness. She urged him to saddle a unicorn and secretly depart on its back to Jericho on 20 January 1929. On 16 August 1929, the two were married before the British Consul in Leipzig.

15

Twilight of a Master

WITHIN LESS THAN a year Crowley had found a new love, a nineteen-year-old German artist called Hanni Jaeger, with whom he journeyed round Europe on funds supplied by Karl Germer. The High Priestess of Voodoo was left to mope in London. On 20 September 1930, Crowley wrote to her:

... you had better get a man who will stand for your secret drinking and your scandalous behaviour. I gave you a great chance in life, and you threw it away. *Tant pis!*

You should get a divorce. I admit what some dithering nincompoops are still imbecile enough to call 'misconduct' on 47 occasions since August 3rd – the fatigues of constant travel must excuse the smallness of the figure – with Hanni Jaeger of Berlin.

It will be no good asking for alimony because we are all in the soup together with the Rt. Hon. Lord Beaverbrook and the British Empire.[1]

Meanwhile fresh financial difficulties had arisen. The wife of Karl Germer – who unlike her husband accepted neither *The Book of the Law* nor Crowley's claim to be the prophet of the new age – objected to the way in which Crowley was spending the considerable sums of money which he had extracted from her and her husband. She wrote to him:

The $15,000 I have given you were spent not in real constructive work but in expensive cigars, cognac, cocktails, taxis, dinners, wives and sweethearts, or anything you desired at the moment. ... I consider you a supremely selfish man. ... You spend as much in a week on cigars and cognac as I do on myself in two months personally. By the time I have paid the household expenses and given the rest to you and Miss Jaeger, there is no more. . . . I am not trying to insult you, but I think you have a Me and God complex. God Almighty Himself would not be as arrogant as you have been, and that is one of the causes of all your troubles.

Suddenly Crowley decided that he must divorce the High Priestess of Voodoo; Hanni was pregnant and wanted to marry him as well as to be his Scarlet Woman. It would be best for 'the Great Work' if he was the plaintiff and his wife the defendant and not the other way round. Israel Regardie, at the time Crowley's secretary, pointed out the difficulties with admirable logic: 'It is too bad that wasn't thought of several months ago when Maria received your letter stating that you had committed adultery umpteen times and that only the rigours of travelling prevented the number being greater. The letter must have caused you a great deal of pleasure when written, but, alas, it prevents you even thinking of being a plaintiff for divorce now. One can't have it both ways.'

The situation eventually resolved itself by the High Priestess of Voodoo being admitted to the mental hospital at Colney Hatch suffering from the delusion that she was 'the daughter of the King and Queen and that she had married her brother, the Prince of Wales'. At around the same time Hanni left him. Crowley awaited eagerly for the appearance of another potential Scarlet Woman. She duly came along in August 1931 in the shape of a thirty-six-year-old woman called Billy Busch. He consecrated her to her office with a sexo-magical act and the two moved into a flat which was as usual paid for with money obtained from Germer and his wife. Billy was however the cause of some disagreement between Crowley and Germer; the latter felt unable to accept her as the equal of Crowley and entitled to the same veneration as him.

Crowley and Billy's life together was a mingling of ecstatic sexual activity and violent quarrels. On one occasion Crowley quarrelled with her in the street and held her against a nearby wall with one hand, while hitting her with the other. She was rescued by some passing Nazi Brownshirts. The ecstatic sexual activity of the two was carefully recorded in Crowley's 'magical record': 'Monday, November 2nd 1931 . . . We went crazy. Instantly we got home I got down on s.w. She pissed gallons – we tore off our clothes and fucked and fucked and fucked. And suddenly she got a jealous fit about 3 cheap whores at Brunnig's and I strangled her. Tuesday 3. Woke early and finished the fuck.' Crowley eventually returned to London. Billy followed him there but in due course Crowley got rid of her as he got rid of all his Scarlet Women.

In May 1933 Crowley sued a Paddington bookseller named Gray for libel. The man put a copy of Crowley's occult novel *Moonchild* in his window with a notice reading 'Aleister Crowley's first novel *The Diary of a Drug Fiend* was withdrawn from circulation after an attack in the sensational press'. Crowley won his case, getting £50 damages together with his costs, the judge ruling that 'There was not the smallest ground for suggesting that any book Mr Crowley had written was indecent or improper. Mr Gray wanted the public to believe that the book to which the label was attached was an indecent book'.

This success inspired Crowley to a further libel action, this time against the publishers Constable who had published an autobiography by Nina Hammett containing the following passage about Crowley's life at Cefalu: 'He was supposed to practise Black Magic there, and one day a baby was said to have disappeared mysteriously. There was also a goat there. This all pointed to Black Magic, so people said, and the inhabitants of the village were frightened of him.' The trial which took place in April 1934 rapidly evolved from being a trial of Constable's for libel to a trial of Aleister Crowley's morals. Crowley came out very badly from his cross-examination, as it was reported in a newspaper of the time:

'Are you asking for damages because your reputation has suffered?'
'Yes.'
'For many years you have been publicly denounced as the worst man in the world?'
'Only by the lowest kind of newspaper.'
'Did any paper call you "The monster of wickedness"?'
'I can't remember.'

'Have you from the time of your adolescence, openly defied all moral conventions?'

'No.'

'And proclaimed your contempt for all the doctrines of Christianity?'

'Not all the doctrines.'

'Did you take to yourself the designation of "The Beast 666"?'

'Yes.'

'Do you call yourself "the Master Therion"?'

'Yes.'

'What does "Therion" mean?'

'Great Wild Beast.'

'Do these titles convey a fair expression of your practice and outlook on life?'

'The "Beast 666" only means "sunlight". You can call me little sunshine.'

Some of Crowley's erotic verse was read out in court and made a bad impression on both judge and jury, as did Betty May's evidence of what she had witnessed at Cefalu. On the fourth day of the case the judge addressed the jury:

I have been over forty years engaged in the administration of the law in one capacity or another. I thought that I knew of every conceivable form of wickedness. I thought that everything which was vicious and bad had been at one time or another produced before me. I have learnt in this case that we can always learn something more if we live long enough. I have never heard such dreadful, horrible, blasphemous and abominable stuff as that which has been produced by the man who describes himself to you as the greatest living poet.

Without retiring the jury returned a verdict against Crowley.

At the end of the trial an incident took place which illustrated the fact that although Crowley had physically degenerated – most of his hair had gone, his teeth were in a bad state and he had grown somewhat obese – he still retained a certain attractiveness for a surprising number of women.

At the end of the case he was walking disconsolately down the street when he was approached by an attractive girl aged only nineteen. She told him that in her view what had happened in court was the worst miscarriage of justice since the crucifixion of Jesus Christ. 'I would like,' she added, 'to bear your child.' Crowley who was never the man to refuse an offer of this sort, went off with the girl, and, nine months later became the father

of a son who was named Aleister Ataturk. It might be thought
that Crowley had taken advantage of a naïve and neurotic young
girl. In fact, however, she was quite experienced in spite of her
age, being already the mother of two illegitimate children, so
she knew what her offer involved.

What was the secret of Crowley's charm for women? In his
early years it can easily be attributed to his good looks, his un-
doubted capacity to fascinate when he cared to exert himself and,
perhaps, his money. But such an explanation does not go far
enough; he retained his attractiveness when he was old, ugly,
and bankrupt. To some extent it may have been his reputation
as the possessor of magical powers that lured women into his net:
power, as a leading diplomat once remarked, has always been a
good aphrodisiac. It seems probable also that his skill as a con-
versationalist, to which even such a brilliant talker as Frank Harris
paid homage, also played a part in his amatory successes. Casanova,
never a physically impressive man, attributed his seductive
abilities to his capacity to talk to women, to make them feel
brilliant, beautiful and, above all, desirable.

Crowley himself attributed his sexual appeal to his smell – or,
rather, to the smell of 'Ruthvah, the perfume of immortality'
which he daily rubbed into his hair, body and head. He instructed
those who wanted to use this unguent that it should be rubbed
well into the skin, particularly into the roots of the hair where
the skin is somewhat elastic, and that this should be so thoroughly
done that the subtle odour of the preparation should be unapparent
to others. The user, he added, is thus armed with a powerful
weapon 'against the deepest elements in the nature of those it is
wished to attract'. The smell of Ruthvah supposedly commanded
obedience from those subjected to it; 'they are all the more
certainly compelled to obey because they do not know they are
being commanded'.

The recipe for Ruthvah, which I give for the sake of anyone
who feels inclined to experiment with it, is simple enough:
compound three parts of civet, two parts of musk and one part of
ambergris.

Crowley was by this time without doubt the best-known

occultist in England; his loss of his case against Constable's only made him more well known than ever. It is not surprising then that throughout the 1930s he continually received letters from strangers who sought his help. Some of these were of splendid eccentricity:

> I am writing to you because I am sure you can help me. . . . When I was three weeks old I met with a shock which has tremendously affected my life. I was lying in my cradle when a hard bowler hat fell off a hat rack and hit me on the temple and rendered me unconscious. The effect of it was that I upset my whole nervous system. Since I can remember I have suffered from excessive perspiration of the hands and feet, extreme nervousness and extreme shyness, and when I reached the age of about fourteen I began to suffer excessive seminal losses, both day and night. . . . I have very great ideals and have a strong desire to do good in the world, for instance putting an end to the White Slave Traffic, stopping any future war, and it is for this reason I would like to develop my psychic power but I cannot do so until I am cured of my nervous condition. Now, Sir, as you are a magician. . . .[2]

Besides answering his correspondence Crowley devoted a great deal of thought to ways of making money to supplement what was given him by his disciples, notably Karl Germer. Some of his ventures of this sort, for example his planned Black Magic Restaurant, never got off the ground. He did however have a certain amount of success with his 'Elixir of Life Pills' which he sold at the rate of 25 guineas for a week's dosage. According to Crowley's case-records those who took these benefited greatly: 'Case 73. Army officer, 54, long service, mostly in India. Had been impotent for over 15 years. . . . I insisted on change of climate before taking the case. His health improved greatly. . . . Potency returned after the first dose, but not satisfactorily. After the fourth he was like an exceptionally strong man of 40. Unfortunately he abused his powers, got into the clutches of a loose woman, and took to drinking heavily.'[3] It is unlikely that this retired army officer, or anyone else who took doses of 'Elixir of Life Pills', realized that they were manufactured from a neutral base combined with Crowley's own semen.

In 1935 the Nazis banned a number of occult organizations,

among them the Brotherhood of Saturn, the OTO and the AA. At the same time Germer's high grade masonic and occult connections attracted the attention of the Gestapo and he was arrested. After some weeks of solitary confinement in the Alexanderplatz prison on a diet of bread and water, during which he was tortured but kept himself sane by reciting the Crowleyan 'Holy Books' (see p. 41) from 'beginning to end and from end to beginning', he was sent to the Esterwegen concentration camp.[4] Before his sudden and unexplained release ten months later he was comforted according to his own account by a vision of his Holy Guardian Angel.[5]

After regaining his freedom Germer lived in Brussels for some years, keeping in touch with both Crowley and, until 1937 when they were finally suppressed, the scattered remnants of the German sex magical groups. He was arrested once more, this time by the Belgians, and deported to France, spending ten months in an internment camp before emigrating to the USA in 1941. From his arrival in America until Crowley's death in 1947 Germer was Grand Treasurer of the OTO, his main tasks being supplying money for Crowley to live on and issue small limited editions of magical books old and new.

His old friend Martha Küntzel had become as great an admirer of Hitler as she was of Crowley and until the outbreak of war in 1939 regularly bombarded Crowley with letters loaded with praises of Hitler. Interestingly enough Crowley and Germer believed that Hitler was Martha Küntzel's 'magical son' and that the former had studied *The Book of the Law*. They supported this extraordinary belief by claiming that in Hitler's conversation, as recorded in Rauschning's *Hitler Speaks*, he frequently either quoted or paraphrased extracts from *The Book of the Law*. Thus when Hitler was reported to have said, 'We are now at the end of the Age of Reason. The intellect has grown autocratic and become a disease of life' he was paraphrasing chapter 2, verses 27–32 of *The Book of the Law*. Crowley's annotated copy of Rauschning, now in the library of the Warburg Institute, contains many examples of similar supposed borrowings from *The Book of the Law*. Alas however the whole theory was destroyed

by Martha Küntzel herself when she wrote to Crowley shortly
before the outbreak of war:

> You are perfectly right when you say I can't think politically. I never cared for
> politics except during the War [of 1914–18] and then since the time of
> Hitler's rising, though late enough, as it was then I began to see that Hindenburg
> was too old to give the helm of the Reich the necessary turn. And then it
> began to dawn on me how much of Hitler's thoughts were as if they had been
> taken from the Law of Thelema. I became his fervent admirer, and am so now,
> and will be to my end. I have ever so often owned to this firm conviction that
> the close identity of Hitler's ideas with what the Book teaches endowed me
> with the strength necessary for my work. I stated this even to the Gestapo some
> years ago. . . . But Germer's letter amused me greatly. Isn't it a lark to hear
> him bring forth his 'theory' about Hitler's 'magic birth'![6]

In spite of this denial there were it must be admitted significant
similarities between the doctrines of Crowley and Hitler. Both
men were drawing upon the daemonic emotional forces which
took refuge in the unconscious during the high noon of European
rationalism.

16

A Magical Revival
and a Death

IN THE LATE 1930s there were indications of a magical revival.
This was centred in California where an OTO lodge, Agapé Lodge,
had come into existence. It was led by W. T. Smith who as long
ago as 1915 had been an initiate of the Vancouver lodge of the
OTO run by C. S. Jones. Smith like all faithful Crowleyans had
broken with Jones after the latter had gone mad; this madness
had taken a most unusual form. Its first sign had been Jones
joining the Catholic Church with the object of converting it to
Crowleyanity. Not having much success with this project he took
to going about wearing only a raincoat which at suitable moments
he would fling aside, exposing himself with the object of showing
that he had given up all Veils of Illusion. After this he underwent
according to his own account a series of greater and greater
initiations which eventually revealed to him that Aiwass, the
entity who had dictated *The Book of the Law*, was a malignant
demon and the enemy of humanity.

W. T. Smith was not a very satisfactory leader of the Agapé
Lodge. He was unable to keep his sexual life and his magical life
separate from one another and seduced Helen, the wife of Jack
Parsons, one of the members of the lodge. One might have
thought that Crowley would have been sympathetic in his
attitude to a slip of this sort, but this was not the case and he
wrote an angry letter to Smith in which he told him that he was
giving the OTO 'the reputation of being that slimy abomination
"a love cult"'. Already in 1915 in Vancouver, all I knew of you
was that you were running a mother and her daughter in double

harness – since then one scandal has followed another'. At this stage of events, in 1942, Crowley came to an odd conclusion based on his study of Smith's horoscope. Smith was not a man at all, although he occupied an ordinary body. He was, potentially at any rate, a god. As such he must leave the Agapé Lodge, occupying himself in future only with such matters as concerned a god. From now on Jack Parsons would direct the affairs of the Californian OTO.[1]

Jack Parsons, born in 1914, was a scientist of genius – he was a brilliant physical chemist who played a part in the foundation of the now world-famous Cal. Tech. He was also strongly sexed – after his wife had transferred her affections to Smith he took her younger sister Maggy as his mistress – and a fanatical believer in Crowley's magick. For three years the Agapé Lodge ran smoothly under Parsons's direction. Each day there was a celebration of Crowley's Gnostic Mass in the lodge's temple, situated in Parsons's home, each month subscriptions from the faithful were forwarded to Germer and from him to Crowley. Then in April 1945 Parsons became acquainted with a science fiction writer who had it would seem, an instinctive capacity for magic. This man – I will call him Frater H. as he has now found fame in another sphere – exerted an extraordinary influence over Parsons, who wrote enthusiastically of him to Crowley in July 1945:

About three months ago I met H. . . . a writer and explorer of whom I had known for some time. . . . He is a gentleman; he has red hair, green eyes, is honest and intelligent, and we have become great friends. He moved in with me about two months ago, and although Maggy and I are still friendly, she has transferred her sexual affections to H.

Although H. has no formal training in Magick, he has an extraordinary amount of experience and understanding in the field. From some of his experiences I deduce he is in direct touch with some higher intelligence, possibly his Guardian Angel. He is the most thelemic person I have ever met and is in complete accord with our own principles. He is also interested in establishing the New Aeon but for cogent reasons I have not introduced him to the Lodge.

We are pooling our resources in a partnership which will act as a limited company to control our business ventures. I think I have made a great gain, and as Maggy and I are the best of friends there is little loss. I cared for her deeply but I have no desire to control her emotions, and I can, I hope, control my own.

I need a magical partner. I have many experiments in mind. . . . The next
time I tie up with a woman it will be on my own terms.

The first experiment which Parsons decided to perform was
to get an elemental, in female human form, who would be his
companion. He decided to do this by the methods laid down in
Of the Secret Marriages of Gods with Men (see p. 100). It will be
remembered that magical operations of this sort are intended to
be solitary, involving 'magical masturbation', but Parsons carried
out the rite in the presence of H., who seems to have played some
part in devising the details of the ceremony employed. The ritual
was repeated for eleven nights and ended with Parsons instructing
the elemental to appear in human form before him as a familiar
spirit and a mate.

At first the only result of the ceremony seemed to have been
a violent wind storm. 'Nothing seems to have happened,' wrote
Parsons despondently to Crowley, 'the wind storm is very
interesting, but that is not what I asked for.' In February 1946
however the elemental duly appeared and on the twenty-third
Parsons wrote an excited letter to Crowley: 'I have my elemental!
She turned up one night after the conclusion of the Operation,
and has been with me since, although she goes back to New York
next week. She has red hair and slant green eyes as specified. If
she returns she will be dedicated as I am dedicated! All or nothing
– I have no other terms. She is an artist, strong minded and
determined, with strong masculine characteristics and a fanatical
independence. . . .'

This letter slightly worried Crowley and in a reply dated 15
March 1946 he wrote: 'I am particularly interested in what you
have written me about the elemental, because for some little time
past I have been endeavouring to intervene *personally* in this
matter on your behalf. I would, however, have you recall Lévi's
aphorism: "The love of the Magus for such things is insensate
and may destroy him". Warn him that because of his sensitiveness
he should be more on his guard than the majority of
people.'

Before this, Parsons had had a difficult time with H. and Maggy.

The money in the joint account of the three – most of which had been supplied by Parsons – had been used to buy a yacht. The idea was that this should be resold and the profit shared between the three of them; but H. and Maggy absconded with the craft. Parsons used magic to bring them back to shore:

H. attempted to escape me by sailing at 5 pm, and I performed a full evocation to Bartzabel [the spirit of Mars, see p. 62] within the Circle at 8 pm. At the same time, so far as I can check, his ship was struck by a sudden squall off the coast, which ripped off his sails and forced him back to port, where I took the boat in custody. . . . I have them [H. and Maggy] well tied up; they cannot move without going to jail. However I am afraid that most of the money [in the joint account] has already been dissipated. I will be lucky to salvage $3,000– 5,000.

Parsons, with remarkable generosity, forgave H. and with the aid of the elemental he had evoked – her name in the world of ordinary people was Marjorie Cameron – began to practise sex magic in the presence of H. with the object of incarnating Babalon see (p. 56) in human form. In March 1946 he reported what had happened to Crowley:

I am under the command of extreme secrecy. I have had the most important – devastating experience of my life between February 2nd and March 4th. I believe it was the result of the IX^0 working with the girl who answered my elemental summons. I have been in direct touch with One who is most Holy and Beautiful as mentioned in *The Book of the Law*. I cannot write the name at present. First instructions were received direct through H., the seer. I have followed them to the letter. There was a desire for incarnation. I do not yet know the vehicle, but it will come to me, bringing a secret sign. I am to act as instructor guardian guide for nine months; then it will be loosed on the world. That is all I can say now. . . .

Crowley was puzzled by all this. 'I thought,' he wrote, 'I had a most morbid imagination, as good as any man's but it seems I have not. I cannot form the slightest idea what you can possibly mean.' To Germer Crowley wrote in even more forthright terms: 'Apparently Parsons or H. or somebody is producing a Moonchild. I get fairly frantic when I contemplate the idiocy of these louts.' Crowley's final judgement of Parsons was expressed in a letter written to Germer on 31 May 1946: 'It seems to me on the information of our Brethren in California that (if we may assume them to be accurate) Frater 210 [Parsons] has committed . . . errors. He has got a miraculous illumination which rimes with nothing, and he has apparently lost all his personal independence. From our brother's[2] account he has given away both his girl and his money – apparently it is the ordinary confidence trick.'

Before and while these curious events were going on in California Crowley was living the life of a retired magician. At the beginning of the war he had been living in Richmond – he had quite enjoyed this as he had congenial neighbours, among them Montague Summers, the writer on Restoration drama, witchcraft and black magic. Then when the worst of the bombing appeared to be over he had removed to London, living at 93 Jermyn Street. In April 1944 fresh bombing led him to leave London and become a guest at the Bell Inn, Aston Clinton. Here he was thoroughly bored. 'A most delightful,' he wrote, 'really old inn, big open fire, food incredibly good. But *nothing* to do and no one to talk to. I shall be forced to work – and at once.'

In January 1945 he moved to Netherwood, a Hastings boarding house run by a man with an eccentric sense of humour – which must have amused Crowley; the 'House Rules' for example read:

> Guests are requested not to tease the Ghosts.
>
> Breakfast will be served at 9 am to the survivors of the Night.
>
> The Hastings Borough Cemetery is five minutes walk away (ten minutes if carrying body), but only one minute as the Ghost flies.
>
> Guests are requested not to cut down bodies from trees.
>
> The Office has a certain amount of used clothing for sale, the property of guests who have no longer any use for earthly raiment.[3]

Crowley was bored at Netherwood. The only things that served to assuage this ennui were letters from – and occasionally meetings with – disciples and increasingly large doses of heroin; his daily consumption rose from three to eleven grains, enough to kill several non-addicts. He died from bronchitis and cardiac degeneration on 1 December 1947. His funeral took place four days later in the chapel of the Brighton Crematorium. The final rites were a sort of magick ceremony with Louis Wilkinson (the novelist Louis Marlowe) reading extracts from *The Book of the Law*, the collects from the Gnostic Mass and Crowley's *Hymn to Pan*. The local paper denounced it as a Black Mass. 'We shall take all necessary steps,' said the chairman of the appropriate Brighton council committee, 'to see such a thing does not happen again.'

How can one sum up the life and personality of Aleister Crowley? Was he, as John Symonds has suggested, a person who made a religion out of his own weaknesses, a case for a psychologist, a false Messiah who has led, and whose writings still lead, many astray? Was he, as Mario Praz described him in *The Romantic Agony*, a 'satanic occultist', or was he, as he himself believed, the prophet of a new age?

It seems to me that there is a certain amount of truth in all these points of view. Thus, as a person who could rationalize any and every one of his actions, he was incapable of self-criticism, of ever admitting that he had done anything wrong. When, for example, he wrote a pornographic work called *White Stains* – almost certainly, it seems to me, an attempt to express his own sexual fantasies – he argued that he was merely writing a tract dealing with the downfall of a man through sexual perversions, a book whose conclusions 'might be approved in any Sunday School'.

As for his status as a false Messiah, or a genuine one, this is a little difficult to pontificate upon. All one can say is that *The Book of the Law*, produced in 1904, and its prophecies of an era of violence, force and fire have provided a better description of what has happened in the last seventy years than the optimistic predictions given by such writers as Shaw and Wells at around the same time.

Crowley as a 'satanic occultist' certainly existed; he identified Aiwass, whom he saw as his own Holy Guardian Angel, with the Christian devil and, it will be remembered, he had once crucified a toad whom he had baptised with the name Jesus Christ. On the other hand he was not *merely* a vulgar satanist and in some of his books, notably *Magick in Theory and Practice*, he had given expression to an occult system and philosophy which was clear, consistent and in some ways beautiful.

He was a man in whom good and evil were as mutually existent, and as closely blended, as in the human race itself.

17

The Aftermath

AFTER CROWLEY'S DEATH California remained for some time the centre of activity of his followers. Jack Parsons continued with his magical experiments and seems to have suffered an inflation of the ego which made him regard himself as the main spiritual opponent of Jesus Christ. In 1948 he took the 'Oath of the Anti-christ' before his old superior W. T. Smith and simultaneously changed his name from Parsons to 'Belarion Armiluss All Dajjal Anti-Christ'. In the following year he issued an occult manifesto called *The Book of Anti-Christ* which consisted of two parts, *The Black Pilgrimage* and *The Manifesto of the Anti-Christ*. The first part dealt with the difficulties he had encountered in both his interior and exterior lives – his disillusionment with ordinary life with its financial and emotional difficulties, the spiritual 'dryness' and sense of abandonment he had suffered. This total disenchantment with life, the loss of money, home, wife and, later, mistress had made him undertake the Black Pilgrimage, a spiritual odyssey which eventually forced him to choose between three possibilities: suicide, a retreat into madness, or taking the 'Oath of the Abyss'. This was a magical adventure essentially identical with the undergoing of the influence of opening oneself to the powers of the demon Choronzon which Crowley had experienced in the Algerian desert.

Not surprisingly Parsons chose the third of these paths and, as a result of this, or so he thought, became transformed into the Anti-Christ. As such, in the second part of his manifesto, he

declared war on 'all authority that is not based on courage and
manhood', demanded an end to 'the authority of lying priests,
conniving judges, blackmailing police', cursed all restriction,
calling for an end to 'conscription, compulsion, regimentation,
and the tyranny of false laws', and claimed that he would spread
Crowley's law amongst all men: 'And in His Law I shall conquer
the world'.

Parsons also believed in the existence of flying saucers, arguing
that they were a mysterious 'engine' mentioned in *The Book of
the Law* and would play a part in converting the world to Crowleyanity. He also produced what he called *The Book of Babalon*, a
fourth chapter of *The Book of the Law* which he had obtained from
some astral being – or his own unconscious mind – which
contained jumbled but obviously deeply felt praises of this
Crowleyan personification of the female elements of the universe:
'She is flame of life; power of darkness; she destroys with a
glance; she may take the soul. She feeds upon the death of men.

'Concentrate all force and being in Our Lady Babalon. Light a
single light on Her altar, saying Flame is Our Lady; flame is Her
hair. I am Flame.'

How Parsons would have gone on developing magically is an
open question; from some of his writings it seems likely that he
would have ended his life as an incurable schizophrenic. His life,
however, ended in 1952 when he accidentally dropped some
mercuric fulminate in his laboratory.

Parsons, with his fourth chapter of *The Book of the Law*, was
regarded as a heretic by the more orthodox Crowleyans who
were led by Karl Germer. He had inherited the chieftainship of
the OTO, the Crowley copyrights and the ashes of his dead Master.
Germer saw his main task as publishing hitherto unprinted
Crowley works – he was responsible for the issue of such books as
The Book of Wisdom and Folly and an enlarged version of Crowley's
kabalistic masterpiece *777* – and binding together the scattered
members of the OTO. To this end he carried on a world-wide
correspondence with various individuals and groups.

A group which met with his particular approval was the
Mysteria Mystica Veritas, the Swiss section of the OTO. This had for

many years enjoyed an extremely quiet existence – in fact one might have regarded it as being almost dormant – until 1943 when a certain Herr Metzger (Frater Paragranus) was initiated into it. Paragranus, a former baker, found occultism much more to his taste than bread making, made a rapid occult development and within a comparatively short time became chief of the Swiss branch of the order.

With time he achieved other occult dignities: he headed a masonic organization; he inherited from a certain Dr Krumm-Heller the chieftainship of an obscure occult society called 'The Ancient Rosicrucian Fraternity', and he became the Patriarch of a French religious organization called the Gnostic Catholic Church. This latter body had had a brief but eventful history. Its real founder seems to have been a French magician called Julius Hussay who got himself a dubious episcopal consecration in 1904, seemingly because he thought it would enhance his magical powers. Hussay gave 'conditional consecration' to several Gnostic bishops. These consecrations were conditional because the persons concerned were already half convinced they were authentic bishops because they had undergone a ceremony of consecration at the hands of A. Doinel, a man who owed his episcopate to two supernatural events. At the first of these Jesus Christ himself had appeared to him and told him that he was, from a spiritual point of view, a bishop; the second took place at a spiritualist seance when the ghosts of two mediaeval Cathar bishops conferred the episcopate upon him.

Amongst those whom Hussay consecrated was an ex-Trappist monk turned occultist named Giraud who in turn consecrated, as Patriarch of the tiny Gnostic Church, Joanny Bricaud, a prolific writer on occultism and the French literature of the decadence. One of Bricaud's followers, and in due course his successor as Patriarch, was Georges Chevillon, murdered by the Gestapo in 1944. It was from him that Frater Paragranus inherited his Patriarchate.

Paragranus found – and still finds – no conflict between his capacities as a disciple of Aleister Crowley and his office of Patriarch. Each Sunday, dressed in episcopal vestments, he celebrates Crowley's Gnostic Mass with, it must be said, the utmost propriety. I, with a friend, attended such a mass in 1971 and was impressed by the aesthetic nature of the ceremony, which was carried out without any of the sexual curiosities that have sometimes accompanied the performance of this rite – in the USA W. T. Smith made an act of cunnilingus the central feature of his version of the Gnostic Mass.

The approval which Germer gave to Herr Metzger and the Swiss OTO was not extended to the German Herr Grosche (Gregor A. Gregorius, to give him his magical alias) who, with the end of the Nazi regime, had refounded the Brotherhood of Saturn – the occult organization whose members, it will be remembered, varied their coital positions according to the disposition of the planets. Grosche had founded a small occult magazine called *Blätter fur Lebenskunst* and the contents of this aroused Germer's wrath: he wrote in a letter to an English disciple of Crowley:

Grosche's manipulations are beginning to become more suspicious. In the June issue of his *Blätter fur Lebenskunst* he prints a childish report on Crowley-Therion, makes him even obtain an audience with the Dalai Lama and other silly things. In the July issue he discloses his game, or the game of those occult forces behind him, more openly. He talks of 'Thelemists' while 'Thelemites' should be, and always has been, 'Thelemiten'. . . . I have no idea of the 'Thelemistic Revelations' from which he quotes (p. 5) the verses VI, 6, 10, 11 and 12. . . . It reads to me at least like the style of the so called Mahatma letters[1]. . . . Magically I see it as the deliberate attempts by the Black Lodge, or whatever lodge, to throw a stick into the wheel of our new serious beginning. . . . Grosche wants to make himself the spokesman for Thelema [i.e. Crowley-anity] in Germany. It may be a deliberate attempt to draw the wind from our sails. It will not succeed, but shows to what current he belongs.

Germer died on 25 October 1962 and was succeeded as world chief of the OTO by Frater Paragranus (Herr Metzger). This succession was announced to the occult world in a manifesto published in the spring of 1963:

We, Grand Secretary General of the Sovereign Sanctuary of the Ordo Templi Orientis, hereby give due Notice to all Sovereign Sanctuaries and Bodies in friendship with the Sovereign Sanctuary of the Ordo Templi Orientis and to all

Members of the said Rite, that the lamented Most Illustrious Frater Superior of the Ordo Templi Orientis, Frater Saturnus (Karl Johannes Germer) Outer Head of the Order, departed this earthly life and was called to the Grand East on October 25th 1962 E.V., and that a convocation of Prince Patriarch Conservators of the said Rite on January 6th 1963 E.V. held in the Abbey of Thelema, Stein, Appenzell unanimously elected the Very Illustrious + H. Josephus M., Frater Paragranus, Grand Master x⁰ of the Ordo Templi Orientis, Sovereign Grand Master General of Ordo Illuminatorum, Sovereign Grand Master General of Fraternitatis Rosicruciana Antiqua, and Sovereign Patriarch of Ecclesiae Gnosticae Catholicae henceforth to be Sovereign Grand Master General, Outer Head of the Order of the Oriental Templars.

The size of occult organizations is often in inverse proportion to the grandeur of their titles and the extravagance of their claims, and many of those who read this manifesto seem to have assumed that 'the Abbey of Thelema' mentioned as existing in the canton of Appenzell was a figment of the imagination of those who produced the manifesto. This was, and is, not so. The Abbey of Thelema and the Swiss OTO are flourishing organizations. The Abbey is a large building set in the outskirts of a small village which nestles in a valley surrounded by mountains. It owns a nearby hotel, run with the aid of immigrant Italian workers, a dairy farm, and the largest collection of beehives I have ever seen. Outside the hotel, as emblems of its management's loyalties to both their country and Crowley, fly three flags: that of Switzerland, that of the canton in which the Abbey is situated and 'the banner of the Rose Cross', a splendidly coloured emblem whose curious design no doubt holds great mystical significance.

The brothers and sisters who are inmates of the Abbey live extraordinarily industrious lives. They not only manage their hotel, but conduct an official Swiss weather observation station which is on the roof of the Abbey, brew mead from the honey produced by their bees, manufacture various medicines according to occult recipes and principles, milk their cows, run a bar and a small cinema – both patronized by the villagers – and carry out numerous magico-religious ceremonies. They also manufacture, in a small workshop that is part of the Abbey buildings, their own paint, and they have an impressively large printing press. On this they produce their monthly magazine, *Oriflamme*, a publication largely devoted to Crowley's life and writings, and various books, most of them German translations of Crowley; they have, for example, published a German edition of Crowley's *Magick in Theory and Practice*. All things considered it is not surprising that the hard work and genuine religious devotion of these Swiss Crowleyans met with Karl Germer's approval.

In England, after Crowley's death, there were several individuals who were members of the OTO but only one person who was chartered by Crowley to conduct a lodge of the OTO. This was a man not usually associated with Crowleyan occultism but a self-styled witch – the late Gerald Gardner, the individual who was largely responsible for the mushroom growth of modern witchcraft. He was on friendly terms with Crowley for some years, was a fourth-degree initiate of the OTO and was authorized by Crowley to set up a 'camp' of the order conferring its first three degrees on those who desired them.[2]

Gardner was not particularly interested in the sexual magic of the OTO but had a strong bent towards flagellation as well as towards occultism. He decided to combine these two tastes in a version of the witch cult which would involve rituals incorporating nudity, scourging and copulation. There is some evidence that he felt the task of composing such rituals beyond his powers and hired, for a suitably large fee, Crowley to do the job.[3] These rituals and instructions for operative witchcraft became collectively known as *The Book of Shadows* and this book is still the basic technical manual used by almost all the members of the cult. It is a curious blend of Crowleyanity on the one hand and the Gnostic survivals recorded by G. C. Leland in his nineteenth-century studies of Italian folklore on the other. This mingling of seemingly incompatible elements into a homogenous whole is well illustrated by the section of *The Book of Shadows* known as 'the Charge':

Listen to the words of the Great Mother. . . .

Whenever ye have need of anything, once in the month, and better it be if the moon is full, then shall ye assemble in some secret place and adore Me who am Queen of all Witcheries. There shall ye assemble, ye who are fain to learn all

sorcery. I shall teach ye things unknown and ye shall be free from all slavery.
As a sign that ye be really free ye shall be naked in your rites and ye shall dance,
sing, make music, make love – all in praise of Me. For Mine is the ecstasy of
spirit and Mine is joy on earth, for my law is Love under Will. [Love under Will
is one of the key phrases of *The Book of the Law*.]

Mine is the secret door of youth, Mine is the Cup of the Wine of Life, Mine
is the Cauldron of Ceridwen, Mine is the Holy Grail.

I am the gracious Goddess who gives the gift of joy unto the heart of Man.
Upon earth I give unimaginable joys; upon death I give peace, rest and ecstasy.
Nor do I demand aught in sacrifice.

Most of this invocation comes from Leland's *Aradia* but there are
elements drawn from Crowley's own writings. Thus the last
paragraph is a slightly modified version of chapter 1, verse 58 of
The Book of the Law.

While the Crowley–Gardner rituals for the various holy days
of the witch calendar vary considerably, that for Candlemas can
be taken as typical and thoroughly in accordance with Crowley's
teachings:

Proceed to the site with a dance step, waving brooms and lighted torches;
the High Priestess carries a broomstick shaped like an erect phallus. All,
dancing, form the Magic Circle. The High Priest enters, in his right hand the
consecrated Magic Sword, in his left hand the wooden image of an erect phallus.
Priest and Priestess exchange the fivefold kiss i.e. breasts, thighs and genitals;
the Priestess then invokes the god into the Priest with the Invocation 'Dread
Lord of Death and Resurrection Lord of Life, Giver of Life, Thou Whose
Name is Mystery of Mysteries, encourage our hearts! Let thy light crystallize
in our blood, bringing to us Resurrection. For there is no part of us that is not
of the gods!' [This phrase was taken by Crowley–Gardner from a Golden
Dawn Ritual.] Descend, we pray thee, upon thy servant and Priest.

Gardner first announced the existence of his witch-cult in a
book entitled *Witchcraft Today*, published by the London firm of
Rider in 1954. The book, which received a good deal of publicity,
resulted in its author receiving a flood of enquiring letters from
would-be witches, both male and female, and many of these
people were eventually initiated by Gardner into his cult. These
supposed witches in their turn initiated others and within a few
years there were groups ('covens') of these cultists in every major

British city. In the same period some Americans obtained a British initiation and Gardnerian witchcraft was soon firmly planted in the USA.

After the death of Gardner in 1964 the cult suffered a good deal of fragmentation and the many covens which exist at the present day can be divided into three main tendencies, all to some extent influenced by Crowley's teachings. The largest of these groups is the 'Alexandrian witches' who have come into existence as the result of the activities of Mr Alec Sanders, a man who has initiated an enormous number of people. According to Mr Sanders's own account he was initiated as a witch by his grandmother when he was only nine years old, the ceremony taking place in a Manchester back kitchen. However, the version of *The Book of Shadows* used by the Alexandrians is identical with the Crowley–Gardner compilation and other ceremonies, conducted by Mr Sanders but not described in his organization's holy book, seem to have been directly derived from Crowley's OTO. Thus, for example, the Alexandrians use certain herbal extracts, which they call 'fluid condensers', as aids in obtaining clairvoyance and other occult powers. Both the names of, and the recipes for preparing these extracts are derived from the writings of Franz Bardon, a German member of the OTO. Alexandrian covens now exist in France, Germany, Britain and the USA.

The second tendency, the pure Gardnerians, seem to be in a state of decline; new initiates are regularly admitted but few of them seem to stay for any length of time. Some of the Gardnerian covens emphasize sex and sado-masochistic activities even more than did Gardner himself; such groups have often been strongly influenced by Crowley and the sexual magic which he taught. The third tendency, the 'robed covens', have – as their name implies – abandoned ritual nudity and sexual practices. Most of these groups do not use *The Book of Shadows* but have evolved their own rites, heavily influenced by the ceremonies of the Golden Dawn and Crowley's non-sexual teachings.

With his obsession with witchcraft and sexual fun-and-games Gardner had not time to run the OTO lodge whose foundation had been authorized by Crowley, and when Germer received a request for a charter from a young English occultist named Kenneth Grant he, after checking that Gardner had no intention of activating his lodge, gave him a charter empowering him to work the first three degrees of the OTO system. All went well for a time but in 1955 Mr Grant transformed his group, which he now called New Isis Lodge, into a full-blown occult organization working eleven Crowley-inspired degrees (initiation degrees 0° to ix° and a group ritual for collective lodge work). At the same time, without seeking Germer's approval, Mr Grant issued a manifesto.

This manifesto is a curious and interesting document. It begins by asserting that a new spiritual influence is affecting the earth, that the 'rays' of this influence come from an 'unexplored source', and that they find their present focus in the planet Isis, which exists beyond the orbit of Pluto; it is almost needless to say that so far orthodox astronomy has failed to find any trace of this planet. The degrees of New Isis Lodge, says the manifesto, have been designed (presumably by Mr Grant himself) with the purpose of enabling individuals to harness the subtle radiations of the new planet.

After detailing at some length the structure of the lodge the manifesto concluded with two statements that would inevitably thoroughly annoy Karl Germer: first of all it stated that the New Isis Lodge possessed secret documents containing knowledge of secret magical formulae implicit in *The Book of the Law* but concealed from 'the eyes of the profane'; and, secondly, it stated that there was a sister-lodge in Germany which dealt with the Saturnian element in the new revelation. This German group, it was added, was controlled by 'the Master G' and was in accord with New Isis Lodge. The 'Master G' was none other than Eugen Grosche, the man who had incurred Germer's hatred and contempt. Mr Grant sent Germer a copy of the Isis manifesto together with a letter in which he said that for reasons of secrecy it was impossible for him to show Germer the new rituals. Germer was incensed. A short but acrimonious correspondence followed which concluded on 20 July 1955 when Germer sent a registered letter to Mr Grant purporting to expel him from the

OTO and withdrawing his authority to work 'a Camp, Lodge, or Temple of the OTO'.

In spite of Germer's anathema, the New Isis Lodge remained in existence for some years, its members frequently experiencing occult excitements. On one occasion, for example, a magical war broke out between Gerald Gardner and Mr Grant. This took place in 1955 and the story has been told in the pages of the occult encyclopedia *Man Myth and Magic* by Mr Grant himself.

The war involved the magical obsession of a young woman named Clanda who claimed to be a 'water witch'. Exactly what she meant by this curious phrase is unclear: she may have merely meant that she had the power of dowsing, of finding water with a forked hazel stick ('water witching' is a phrase used as equivalent to dowsing in many American rural dialects); on the other hand she may have been claiming to have certain physical and psychic attributes which enabled her to control water spirits – such a theory is strengthened by the fact that Mr Grant found her appearance to be suggestive of that traditionally associated with a mermaid.

Clanda had been a member of Gerald Gardner's witch-cult but had found that she was making little magical progress towards the end she desired – that of becoming 'a Priestess of the Moon'. She transferred her allegiance to New Isis Lodge, a move that Gardner believed had also been made by some of his other witches. Gardner, in short, came to believe that Mr Grant was 'stealing' his witches and decided to launch a magical attack on him. Interestingly enough Gardner did not feel enough confidence in his own occult powers to do this, but employed the services of an occultist and painter named Austin Osman Spare.

Spare, born on the last day of 1888, the son of a London policeman, had been 'discovered' as a painter at a very early age and by 1909 enjoyed a fair reputation amongst the art critics of his time. At around the same date he joined Aleister Crowley's AA and learned that organization's versions of yoga and the magic of the Golden Dawn. Long before that, however, he had started learning some variety of witchcraft from an old fortune-teller called Mrs Paterson. According to Spare Mrs Paterson had great skill in divination and could immediately discern and express the essential character of a person before going into details of his or her future. Apart from this, claimed Spare, she possessed the magical ability to materialize her thoughts, or those of others, to visible appearance. Spare acquired this ability from her but could only exercise this faculty in an erratic and uncontrolled fashion.

As early as 1909–10 Spare produced *The Book of Pleasure*, a work which combined the magic he had learned from Crowley and Mrs Paterson with a weird occult draughtmanship of his own. In this and succeeding works he elaborated a new occult synthesis which he called Zos and Zoz. There were many points of interest in this new magical system. Like most who practise magic in a serious way Spare felt that any desire deeply felt in the inmost consciousness was capable of fulfilment. He designed various techniques for obtaining this realization of desires of an altogether simpler nature than the traditional methods of ceremonial magic. These involved painting certain strange sigils and talismans designed by Spare himself and the use of what he called 'the alphabet of desire'. To manufacture a sigil in the alphabet of desire is simple enough. A sentence, as brief and to the point as possible, and expressive of the inner desire, is written out in full. Then, so that no letters are repeated, certain excess letters are crossed out. The remaining letters are combined into a sigil, resulting in a sort of involved monogram. The sigil is then stared at by the magician who lets it sink into the subconscious and then forgets, as far as is possible to do so, the original desire, leaving 'the god within' – the divine element supposedly existing at the core of every human personality – to work undisturbed towards the wished-for end.

By the time Gardner contacted Spare for his aid in getting back his lost witch the latter was almost forgotten as both artist and occultist. He was living in poverty in a depressing South London flat earning money by doing quick portrait sketches for small sums in local pubs. For a fee he agreed to manufacture a talisman which would 'restore lost property to its rightful place'. Gardner left Spare unaware of the exact nature of the 'lost property' to be restored and at whom the talisman was aimed as he knew that

Spare was on friendly terms with Mr Grant, the latter being an enthusiastic admirer of the former's philosophy and artistic work. The talisman was duly prepared, taking the form of a picture of what Spare described as 'a sort of amphibious owl with the wings of a bat and talons of an eagle'. Before long the New Isis Lodge experienced, so it would seem, the evil effects of the talisman.

At the time, New Isis Lodge met in a weirdly decorated room situated in an Islington house owned by a furrier who was also that rare twentieth-century phenomenon, a practising alchemist; subsequently he wrote a modern text book on the subject, of which contemporary adepts of that strange art have the highest opinion. The owner did not live in the house, using it solely for his own alchemical activities and the magical rites of his friends. On the evening in question the room used by the New Isis Lodge was theatrically magnificent. The only illumination came from two enormous candles situated on either side of an altar on which lay, fully extended, Clanda the water-witch. The air was blue with the smoke of the incense of Black Isis – storax, olibanum, onycha and galbanum – and its smell blended weirdly with the musty smell of rotten wood that is so typical of old, empty houses. Through the haze of the incense moved four violet-robed and cowled members of the lodge. As it was the Black Isis, the dark manifestation of the goddess more usually associated with light, that was being invoked, an extremely powerful manifestation of her presence was expected by the assembled magicians.

A series of mesmeric-type passes, designed to concentrate occult power in the chakras – the supposed centres of psycho-spiritual activity in the subtle body – were made over Clanda's extended form. Following these she was supposed to lie passively. Instead she suddenly sat up, her body rigid and sweating, her eyes with an hypnotized glaze to them.

The magicians sensed a cold wind blowing across the room and at the same time heard, either physically or clairaudiently – it is not clear which – a curious sound as of scrabbling talons coming from a heavily curtained window.

Meanwhile Clanda exhibited all the signs of extreme terror. Her body shook with convulsions, she swayed with fear and heard the flutter of immense wings. Subjectively, undetected by the four magicians who were conducting the ceremony, she saw the curtains swing apart, a huge bird wing its way into the room and clutch its talons into her. The bird then lifted her into the air – at least this was her impression – and carried her out into the night. She saw, far below her, roof-tops, the steeples of churches, busy streets and a dark vapour curling round a Thames wharf in the far distance. While all this was going on, while she was enduring this extraordinary dissociation of consciousness, her physical body lay unconscious upon the altar on which it lay.

She struggled against the claws which gripped her, seemed to escape, and felt herself falling back onto the altar. The observers of the lodge merely saw her come back to full consciousness, crying, thoroughly confused and betraying every sign of deep mental disturbance. She shuddered with fear as she looked at the window through which she had discerned the ghostly bird coming at her; its curtains fluttered as though some entity was still trying to obtain ingress at the window.

A physical aspect of the event which had now taken place became apparent. On the frosted window – it was a cold and snowy night – were marks seemingly made by the claws of an enormous bird. Even more alarming, on the window sill was a curious deposit, a 'gelatinous substance, resembling seaweed' which heaved gently up and down as though breathing. In spite of this curious happening Gardner did not obtain his desire; far from returning to Gardner Clanda emigrated to New Zealand and drowned. Were the water spirits reclaiming their own? According to Mr Grant after the manifestation of Spare's bird, a strong smell of the sea lingered round the temple for many days.

In America, as in England, a Crowleyan organization that was not regarded as orthodox by Karl Germer was active. This was the 'Great Brotherhood of God', a fraternity which owed its existence to the activities of C. F. Russell (Frater Genesthai) the American ex-naval man who had for a time resided at Crowley's Abbey in Cefalu (see p. 134).

The brotherhood had started life as the Choronzon Club, a

society whose advertisements had begun to appear in the occult press as early as 1931:

A short-cut to Initiation
The Choronzon Club
Box ABC, Chicago Illinois

The Choronzon Club, which changed its name to the Great Brotherhood of God at some time in the 1930s, taught strange variations of the magic of both the OTO and the Golden Dawn. Choronzon, it will be remembered, was the 'mighty devil' whom Crowley had evoked and fought with in the Algerian desert and whom he considered the spiritual embodiment of all that is dispersed, deformed, unbalanced and chaotic. It was a curious thing, therefore, to name an occult body after this demon. Some have suggested that Russell was dabbling with satanism; certainly he was turning the Golden Dawn system upside down. Thus the pentagrams – the five-pointed stars supposedly endowed with magical powers – which he taught his followers were the same as those used in the Golden Dawn but drawn the opposite way up; that is to say they had two points rather than one at the top of the figure. Most occultists regard a pentagram drawn in this way as a symbol of evil, a representation of the triumph of matter over spirit – a rather more sophisticated equivalent of the mumbling of the Lord's Prayer backwards, as supposedly indulged in by evilly disposed peasant witches, the servants of Satan.

Russell had his own interpretation of *The Book of the Law*, different in many ways to that of Crowley, and claimed that the latter had failed to carry out his own teaching that the 'pairs of opposites' – the contradictory elements present in every human being – should be 'slain', that is, resolved in a higher dialectical unity.

Russell also varied some of the sex-magic techniques taught by the OTO. He abandoned the magic taught in the VIII° – this was, of course, 'magical masturbation' – and replaced it with what he called Dianism. This is the practice usually known as Karezza, sexual intercourse often continued for some hours but never reaching the point of orgasm. This practice is not regarded with favour by most sexologists but Russell taught his followers to engage in it until they reached what he called 'the borderland state'. By this was meant a hallucinatory trance in which both participants in the sexual act regarded each other as the personification of his or her own Holy Guardian Angel. After the initiate had mastered Dianism and had his or her proficiency in it tested by another member of the brotherhood the IX° techniques of the OTO were taught in orthodox fashion. The test for perfection in the practice of Dianism was no mere formality. The late Louis Culling, one of the earliest initiates of the sect, underwent an 'examination' in the subject which involved him paying the travelling expenses of his female companion from the order's headquarters in Chicago to San Diego in California. According to his own account he passed the test with ease, engaging in copulation for three hours without reaching orgasm.

From whence Russell derived his Karezza is something of a mystery. It bears some resemblance to the sexo-yogic techniques of Buddhist tantrism but it seems likely that Russell was uninfluenced by oriental sources. It is clear that he was influenced, to some extent at least, by *The Heavenly Bridegroom*, a book by Ida Craddock which not only advocated Karezza but argued that the use of this method was the solution to all sexual and emotional problems.

The organization of Russell's brotherhood was similar in some respects to the cell-system used by communists in countries where their party was illegal. Those initiates who were introduced to the order by Russell were appointed as 'Neighbourhood Primates'. These led local groups and were the only members directly in contact with headquarters. Their task was to recruit and train members of their local groups in the techniques of sexual magic. This cellular form of organization was probably introduced in order to reduce to a minimum the amount of sexual instruction passing through the mails; at the time the brotherhood had been founded the United States postal authorities were applying a rigidly puritanical interpretation of the laws against sending obscene matter through the mails.

The Neighbourhood Primates were given financial incentives to build up their local following. Of the initiation fee of $5 paid by each new member only half had to be forwarded to the headquarters, the remainder being retained by the Neighbourhood Primate. This policy seems to have met with success: soon there were local chapters of the brotherhood in all larger American population centres and some of these had quite a considerable membership. Thus in Los Angeles there were 75 members and in Denver 125, surprisingly large figures never attained by the OTO itself.

In 1938 the brotherhood very much reduced the scope of its activities but Russell continued to run a neo-Gnostic cult concerned with sexual magic. In 1969 and 1971 the 'Great Brotherhood of God' enjoyed a resurgence of activity when one of its initiates, the late Louis T. Culling, a former astrologer and performer on the electric organ, published all the secrets of the order in two books, *The Complete Magick Curriculum of the Secret Order G.B.G.* and *A Manual of Sex Magick*. These books had a surprisingly wide sale and influenced groups of people, most of them fairly young, who either organized themselves into lodges under Mr Culling's leadership or formed their own groups for the study of sex magic and Crowley's *The Book of the Law*.

There was nothing at all sinister about the Russell–Culling brotherhood and what it taught from the point of view of anyone who does not regard the practice of sex magic as evil in itself. In the 1960s, however, there were unorthodox Crowleyan groups active in the USA whose leading members were alleged to have engaged in practices involving sadism, blood sacrifice and bizarre sexuality. Similar allegations have recently been made about the activities of English occult groups supposedly deriving from the OTO and, according to a number of press reports which appeared in the early spring of 1986, the leaders of these groups conduct initiation rituals which involve urine drinking and other scatological practices, the maltreatment of animals, perverse sexual couplings, and the use of dangerous drugs.

These and other similar stories seem to have been very largely derived from the fantasies of disturbed individuals, most notably

Mr Derry Mainwaring-Knight, a confidence trickster of genius who managed to convince a number of wealthy evangelical Christians of the existence of a vast Satanic conspiracy. This conspiracy, so it was asserted, had some sort of connection with Crowley and the OTO, involved a large number of fairly ordinary individuals – amongst them the present writer and an Essex traffic policeman who had the temerity to breathalyse Mr Mainwaring-Knight – and was led by such politicians as Lord Whitelaw, Mr Enoch Powell and Mr Leo Abse.

It was necessary, Mr Mainwaring-Knight informed his dupes, for him to buy various items of Satanic regalia, including a sceptre, a chalice, and a golden throne which was kept, surrounded by water, in a luxurious flat in Pall Mall, and ritually destroy them. This, so he said, would free him from various oaths he had taken and, more important, destroy the worldwide network of Satanic groups which was busily plotting the destruction of all law and morality. It was also essential, explained Mr Mainwaring-Knight, that he himself should drive a Rolls-Royce equipped with a radio telephone – Satanists, he said, are even more impressed by the material trappings of wealth than are the rest of us.

Improbable as this story was, a number of wealthy and dedi-cated Christians found it sufficiently plausible to hand over to Mr Mainwaring-Knight a sum of money in the region of a quarter of a million pounds.

The Satanic conspiracy, so at least some of those who contri-buted money understood, was spearheaded by the OTO with which Mr Mainwaring-Knight claimed to have a long-standing family connection – his late grandmother, he explained, had posed as an enthusiastic Christian but had in reality been a sorceress, an associate of Aleister Crowley, and the High Priestess of an OTO temple which operated in Southend-on-Sea.

Not all of those approached for moral and financial support by Mr Mainwaring-Knight were prepared to give uncritical credence to the stories they were told, and one Anglican cleric, a man with considerable knowledge of occult history, pointed out that it was impossible to reconcile aspects of the 'Satanic OTO conspiracy' story with certain factual information given in a book edited by the present writer.

Mr Mainwaring-Knight provided a suitable answer. King's writings, he said, 'mustn't be taken seriously'; for King was a whitewasher, a man whose words, so it was implied, were dictated by Lucifer himself. Subsequently Mr Mainwaring-Knight, possibly feeling that Satan would have chosen a better amanuensis than myself, amended his story. He had gone along, he said, with the idea that it was the OTO which headed the conspiracy, but in reality the OTO was a mere subsidiary of 'the Sons of Lucifer', an occult society of such secretiveness that no one had ever heard of it, clear proof of its power and wickedness.

The evidence given at the trial of Mr Mainwaring-Knight, which ended in him being sentenced to a period of seven years' imprisonment, was bizarre and, on occasion, funny. Thus the Reverend John Baker, the rector of the East Sussex parish of Newick, gave evidence that the mere mention of 'five objects used in Satanic rites' could threaten the lives of various opponents of Lucifer, including himself, and that he had seen Mr Mainwaring-Knight possessed by a devil which 'in a strange voice' said of Mr Mainwaring-Knight: 'You cannot have him, he belongs to Lucifer, he was dedicated by sacrifice as a child and he is a master of the occult.'

Other evidence was somewhat more mundane and, as the trial ran its lengthy course, it became apparent that the money donated to Mr Mainwaring-Knight had been expended, not on the purchase of satanic regalia, but on cars, prostitutes, and other delights which pertain to the World and the Flesh rather than the Devil. This did not prevent some newspapers from publishing, once the trial was over, background stories describing the iniquities practised by the OTO and other alleged diabolists.

There would seem to be very little truth in such stories as far as either groups with an authentic OTO derivation or more obscure and insignificant occult societies are concerned. The former groupings are, of course, as anti-Christian as was Crowley himself, but it would be impossible to substantiate claims that they celebrate 'the Black Mass' and other evil rites. There are, it is true, tiny 'Satanic' associations whose members profess to admire Crowley's writings but have no connection with the OTO; the activities of these

groups rarely seem to involve anything more than a certain amount
of childish blasphemy combined with group sex – all very
reprehensible, no doubt, but not much more so than the activities
of suburban wife-swappers and other 'swingers'.

There are also persistent rumours of the existence of the
diabolist 'temples', some of them falsely claiming to be OTO, which
are involved in sado-masochism, the trade in hard drugs, and even
the activities of the neo-Nazi lunatic Right. The origins of such
stories lie in the statements made by a number of individuals who
claim to have been members of such cults and to be struggling to
escape from the Devil's influence. A number of committed
Christians have found such claims credible. Others are inclined to
attribute them to gross exaggeration, hysteria, and even psychosis
– there are some individuals who claim that their minds are tele-
pathically controlled by the OTO just as there are others who claim
that a similar control is being exerted by extra-terrestrial beings.

There can be no certainty about the extent of the perversities
engaged in by eccentric individuals or cults. What seems beyond
question, however, is that the idea that the OTO, or the 'Sons of
Lucifer', or some other secret society, is at the head of a
worldwide, rich, and powerful conspiracy which strives to
overthrow morality in general, and Christian morality in particular,
remains what it always has been, a myth born of human fantasy,
ignorance and gullibility. This does not mean, of course, that there
may not exist unorthodox Crowleyan groups which engage in
activities which most of us would regard as silly, undesirable, or
even dangerous.

Apart from organized Crowleyan activity, both orthodox and
heterodox, the thirty years since Crowley's death had witnessed
a growing interest in magic in general and Crowley's life and
writings in particular. This interest began with the publication
of John Symonds' biography of Crowley in 1951. For although
the book was generally hostile towards its subject it reflected
Crowley's contempt for orthodox religious belief and ordinary
standards of behaviour in a way that attracted those people,
mostly members of the younger generation, who were repelled

by the grimly Puritan austerities of the 1940s. Crowley's published writings, some of which had long been available at waste-paper prices, began to be seriously collected and individuals and small groups commenced to study and practise magick.

Thus, throughout the 1950s, interest in Crowley continued to expand slowly, mainly amongst those who felt themselves at odds with western society and its ethical values. In the next decade this growth speeded up. Crowley's philosophy and his recorded activities – not least his libertarian attitudes towards sex and the use of drugs – appealed to many of the 'beats', the 'hippies', and the 'flower children', who came to regard the 'Great Beast' as the prophet of their counter-culture, their irrationalist ways of looking at the world, and their rebellion against all the values their parents held sacred. Crowley's long unavailable works began to be reprinted; tattered manuscripts were dug out of private collections and published for the first time; references to Crowley began to appear in science fiction and fantasy literature – in the pages of Heinlein's *Stranger in a Strange Land*, for example. Even the Beatles fell under the charm of Crowley, putting his photograph as 'one of the people we like' on the cover of their LP record entitled *Sergeant Pepper*. Other rock musicians also admired Crowley: one of them, a now dead bandleader, claimed to be Crowley's bastard son; while Jimmy Page, lead guitarist of the world-famous Led Zeppelin, bought Crowley's old Scottish home and spent a considerable sum on its restoration.

Today the flower children and the beats have almost all gone. Some have died, some are living simple lives in communes, and some – the overwhelming majority – have rejoined society. But, paradoxically, the interest in Crowley survives. Dead, he has far more disciples than he ever did when alive, and it seems unlikely that we have heard the last of the Beast 666 and his followers.

Notes

1 THE MAGICAL DECADE

1 *Crowley on Christ* (C. W. Daniel, London 1974), p. 138.

2 Presumably in imitation of Liane de Pougy, the notorious actress-harlot. In spite of Pollitt's cross-dressing there is no doubt that he played the active part in his relationship with Crowley.

3 Crowley's *Confessions* (Mandrake Press 1929), vol. 1, ch. 13.

4 She was initiated in 1888 but her membership 'went into abeyance' in November 1889. In his *Magicians of the Golden Dawn* (1972) Ellic Howe has suggested that Oscar objected to his wife becoming a practising magician.

5 *Dogma and Ritual of High Magic* and *History of Magic* (Paris 1854–6).

6 In the form of a letter to A. J. A. Symons.

2 THE GOLDEN DAWN

1 A catalogue of Hockley's library was issued after its owner's death by George Redway, an occult publisher and bookseller who disposed of it on behalf of Hockley's heirs. While this catalogue contains many items of manuscript none of them can be identified with the mysterious cipher documents.

2 Strictly speaking they were not *cipher* manuscripts although they always seem to be referred to as such. In reality they are in a simple alphabetic code of sixteenth-century origin.

3 Westcott produced both letters supposedly received by him from a German Rosicrucian initiate called Anna Sprengel and a charter, alleged to be from the same source, authorizing the foundation of the 'Isis-Urania Temple'. Ellic Howe has proved that both letters and charter were crude forgeries, probably produced by Westcott himself.

4 *Vestigia* is a contraction of '*Vestigia nulla retrorsum*' ('I never retrace my steps') the occult motto of Mathers's French wife Moina, the sister of the philosopher Bergson.

5 As a freemason.

6 This reference is to the masonic *Societas Rosicruciana in Anglia*.

7 The *Kabalah Denudata* (vol. I, 1677; vol. II, 1684), an extraordinary medley of late and early kabalistic tracts compiled by the Christian kabalist Knorr von Rosenroth, exerted a profound effect upon Western mysticism. Contrary to what is implied by Westcott, Mathers's *Kabalah Unveiled* is not a translation of the complete work but only of three of its longer tracts.

8 This memorandum is as reproduced by Ellic Howe, op. cit., pp. 37–8.

9 Or so Yeats said. It would be surprising however if they had not met previously in the circle of Madame Blavatsky, for both were active in this at the same period.

10 Crowley in fact claimed to be the reincarnation of the eighteenth-century charlatan Count Cagliostro.

11 Crowley's description of Yeats's alleged occult attack and its defeat can be found in the short story *At the Fork of the Roads* included in the *Equinox*, No. 1 (March 1909).

12 Crowley's *Confessions* (Mandrake Press 1929), vol. 1, ch. 21.

13 The full text of this rite can be found in vol. 2 of Israel Regardie's *Golden Dawn* (Aires Press, Chicago 1937–40) while a somewhat abbreviated version of it was included by Crowley in the *Equinox*, No. 3 (March 1910).

3   THE BOOK OF THE LAW

1 In fact he first of all went to New York but disliked it so much that he quickly departed for Mexico.

2 This was an adaptation by Mathers of an 1852 English translation of a late Graeco-Egyptian magical text.

3 Probably by the invocation in *Liber Israfel*, a magical text published by Crowley in the *Equinox*, No. 7.

4 Mr and Mrs Horos, the 'evil *Adepts*', had in 1901 been sentenced to terms of penal servitude for fraud and rape.

5 This note is dated for the festival of Corpus Christi 1903. If this dating is correct – and Crowley's dating was usually so – it would seem that he had made a final break with Mathers almost a year before the reception of *The Book of the Law*. It should be noticed that in his edition of the *Goetia* Crowley already claimed the headship of the Rosicrucian Order, referring to himself as 'our illustrious and ever-Glorious Frater, ye wise Perdurabo, that Myghte Chiefe of ye Rosy-Cross Fraternitye'.

4   TOWARDS THE SILVER STAR

1 Fuller was about the only Englishman whom Hitler really liked. He was a guest at the small tea-party which Hitler gave to celebrate his fiftieth birthday.

2 Neuburg was of course recording what had taken place on the previous night. The Bornless One ritual referred to is identical with the Preliminary Invocation of the *Goetia* referred to in the preceding chapter.

3   I have not been able to get access to the original of this and have relied
on the quotations made from it in Jean Overton Fuller's biography of Neuburg.

5   CHORONZON

1   Dee and Kelley on the other hand seem to have thought they were
physical places; in this connection see Meric Casaubon's *True and Faithful
Relation* (1659).

2   On the other hand I can find no trace of Crowley using certain 'pyramids'
derived from the Enochian system for 'skrying in the spirit vision', a popular
Enochian technique with the adepts of the Golden Dawn.

3   An alternative and thoroughly satanic translation can be found in Anton
La Vey's *Satanic Bible* (Avon Books, 1970).

4   A Golden Dawn symbol.

5   *The Vision and the Voice* (Barstow, California 1953).

6   Op. cit.

7   In his *The Eye in the Triangle* (Minnesota 1970).

8   Traditionally the words with which Adam opened the gates of hell.

6   THE RITES OF ELEUSIS

1   An evocation of Bartzabel, presumably bearing some likeness to the rite
used by Neuburg, was included in the *Equinox*, No. 9.

2   They were later published in the *Equinox*, No. 6.

7   BOOK FOUR

1   A slightly fictionalized version of this party is given in Crowley's novel
Moonchild (Mandrake Press 1929).

2   Aba, transliterated into Hebrew as Aleph, Beth, Aleph, becomes four
by gematria as follows: Aleph = 1, Beth = 2, Aleph = 1, total = 4.

3   This, which Crowley regarded as being the best type of incense for all
magical workings where a physical plane manifestation was desired, was compounded of one part of lignum aloes, two parts of storax and four parts of
olibanum.

4   Crowley had also performed various banishing rituals and recited the
Preliminary Invocation of the *Goetia*.

5   *Book Four*, parts I and II, are included in the omnibus Crowley volume
Magick (Routledge & Kegan Paul, London 1973).

6   Both the third and fourth parts of *Book Four* were eventually completed.
The former, entitled *Magick in Theory and Practice*, was published by Lecram of
Paris in 1929 while the latter, the commentary on *The Book of the Law*, was
published posthumously in 1973 by '93 Publishers' of Canada.

7   Elliot O'Donnell, *Rooms of Mystery* (Philip Allan, Oxford 1931).

8   Harry Kemp in the *World Magazine* (August 1914), as quoted by John
Symonds in *The Great Beast* (Macdonald, London 1971).

8   WESTERN TANTRISM

1   This for reasons of space is a simplified exposition of sex magic techniques. Those who want to study them in detail are referred to *A Manual of Sex Magick* by Louis Culling (St Paul, Minnesota 1971), to the chapter entitled 'The Mass of the Holy Ghost' in Dr Israel Regardie's *The Tree of Life* (Samuel Weiser, New York 1969) and to the *Secret Rituals of the O.T.O.* (C. W. Daniel, London 1973).

2   The detailed record of these is contained in two manuscripts *The Book of the High Magick Art* and *The Esoteric Record*. I must thank Gerald Yorke for giving me access to typescripts of these MSS in 1966 and 1967. Both these records were compiled by Neuburg.

3   Published in a limited edition of ninety-three copies of the magazine *Sothis* (St Albans 1976).

4   *Lampada tradam* = 'I carry the torch.'

9   THE DEPARTURE AND LATER LIFE OF NEUBURG

1   The drawing is reproduced opposite p. 112 of C. R. Cammell's *Aleister Crowley* (Richards Press 1951).

2   Jean Overton Fuller reproduced this in her *The Magical Dilemma of Victor B. Neuburg* (W. H. Allen, London 1965).

3   Statement of Dame Rebecca West, who had been a fellow student of Joan Hayes, in Fuller, op. cit.

4   Fuller, op. cit.

5   Cammell, op. cit.

6   As quoted by Jean Overton Fuller, op. cit.

7   Presumably Neuburg's statement that he was once a goat was the origin of the absurd story, still repeated in some occult circles, that he had at one time been changed into a camel by Crowley's magic.

8   According to Mr Kenneth Grant's article on 'Spirits and Forces' in *The Encyclopedia of the Unexplained* (Routledge & Kegan Paul, London 1974) Heseltine's death was connected with his magical practices. It would seem that he invoked an Abramelin demon, by tracing its magical square on his arm, with the object of getting his wife to return to him. This she did – and a short time later shot himself, allegedly the victim of the demon who had by now turned against him.

9   For a fuller account of Neuburg's discovery of Thomas see Jean Overton Fuller, op. cit.

10   SEXUAL WISDOM

1   There are five of these instructional documents: *Of the Nature of the Gods; Of the Secret Marriages of Gods with Men; Liber Agapé – the Book of the Unveiling of the Sangraal; De Arte Magica; Of the Homunculus*. Of these all except *De Arte Magica* are included in *The Secret Rituals of the O.T.O.* (C. W. Daniel, London; Samuel Weiser, New York, 1973). *De Arte Magica* was published as a short

pamphlet (Level Press, San Francisco n.d.) and appears as an appendix to
Crowley on Christ, op. cit.

It is worth adding that there have been so many of Crowley's writings
published for the first time in the last few years that a good deal of biblio-
graphical confusion has been created. An excellent guide through this jungle of
small editions is provided by *The Crowley Cross-Index* published by the magazine
Agapé (7 Turner's Tower, Faulkland, Nr Bath, Avon, England).

2   *The Secret Rituals of the O.T.O.*, p. 172.

3   Ibid., p. 178.

4   Ibid., p. 180.

5   The reference is to Burton's book *The Jew, The Gypsy and El Islam*,
published posthumously in 1898 but excluding the middle section which dealt
with alleged ritual murder among the Sephardic Jews of Damascus and the
murder of a certain Padro Tomaso in 1840.

6   *The Secret Rituals of the O.T.O.*, p. 193.

7   Ibid., pp. 198–9.

8   Ibid., p. 201.

9   Published by Level Press (San Francisco, n.d.), and also published as an
appendix to *Crowley on Christ*, op. cit.

10   That 'a drop of semen equals an ounce of blood' was a belief enshrined
in Victorian sexo-medical folklore.

11   *The Secret Rituals of the O.T.O.*, pp. 233–9.

12   Crowley's novel *Moonchild*, op. cit., is concerned with the creation of
just such an homunculus.

11   AMERICA

1   *Rex de Arte Regia* is included in *The Magical Record of the Beast 666* (vol. 1)
(Duckworth, London 1972).

2   Eventually Jones was to discover 'the Key of it All'; to make certain
discoveries about the kabalistic importance in *The Book of the Law* of the words
AL (God) and LA (not).

3   A fuller account of the 'Amalantrah working' can be found in John
Symonds' *The Great Beast* (Macdonald 1971). The Crowleyan magazine *Sothis*
(St Albans) has announced that it will be publishing the full record of these
workings but at the time of writing this has not yet appeared.

4   Seabrook's account is slightly muddled; it is clear from Crowley's
Confessions that at the time of the red paint incident Crowley had already spent
some time in his island and had only temporarily (19–21 August 1918) gone to
New York on OTO business.

5   Seabrook's own account of this incident, together with the story of how
he and Crowley once tried to carry on a conversation with one another by
barking like dogs will be found in his *Witchcraft* (Sphere Books 1970).

6   The *King Khang King* was published privately by Crowley in 1939. The

Tao Teh King was published posthumously in 1976 (Askin Publishers, London; Samuel Weiser, New York) with an introduction by Stephen Skinner.

12 LEAH HIRSIG

1 According to Seabrook, op. cit., this mark was not painted upon her but had been branded with the red-hot point of a Chinese sword.

2 As quoted by Symonds, op. cit.

3 Crowley, who used the nineteenth-century translation of it made by James Legge, always called the book the *Yi King*.

4 At the time of writing the best account of Crowley's Cefalu period is contained in Symonds, op. cit. I understand that two publishing firms, Duckworth and Neville Spearman, are planning to publish Crowley's 'magical record' for the Cefalu years.

5 As quoted by Symonds, op. cit.

6 Ninette it will be remembered, was pregnant.

13 THE END OF THE ABBEY

1 The full text of this sad but amusing letter may be found in Symonds, op. cit.

2 Almost the full text of Loveday's account of his first week at Crowley's Abbey can be found in Symonds, op. cit.

3 What Betty May actually heard was '*Ateh Aiwass Malkuth ve-Geburah, ve-Gedulah, le-olahm, Amen*'. This is Hebrew of a sort and means, 'Unto Thee O Aiwass be the Kingdom, the Power and the Glory unto Eternity, Amen'.

14 WANDERINGS OF A MAGICIAN

1 A more complete version of this letter will be found in Symonds, op. cit.

2 See article 'German Occult Groups' by Ellic Howe in *Encyclopedia of the Unexplained* (Routledge & Kegan Paul, London 1974).

3 In astrology an 'aspect by transit' is formed when the sun, the moon, or one of the planets is in a position where it forms a significant angle (an aspect) with the position the same or another heavenly body was in at the moment of birth.

4 The full text of this document can be found in Francis King, *Sexuality, Magic and Perversion* (Citadel Press, New Jersey 1972). According to Ellic Howe, 'By comparison with the Golden Dawn material published by Dr Israel Regardie . . . the magical and occult pabulum offered by the Fraternitas Saturni was even more complex and in some ways more sophisticated'.

15 TWILIGHT OF A MASTER

1 The full text of this letter can be found in Symonds, op. cit.

2 A more complete version of this letter will be found in Symonds, op. cit.

3 Another case-history will be found in Symonds, op. cit.

4 After his release he described his experiences in a book entitled *I Was*

a Prisoner; he never found a publisher for this but several copies survive in typescript.

5   See Francis King, op. cit., p. 120.

6   See Francis King, *Satan and Swastika* (Mayflower 1975), pp. 139–42.

16   A MAGICAL REVIVAL AND A DEATH

1   To ensure that Smith should fully achieve the status of a god Crowley wrote a full instruction for him (*Liber Apotheosis*) giving details of the process to be followed. An excerpt from this was published in Kenneth Grant's book *The Magical Revival* (Muller, London, 1972). Smith religiously followed the course charted for him by Crowley but without success; his last letter to Crowley was one of utter despondency.

2   'Our brother' was the late Louis Culling, an occultist, astrologer and electric organist. The individual referred to as 'Frater H.' was the late L. Ron Hubbard, the originator of the cults of dianetics and scientology.

3   As quoted by John Symonds, op. cit.

17   THE AFTERMATH

1   This is a reference to the letters allegedly sent to Madame Blavatsky by Himalayan supermen called Mahatmas. It is now generally accepted that these letters were in reality written by Blavatsky herself.

2   This authorization, in the form of a solemn charter, was on view at the Castletown (Isle of Man) Museum of Witchcraft until the entire collection was purchased by the Ripley 'Believe it or Not' organization. There are rumours, probably correct, that Gardner paid Crowley a considerable sum for his charter.

3   At least one prominent American member of the witch cult has affirmed that he has seen a copy of these rituals, collectively known as *The Book of Shadows*, in Gardner's collection of witchcraft and magical material.

A Note on Further Reading

THE GENERAL BACKGROUND TO CROWLEY'S OCCULT
LIFE AND DEVELOPMENT

Cavendish, Richard, *The Black Arts* (Routledge & Kegan Paul, Ltd., 1967). An introduction to all aspects of the 'occult sciences' written from a non-partisan point of view and for the general rather than the occult specialist.

—, *History of Magic* (Weidenfeld and Nicolson Ltd., 1977). A short work, but one which provides the only reliable general history of magic and magicians through the ages.

Howe, Ellic, *The Magicians of the Golden Dawn* (Routledge, 1972). A somewhat hostile but brilliantly researched account of the Golden Dawn and its history.

Regardie, Israel, *The Golden Dawn* (Aries Press, 4 volumes, 1937–40). This work, now available as four volumes in one from Llewellyn Publications, is essential study-material for anyone who wants to fully understand the intricacies of the occult system taught by MacGregor Mathers and his Golden Dawn associates.

—, *The Tree of Life* (Rider, 1932). Now re-issued by Samuel Weiser of New York in paperback form this is undoubtedly the best introduction to ritual magic ever written by a practising occultist.

CROWLEY'S LIFE AND PSYCHO-SPIRITUAL DEVELOPMENT

Burnett-Rae, Alan, *Aleister Crowley: A Memoir of 666* (Victim Press, 1971). Amusing memories of a former landlord of Crowley's.

Cammell, C. R., *Aleister Crowley* (Richards Press, 1951). A memoir rather than a biography, this book throws an interesting light on some periods of Crowley's life.

Fuller, J. F. C., *The Star in the West* (Walter Scott Publishing Co., 1907). In spite of all its critical and stylistic extravagances this work is still the only one to attempt a religio-philosophical analysis of Crowley's early writings, particularly his poetry.

Fuller, Jean Overton, *The Magical Dilemma of Victor B. Neuburg* (W. H. Allen & Co. Ltd., 1965). Written from the point of view of extreme hostility to Crowley and his ideas this book nevertheless throws much light on the relationship between Neuburg and his teacher.

Regardie, Israel, *The Eye in the Triangle* (Llewellyn Publications, 1970). A superb study of Crowley's occult development between 1898 and 1914. An invaluable work for the occult student.

Symonds, John, *The Great Beast* (Macdonald, 1971). A very full biography written from an unsympathetic standpoint. Deals with Crowley not only as a magician but as a mountaineer, traveller, painter and poet.

A SELECTION OF CROWLEY'S OWN WRITINGS

Crowley, Aleister, *Confessions* (Hill and Wang, 1970). Crowley's inevitably biased and one-sided account of his own life until *circa* 1920.

—, *Equinox* (various publishers, eleven numbers 1909–19). Most of the contents of this voluminous publication were written by Crowley himself. The articles and poetry cover almost every aspect of magic, 'magick', and mysticism.

—, *Magick* (Routledge, 1973). Contains 'Part One of Book Four' – perhaps the best ever written introduction to yoga – 'Part Two of Book Four', a somewhat confused and confusing essay

on magic, and *Magick in Theory and Practice*, Crowley's *magnum opus*.
—, *Secret Rituals of the O.T.O.* (C. W. Daniel and S. Weiser, 1973). The basic rituals and instructional material of Crowley's sex-magical occult fraternity.

MISCELLANEOUS MATERIAL

Drury, Neville and Skinner, Stephen, *The Quest for Abraxas* (Spearman, 1972). Admirably illustrates Crowley's influence on the occultists of the 1970s.
Grant, Kenneth, *The Magical Revival* (Muller, 1972).
—, *Aleister Crowley and the Hidden God* (Muller, 1973).
—, *Cults of the Shadow* (Muller, 1975). These three books are informative about Crowleyan derivatives and contain a certain amount of Crowley material not published elsewhere. They make worthwhile reading for the occult specialist. Mr Grant is an admirer and disciple of Crowley and writes from that very specific point of view. Some of his interpretations of Crowleyan theory – notably his idea about the XI° of the OTO – are considered extremely unorthodox by other followers of Crowley.
Russell, C. F., *Znuss is Znees* (privately printed, 1970). An interesting account by an ex-disciple combined with a good deal of curious mathematics.

RECENT PUBLICATIONS OF RELEVANCE TO CROWLEY'S OCCULTISM

Cavendish, Richard, *The Magical Arts* (Arkana, 1984). A new version of this author's *The Black Arts*.
D'Arch Smith, Timothy, *The Books of the Beast* (Aquarian Press, 1987). Contains a lengthy and informative study of Crowley's use of books as 'magical talismans'.
King, Francis, *Tantra for Westerners* (Aquarian Press, 1986).
MacGregor Mathers, S. L., *Astral Projection, Ritual Magic, and Alchemy* (Aquarian Press, 1987). Golden Dawn instructional material which deeply influenced Crowley's 'Magick'.
Regardie, Israel, *The Complete Golden Dawn System of Magic* (Falcon Press, Arizona, 1984).
Suster, Gerald, *Hitler and the Age of Horus* (Sphere Books, 1981).

Index

Bestselling Non-Fiction

☐ The Alexander Principle	Wilfred Barlow	£2.95
☐ The Complete Book of Exercises	Diagram Group	£4.95
☐ Everything is Negotiable	Gavin Kennedy	£2.95
☐ Health on Your Plate	Janet Pleshette	£2.50
☐ The Cheiro Book of Fate and Fortune	Cheiro	£2.95
☐ The Handbook of Chinese Horoscopes	Theodora Lau	£2.50
☐ Hollywood Babylon	Kenneth Anger	£7.95
☐ Hollywood Babylon II	Kenneth Anger	£7.95
☐ The Domesday Heritage	Ed. Elizabeth Hallam	£3.95
☐ Historic Railway Disasters	O. S. Nock	£2.50
☐ Wildlife of the Domestic Cat	Roger Tabor	£4.50
☐ Elvis and Me	Priscilla Presley	£2.95
☐ Maria Callas	Arianna Stassinopoulos	£2.50
☐ The Brendan Voyage	Tim Severin	£3.50

ARROW BOOKS, BOOKSERVICE BY POST, PO BOX 29, DOUGLAS, ISLE OF MAN, BRITISH ISLES

NAME ....

ADDRESS ....

....

....

Please enclose a cheque or postal order made out to Arrow Books Ltd. for the amount due and allow the following for postage and packing.

U.K. CUSTOMERS: Please allow 22p per book to a maximum of £3.00.

B.F.P.O. & EIRE: Please allow 22p per book to a maximum of £3.00.

OVERSEAS CUSTOMERS: Please allow 22p per book.

Whilst every effort is made to keep prices low it is sometimes necessary to increase cover prices at short notice. Arrow Books reserve the right to show new retail prices on covers which may differ from those previously advertised in the text or elsewhere.

Bestselling Non-Fiction

☐ The Gradual Vegetarian	Lisa Tracy	£2.95
☐ The Food Scandal	Caroline Walker & Geoffrey Cannon	£3.95
☐ Harmony Rules	Gary Butt & Frena Bloomfield	£2.25
☐ Everything is Negotiable	Gavin Kennedy	£2.95
☐ Hollywood Babylon	Kevin Anger	£7.95
☐ Red Watch	Gordon Honeycombe	£2.75
☐ Wildlife of the Domestic Cat	Roger Tabor	£4.50
☐ The World of Placido Domingo	Daniel Snowman	£4.95
☐ The Sinbad Voyage	Tim Severin	£2.75
☐ The Hills is Lonely	Lillian Beckwith	£1.95
☐ English Country Cottage	R. J. Brown	£3.50
☐ Raw Energy	Leslie & Susannah Kenton	£2.95

ARROW BOOKS, BOOKSERVICE BY POST, PO BOX 29, DOUGLAS, ISLE OF MAN, BRITISH ISLES

NAME ....

ADDRESS ....

....

....

Please enclose a cheque or postal order made out to Arrow Books Ltd. for the amount due and allow the following for postage and packing.

U.K. CUSTOMERS: Please allow 22p per book to a maximum of £3.00.

B.F.P.O. & EIRE: Please allow 22p per book to a maximum of £3.00.

OVERSEAS CUSTOMERS: Please allow 22p per book.

Whilst every effort is made to keep prices low it is sometimes necessary to increase cover prices at short notice. Arrow Books reserve the right to show new retail prices on covers which may differ from those previously advertised in the text or elsewhere.

Bestselling Fiction

☐ Toll for the Brave	Jack Higgins	£1.75
☐ Basikasingo	John Matthews	£2.95
☐ Where No Man Cries	Emma Blair	£1.95
☐ Saudi	Laurie Devine	£2.95
☐ The Clogger's Child	Marie Joseph	£2.50
☐ The Gooding Girl	Pamela Oldfield	£2.75
☐ The Running Years	Claire Rayner	£2.75
☐ Duncton Wood	William Horwood	£3.50
☐ Aztec	Gary Jennings	£3.95
☐ Enemy in Sight	Alexander Kent	£2.50
☐ Strumpet City	James Plunkett	£3.50
☐ The Volunteers	Douglas Reeman	£2.50
☐ The Second Lady	Irving Wallace	£2.50
☐ The Assassin	Evelyn Anthony	£2.50
☐ The Pride	Judith Saxton	£2.50

ARROW BOOKS, BOOKSERVICE BY POST, PO BOX 29, DOUGLAS, ISLE
OF MAN, BRITISH ISLES

NAME ....

ADDRESS ....

....

....

Please enclose a cheque or postal order made out to Arrow Books Ltd. for the amount
due and allow the following for postage and packing.

U.K. CUSTOMERS: Please allow 22p per book to a maximum of £3.00.

B.F.P.O. & EIRE: Please allow 22p per book to a maximum of £3.00.

OVERSEAS CUSTOMERS: Please allow 22p per book.

Whilst every effort is made to keep prices low it is sometimes necessary to increase cover
prices at short notice. Arrow Books reserve the right to show new retail prices on covers
which may differ from those previously advertised in the text or elsewhere.

A Selection of Arrow Bestsellers